The Complete Mediterranean Diet
Cookbook for Beginners 2023

2000 Days of Quick, Delicious and Healthy Mediterranean Recipes to Help You Build New Healthy Habits with 30-DAY MEAL PLAN

Kassandra M. Barrows

Table of Contents

Chapter 4 Poultry — 33

Chapter 5 Beef, Pork, and Lamb — 40

Chapter 6 Fish and Seafood — 47

Chapter 7 Snacks and Appetizers   54

Chapter 8 Vegetables and Sides   61

Chapter 10 Desserts 79

Chapter 11 Salads 86

Chapter 12 Pizzas, Wraps, and Sandwiches 92

Chapter 13 Pasta 97

Chapter 14 Staples, Sauces, Dips, and Dressings 103

Appendix 1: Measurement Conversion Chart 107

Appendix 2: The Dirty Dozen and Clean Fifteen 108

INTRODUCTION

Welcome to the captivating world of Mediterranean cuisine, where vibrant flavors, wholesome ingredients, and a profound respect for the connection between food and well-being intertwine. In this Mediterranean diet cookbook, I am delighted to guide you on a culinary journey that not only tantalizes your taste buds but also nourishes your body, mind, and soul.

The Mediterranean diet has garnered worldwide recognition for its remarkable health benefits and its ability to promote longevity and vitality. Originating from the sun-drenched lands of Greece, Italy, Spain, and other Mediterranean countries, this way of eating embraces the abundance of nature, celebrates the joy of communal dining, and emphasizes the importance of balance and moderation.

As the author of this cookbook, I have been captivated by the Mediterranean diet's rich heritage and its profound impact on well-being. Through these pages, I invite you to embark on a culinary adventure that transcends mere recipes—it is an exploration of a lifestyle deeply rooted in tradition, culture, and a deep appreciation for the simple pleasures of life.

In the first section of this cookbook, we will delve into the heart of the Mediterranean diet, understanding its core principles and how they contribute to a vibrant and healthy life. We will explore the importance of fresh, seasonal ingredients, the balance between food groups, and the art of portion control. You will gain a comprehensive understanding of how the Mediterranean diet nourishes your body and promotes optimal health.

Next, we will embark on a sensory journey as we explore the Mediterranean flavors that make this cuisine so alluring. From the piquant notes of sun-ripened tomatoes and fragrant basil to the tangy zest of citrus fruits and the earthy aroma of olive oil, each dish tells a story of the sun-soaked Mediterranean landscape. Together, we will uncover the secrets of Mediterranean herbs and spices, the versatility of wholesome grains and legumes, and the delight of succulent seafood and tender meats.

In the heart of this cookbook, we will dive into a treasure trove of traditional Mediterranean dishes. From classic Greek moussaka to hearty Italian pasta dishes, from Spanish paella to Turkish kebabs, each recipe will transport you to the heart of the Mediterranean, allowing you to savor the authentic flavors and experience the culinary heritage of this extraordinary region. With detailed instructions and helpful tips, you will confidently master the art of Mediterranean cooking in your own kitchen.

As we progress further, we will explore the concept of seasonal eating and the joy of embracing local produce. We will celebrate the bounties of each season, discovering the delights of fresh fruits and vegetables that grace our tables throughout the year. By understanding the importance of eating in harmony with nature, we not only support our health but also cultivate a sustainable and eco-conscious approach to nourishment.

But the Mediterranean diet is not merely about what we eat—it encompasses a holistic lifestyle that promotes physical activity, mindfulness, and the nurturing of social connections. We will discover the joy of leisurely walks along the Mediterranean shores, the tranquility of mindful eating, and the pleasure of sharing meals with loved ones. By embracing the Mediterranean way of life, we unlock a pathway to greater happiness, contentment, and overall well-being.

In this cookbook, you will find a collection of delectable recipes, insightful tips, and practical guidance that will empower you to embrace the Mediterranean diet and its lifestyle fully. Whether you are seeking to improve your health, explore new flavors, or simply embark on a culinary adventure, this cookbook will be your trusted companion on your journey.

So, immerse yourself in the vibrant flavors, nourishing ingredients, and enchanting traditions of the Mediterranean diet. Allow the Mediterranean sun to infuse your dishes with warmth and vitality, and let the communal spirit of Mediterranean dining bring joy to your table. Together, let us savor the tastes of the Mediterranean and embark on a culinary journey that nurtures not only our bodies but also our souls. Bon appétit!

Chapter 1 All about Mediterranean Diet

What is Mediterranean Diet

The Mediterranean diet is more than just a way of eating—it is a lifestyle rooted in the rich culinary traditions and cultural heritage of the Mediterranean region. It is a way of nourishing the body while embracing the joys of food, community, and a balanced approach to life. The Mediterranean diet is renowned for its numerous health benefits, including reducing the risk of heart disease, promoting weight management, and enhancing overall well-being.

At its core, the Mediterranean diet emphasizes an abundance of fresh, whole foods that are minimally processed and rich in nutrients. The foundation of this diet is plant-based, with a focus on fruits, vegetables, legumes, whole grains, nuts, and seeds. These nutrient-dense foods provide a wide range of vitamins, minerals, fiber, and antioxidants that support optimal health.

Another key aspect of the Mediterranean diet is the consumption of healthy fats, primarily from sources such as olive oil, avocados, and nuts. These fats are an essential part of the diet and contribute to cardiovascular health, brain function, and the absorption of fat-soluble vitamins.

In addition to plant-based foods and healthy fats, the Mediterranean diet includes moderate amounts of lean proteins, such as fish, poultry, and eggs. These proteins provide essential amino acids and omega-3 fatty acids, which are beneficial for heart health and brain function. Dairy products, including yogurt and cheese, are also consumed in moderation.

One of the distinguishing features of the Mediterranean diet is its limited consumption of red meat and processed foods. Red meat is enjoyed occasionally, while processed foods high in added sugars and unhealthy fats are minimized. This emphasis on whole, unprocessed foods contributes to the overall nutritional profile of the diet and helps maintain a healthy weight.

The Mediterranean diet is not just about what we eat, but also how we eat. It encourages mindful eating, savoring each bite, and paying attention to hunger and fullness cues. Meals are typically enjoyed in the company of others, fostering a sense of community and connection. The Mediterranean lifestyle also promotes regular physical activity, such as walking, swimming, or gardening, which contributes to overall well-being and weight management.

Numerous scientific studies have demonstrated the health benefits of the Mediterranean diet. Research has shown that following this dietary pattern can reduce the risk of chronic diseases, including cardiovascular disease, type 2 diabetes, certain types of cancer, and neurodegenerative conditions like Alzheimer's disease. The Mediterranean diet's emphasis on whole, nutrient-dense foods, along with its favorable balance of macronutrients, contributes to these positive health outcomes.

Beyond its physical benefits, the Mediterranean diet is a way of life that celebrates the pleasures of food, the importance of social connections, and the harmony between nature and our well-being. It encourages us to slow down, appreciate the quality of ingredients, and find joy in preparing and sharing meals with loved ones. This holistic approach to food and lifestyle sets the Mediterranean diet apart and has contributed to its growing popularity worldwide.

In conclusion, the Mediterranean diet is a flavorful and nutritious way of eating that embraces whole, unprocessed foods, emphasizes plant-based ingredients, and encourages a balanced and mindful approach to meals. By adopting the Mediterranean diet and lifestyle, we can nourish our bodies, promote overall well-being, and enjoy the simple pleasures of food and community. So, let us embark on this culinary journey and discover the beauty and benefits of the Mediterranean diet together.

Key Components of Mediterranean Diet

The Mediterranean diet is renowned for its emphasis on wholesome, nutrient-dense foods that promote optimal health and well-being. It embraces a diverse range of food groups and flavors, creating a balanced and enjoyable way of eating. Let's explore the key components of the Mediterranean diet and how they contribute to its remarkable health benefits.

♦ Abundance of Fruits and Vegetables: Fresh fruits and vegetables take center stage in the Mediterranean diet. These vibrant and colorful foods provide an array of vitamins, minerals, antioxidants, and fiber. They are essential for maintaining overall health, supporting digestion, and reducing the risk of chronic diseases. The Mediterranean diet encourages incorporating a variety of fruits and vegetables into meals and snacks throughout the day.

♦ Whole Grains and Legumes: Whole grains, such as whole wheat, barley, oats, and brown rice, are staples of the Mediterranean diet. These grains are a great source of complex carbohydrates, fiber, and essential nutrients. Legumes, including beans, lentils, and chickpeas, are also integral to the diet, offering plant-based protein, fiber, and micronutrients. These foods provide sustained energy, support digestive health, and contribute to satiety.

♦ Healthy Fats: The Mediterranean diet promotes the consumption of healthy fats, particularly monounsaturated fats found in olive oil, avocados, and nuts. These fats have been associated with improved heart health, reduced inflammation, and enhanced cognitive function. Olive oil, in particular, is a key component of the diet and is used as the primary source of fat for cooking and dressing dishes.

♦ Lean Proteins: The Mediterranean diet includes moderate amounts of lean proteins, such as fish, poultry, and eggs. Fish, especially fatty fish like salmon, sardines, and mackerel, are rich in omega-3 fatty acids, which have been linked to numerous health benefits, including reducing the risk of heart disease. Poultry and eggs provide high-quality protein and essential nutrients.

♦ Moderate Consumption of Dairy: Dairy products, such as yogurt and cheese, are enjoyed in moderation in the Mediterranean diet. These foods are excellent sources of calcium, protein, and probiotics, which support bone health and gut health. However, it is important to choose high-quality, minimally processed dairy products and consume them in appropriate portion sizes.

♦ Limited Red Meat and Sweets: Red meat, such as beef and lamb, is consumed sparingly in the Mediterranean diet. Instead, the focus is on leaner sources of protein like fish and poultry. Sweets and desserts are also enjoyed in moderation, usually on special occasions. The Mediterranean diet promotes the idea of indulging in small portions of high-quality, homemade treats rather than regularly consuming processed sweets.

◆ Plenty of Herbs and Spices: Herbs and spices play a vital role in Mediterranean cuisine, adding depth and flavor to dishes. They are used liberally to season foods instead of relying on excessive salt or unhealthy condiments. Common herbs and spices include basil, oregano, parsley, garlic, cumin, and cinnamon, each offering their unique health-promoting properties.

◆ Hydration through Water and Moderate Wine Consumption: Staying hydrated is essential for overall health, and the Mediterranean diet emphasizes drinking plenty of water throughout the day. In addition, moderate consumption of red wine is often associated with the Mediterranean diet. Red wine, when enjoyed in moderation, has been linked to certain health benefits due to its antioxidant content, particularly resveratrol.

These key components of the Mediterranean diet work synergistically to provide a wide range of nutrients, promote satiety, and support overall health. By embracing these principles and incorporating them into our daily lives, we can experience the remarkable benefits of the Mediterranean diet and enjoy a delicious, balanced approach to eating.

Benefits of Following a Mediterranean Diet

Following a Mediterranean diet offers a multitude of benefits for both physical and mental well-being. This dietary pattern, inspired by the traditional eating habits of Mediterranean countries, has been extensively studied and recognized for its positive impact on health. Let's explore the remarkable benefits of embracing a Mediterranean diet:

♦ Heart Health: The Mediterranean diet is renowned for its ability to promote heart health. It emphasizes the consumption of heart-healthy fats, such as monounsaturated fats found in olive oil and omega-3 fatty acids from fish. These fats have been shown to reduce bad cholesterol levels, lower blood pressure, and decrease the risk of heart disease and stroke.

♦ Reduced Risk of Chronic Diseases: Following a Mediterranean diet has been associated with a lower risk of chronic diseases, including type 2 diabetes, certain types of cancer (such as breast and colorectal cancer), and neurodegenerative conditions like Alzheimer's disease. The abundance of plant-based foods, antioxidants, and anti-inflammatory compounds found in the diet contribute to these protective effects.

♦ Weight Management: The Mediterranean diet offers a balanced approach to weight management. It focuses on whole, nutrient-dense foods that are naturally lower in calories while providing high levels of satiety due to their fiber content. Additionally, the inclusion of healthy fats and lean proteins helps to control appetite and promote a sustainable approach to weight loss or maintenance.

♦ Improved Cognitive Function: The Mediterranean diet has been linked to better cognitive function and a reduced risk of cognitive decline. The combination of antioxidant-rich fruits and vegetables, omega-3 fatty acids from fish, and healthy fats like olive oil provides nourishment for the brain. This can help preserve memory, enhance cognitive performance, and reduce the risk of age-related cognitive impairment.

♦ Enhanced Gut Health: The Mediterranean diet, with its emphasis on whole grains, legumes, fruits, vegetables, and fermented dairy products like yogurt, promotes a healthy gut microbiome. The fiber-rich foods support the growth of beneficial gut bacteria, contributing to improved digestion, immune function, and overall gut health.

♦ Anti-Inflammatory Effects: Chronic inflammation is a significant contributor to many diseases. The Mediterranean diet, with its emphasis on whole foods and the presence of anti-inflammatory compounds, helps to combat inflammation in the body. The combination of antioxidants, monounsaturated fats, omega-3 fatty acids, and phytochemicals found in the diet work synergistically to reduce inflammation and promote overall well-being.

♦ Longevity: Studies consistently show that adhering to a Mediterranean diet is associated with increased longevity. The diet's protective effects against chronic diseases, heart health benefits, and overall nutrient-rich profile contribute to a longer and healthier life.

♦ Mental Well-being: The Mediterranean diet not only supports physical health but also positively impacts mental well-being. The inclusion of nutrient-dense foods and healthy fats helps support brain function, mood stability, and emotional well-being. Additionally, the social aspect of the Mediterranean lifestyle, with its emphasis on communal meals and social connections, contributes to a sense of belonging and happiness.

In summary, the Mediterranean diet offers a host of benefits, including improved heart health, reduced risk of chronic diseases, weight management, enhanced cognitive function, better gut health, anti-inflammatory effects, increased longevity, and positive mental well-being. By embracing the Mediterranean way of eating, you can nourish your body and enjoy a vibrant and fulfilling life.

What to Eat and Avoid on Mediterranean Diet

Foods to Eat

The Mediterranean diet is renowned for its emphasis on fresh, whole foods that are abundant in the Mediterranean region. This dietary pattern emphasizes the consumption of nutrient-dense ingredients that promote optimal health and well-being. Let's explore the wide variety of foods that are commonly enjoyed as part of the Mediterranean diet:

♦ Fruits and Vegetables: A wide array of fruits and vegetables are at the heart of the Mediterranean diet. Fresh, seasonal produce such as tomatoes, cucumbers, spinach, kale, eggplant, oranges, grapes, and figs are commonly enjoyed. These vibrant foods provide an abundance of vitamins, minerals, antioxidants, and fiber.

♦ Whole Grains: Whole grains like whole wheat, oats, barley, farro, brown rice, and couscous are staples of the Mediterranean diet. These grains are rich in fiber, vitamins, minerals, and complex carbohydrates. They provide sustained energy and contribute to feelings of satiety.

♦ Legumes: Legumes are a crucial part of the Mediterranean diet, including beans, lentils, chickpeas, and peas. These plant-based protein sources are rich in fiber, minerals, and antioxidants. Legumes are versatile ingredients that can be incorporated into soups, stews, salads, and side dishes.

♦ Healthy Fats: The Mediterranean diet emphasizes the consumption of healthy fats. Extra virgin olive oil is a primary source of fat, used for cooking, dressing salads, and drizzling over dishes. Other sources of healthy fats include avocados, nuts (such as almonds, walnuts, and pistachios), and seeds (like flaxseeds and chia seeds).

♦ Fish and Seafood: Fish and seafood are key components of the Mediterranean diet, providing lean protein and omega-3 fatty acids. Fatty fish like salmon, sardines, mackerel, and trout are particularly rich in these heart-healthy fats. Aim to include fish in your meals a few times per week.

♦ Poultry and Eggs: Poultry, such as chicken and turkey, is consumed in moderation in the Mediterranean diet. Eggs are also enjoyed as a source of protein and nutrients. Opt for lean cuts of poultry and pasture-raised or omega-3 enriched eggs whenever possible.

♦ Dairy Products: Dairy products like Greek yogurt and cheese are consumed in moderation in the Mediterranean diet. Greek yogurt is often preferred due to its higher protein content and probiotic benefits. Cheese, such as feta or goat cheese, is used to enhance the flavors of various dishes.

♦ Herbs and Spices: Herbs and spices play a vital role in Mediterranean cuisine, providing depth and flavor to dishes. Commonly used herbs include basil, oregano, rosemary, thyme, and mint. Spices like garlic, cinnamon, cumin, and paprika add a distinctive Mediterranean touch to recipes.

♦ Nuts and Seeds: Nuts and seeds are a nutritious and satisfying snack in the Mediterranean diet. Almonds, walnuts, pistachios, sesame seeds, and flaxseeds are excellent sources of healthy fats, protein, and fiber. They can be enjoyed on their own, added to salads, or used in cooking and baking.

♦ Hydration: While not a specific food, hydration is a fundamental aspect of the Mediterranean diet. Water is the primary beverage, and it is recommended to stay hydrated throughout the day. Herbal teas, such as chamomile or mint, are also commonly enjoyed.

These are just a few examples of the wide variety of foods enjoyed in the Mediterranean diet. The key is to prioritize whole, unprocessed foods, emphasize plant-based ingredients, and enjoy a diverse range of flavors and textures. By incorporating these foods into your daily meals, you can experience the many health benefits and delicious flavors of the Mediterranean diet.

Foods to Avoid

While the Mediterranean diet promotes the consumption of wholesome, nutrient-dense foods, it also suggests minimizing or avoiding certain foods that are less beneficial to overall health. By being mindful of these food choices, you can fully embrace the Mediterranean lifestyle. Here are some foods to limit or avoid when following the Mediterranean diet:

♦ Processed Meats: Highly processed meats like sausages, hot dogs, bacon, and deli meats should be limited or avoided. These meats often contain high levels of sodium, unhealthy fats, and preservatives that can have negative effects on health.

♦ Red and Processed Meats: While small amounts of lean, unprocessed red meat can be included in moderation, it is recommended to limit the consumption of red meat overall. Processed meats, such as sausages and cured meats, should be avoided due to their link to increased risks of certain diseases.

♦ Refined Grains: Refined grains, such as white bread, white rice, and refined pasta, have undergone processing that removes many beneficial nutrients and fiber. Instead, choose whole grains like whole wheat bread, whole grain pasta, and brown rice, which provide more fiber and nutrients.

♦ Added Sugars and Sweets: The Mediterranean diet emphasizes limiting the consumption of added sugars and sugary treats. This includes avoiding sugary beverages, processed snacks, candy, pastries, and desserts. Instead, opt for natural sources of sweetness like fresh fruit.

♦ Sodas and Sweetened Beverages: Sugar-sweetened beverages, including soda, fruit juices with added sugars, and energy drinks, should be avoided. These beverages are high in added sugars and provide little to no nutritional value. Water, herbal teas, and unsweetened beverages are preferable options.

♦ Trans Fats: Trans fats, commonly found in processed foods, fried foods, and certain margarines, have been linked to an increased risk of heart disease. It is best to avoid or minimize the consumption of foods containing trans fats and opt for healthier fat sources like olive oil and nuts.

♦ Excessive Salt: While a moderate amount of salt is acceptable, it's important to avoid excessive salt intake. Processed foods, canned soups, and packaged snacks often contain high amounts of sodium. Instead, use herbs, spices, and other seasonings to enhance the flavors of your dishes.

♦ Highly Processed and Fast Foods: Highly processed and fast foods are typically high in unhealthy fats, added sugars, sodium, and artificial additives. These foods often lack essential nutrients and contribute to poor health outcomes. It's best to prioritize fresh, whole foods prepared at home whenever possible.

Remember, the Mediterranean diet focuses on nourishing your body with whole, unprocessed foods that promote optimal health. By minimizing or avoiding these less beneficial foods, you can fully embrace the Mediterranean way of eating and experience its numerous health benefits.

Frequently Asked Questions

♦ Is the Mediterranean diet suitable for everyone?

Yes, the Mediterranean diet is generally considered suitable for people of all ages and backgrounds. It provides a balanced approach to nutrition and focuses on whole, nutrient-dense foods. However, it's always a good idea to consult with a healthcare professional before making significant changes to your diet, especially if you have specific health concerns or dietary restrictions.

♦ Can I lose weight on the Mediterranean diet?

The Mediterranean diet has been associated with weight loss and weight management. By emphasizing whole, unprocessed foods and encouraging portion control, it can help promote a healthy body weight. However, individual results may vary, and weight loss depends on various factors such as calorie intake, physical activity level, and overall lifestyle choices.

♦ Is the Mediterranean diet expensive?

The Mediterranean diet can be affordable and cost-effective, as it emphasizes whole, unprocessed foods that are widely available. By prioritizing seasonal, locally sourced ingredients and planning meals in advance, you can make the Mediterranean diet more budget-friendly. It's also important to remember that the diet encourages moderation, so you don't need to buy excessive amounts of expensive ingredients.

♦ Can I follow the Mediterranean diet if I have dietary restrictions?

Yes, the Mediterranean diet can be adaptable to different dietary restrictions. It offers a wide variety of plant-based options for vegetarians and vegans. For those with gluten intolerance, there are many gluten-free whole grains available. However, if you have specific dietary restrictions or allergies, it's essential to carefully read labels and make appropriate substitutions to ensure compliance with your dietary needs.

♦ Can I eat out while following the Mediterranean diet?

Yes, you can eat out and still adhere to the principles of the Mediterranean diet. Look for restaurants that offer Mediterranean-inspired dishes or focus on fresh, seasonal ingredients. Choose grilled or baked options, prioritize vegetables, and be mindful of portion sizes. You can also request modifications, such as swapping out sides or dressings, to make your meal more in line with the Mediterranean diet.

♦ Are there any health benefits to the Mediterranean diet?

Yes, the Mediterranean diet has been extensively studied and has been associated with numerous health benefits. It has been linked to a reduced risk of heart disease, stroke, type 2 diabetes, certain cancers, and cognitive decline. The diet's emphasis on whole, nutrient-dense foods, healthy fats, and antioxidants contributes to its positive impact on overall health and well-being.

♦ Can I still enjoy desserts on the Mediterranean diet?

While the Mediterranean diet encourages moderation, it is not focused on indulging in sweets and desserts regularly. However, there are many delicious Mediterranean-inspired dessert options that use ingredients like fruits, nuts, and honey. These options offer a healthier alternative to traditional sugary treats, allowing you to satisfy your sweet tooth while still adhering to the principles of the diet.

Remember, the Mediterranean diet is not a strict set of rules but rather a flexible and balanced approach to eating. It's about embracing whole, unprocessed foods, enjoying the pleasures of the table, and adopting a mindful, sustainable lifestyle. If you have specific questions or concerns, it's always a good idea to consult with a healthcare professional or registered dietitian who can provide personalized guidance based on your unique needs and goals.

Eating out can be an enjoyable experience, even when following a Mediterranean diet. While it may require some mindful choices, there are plenty of ways to stay true to the principles of the Mediterranean diet while dining at restaurants. Here are some helpful tips for eating out:

♦ Research the Restaurant: Before heading out, take some time to research the restaurant you plan to visit. Look for establishments that offer Mediterranean-inspired or healthy menu options. Many restaurants now provide their menus online, allowing you to review the options in advance and make a more informed choice.

♦ Choose Grilled, Steamed, or Baked: When selecting your main dish, opt for grilled, steamed, or baked preparations instead of fried or breaded options. These cooking methods retain more of the natural flavors and nutrients of the food while reducing the added fats and calories.

♦ Prioritize Vegetables and Salads: Look for dishes that feature an abundance of vegetables or include a side salad. Vegetables are a cornerstone of the Mediterranean diet, providing a wide range of nutrients, fiber, and antioxidants. Request dressings and sauces on the side to control the amount you consume.

♦ Request Substitutions: Don't be afraid to ask for substitutions or modifications to your meal. For example, you can replace French fries with a side of steamed vegetables or opt for whole grain bread instead of white bread. Most restaurants are accommodating and willing to make adjustments to meet your dietary preferences.

♦ Control Portion Sizes: Restaurant servings can often be larger than what we need. Consider sharing a dish with a dining companion or ask for a takeout container at the beginning of the meal to portion out an appropriate serving size. This way, you can enjoy your meal without overindulging.

♦ Be Mindful of Sauces and Dressings: Many sauces and dressings can be high in unhealthy fats, added sugars, and sodium. Request sauces and dressings on the side so that you can control the amount you use or opt for lighter options like vinaigrettes or olive oil-based dressings.

♦ Choose Whole Grains: If the restaurant offers whole grain options, such as whole wheat bread or brown rice, choose those over refined grains. Whole grains provide more fiber and nutrients, keeping you fuller for longer and contributing to a more balanced meal.

♦ Enjoy the Social Aspect: The Mediterranean diet is not just about the food but also about the enjoyment of meals with family and friends. Embrace the social aspect of dining out, engage in conversation, and savor each bite mindfully. Eating slowly and paying attention to your body's signals of fullness can help prevent overeating.

♦ Hydration is Key: Opt for water or unsweetened beverages to stay hydrated. Avoid sugary sodas and opt for herbal teas, sparkling water, or infused water for a refreshing and healthier choice.

♦ Be Flexible and Enjoy the Experience: While it's important to make mindful choices, it's also essential to be flexible and enjoy the dining experience. If you can't find a perfect Mediterranean option, choose the best available option and focus on the overall balance of your diet.

Remember, the Mediterranean diet is a flexible and adaptable way of eating. By applying these tips and making conscious choices, you can maintain your commitment to the Mediterranean lifestyle while enjoying the experience of eating out.

30 Days Mediterranean Diet Meal Plan

DAYS	BREAKFAST	LUNCH	DINNER	SNACK/DESSERT
1	Spinach Pie	Greek Bean Soup	Citrus Fennel Salad	Nut Butter Cup Fat Bomb
2	Peachy Green Smoothie	Sesame-Ginger Broccoli	Chopped Greek Antipasto Salad	Ricotta Cheesecake
3	Mediterranean Muesli and Breakfast Bowl	Zesty Cabbage Soup	Pistachio-Parmesan Kale-Arugula Salad	Strawberry-Pomegranate Molasses Sauce
4	Broccoli-Mushroom Frittata	Roasted Harissa Carrots	Turkish Shepherd'S Salad	Blueberry Panna Cotta
5	Enjoy-Your-Veggies Breakfast	Garlicky Broccoli Rabe with Artichokes	Greek Village Salad	Creamy Spiced Almond Milk
6	Greek Yogurt and Berries	Roasted Vegetables with Lemon Tahini	Italian Coleslaw	Individual Apple Pockets
7	Strawberry Collagen Smoothie	Baba Ghanoush	Toasted Pita Bread Salad	Apple and Brown Rice Pudding
8	Ricotta and Fruit Bruschetta	Honey and Spice Glazed Carrots	Superfood Salmon Salad Bowl	Greek Yogurt Ricotta Mousse
9	Red Pepper and Feta Egg Bites	Greek Stewed Zucchini	Italian White Bean Salad with Bell Peppers	Strawberry Ricotta Parfaits
10	Breakfast Pita	Indian Eggplant Bharta	Beets with Goat Cheese and Chermoula	Grilled Peaches with Greek Yogurt
11	Buffalo Egg Cups	Zucchini Pomodoro	Spanish Potato Salad	Slow-Cooked Fruit Medley
12	Morning Buzz Iced Coffee	Caesar Whole Cauliflower	Traditional Greek Salad	Lemon Berry Cream Pops
13	Cauliflower Avocado Toast	Hearty Minestrone Soup	Wilted Kale Salad	Banana Cream Pie Parfaits
14	Mushroom-and-Tomato Stuffed Hash Browns	Rosemary-Roasted Red Potatoes	Arugula and Fennel Salad with Fresh Basil	Blueberry Pomegranate Granita
15	Quinoa and Yogurt Breakfast Bowls	Artichokes Provençal	Fruited Chicken Salad	Chocolate Turtle Hummus
16	Spinach and Feta Egg Bake	Parmesan-Thyme Butternut Squash	Red Pepper, Pomegranate, and Walnut Salad	Vanilla-Poached Apricots
17	Herb & Cheese Fritters	Spinach and Sweet Pepper Poppers	No-Mayo Florence Tuna Salad	Honey Ricotta with Espresso and Chocolate Chips
18	Breakfast Hash	Superflax Tortillas	Tabbouleh	Lemon Fool

DAYS	BREAKFAST	LUNCH	DINNER	SNACK/DESSERT
19	Almond Date Oatmeal	Lemony Orzo	Baked Falafel Sliders	Chocolate-Dipped Fruit Bites
20	Mexican Breakfast Pepper Rings	Toasted Grain and Almond Pilaf	Linguine and Brussels Sprouts	Greek Island Almond Cocoa Bites
21	Mediterranean Frittata	Ratatouille	Stuffed Portobellos	Figs with Mascarpone and Honey
22	Garlicky Beans and Greens with Polenta	Garlicky Sautéed Zucchini with Mint	Crispy Tofu	Steamed Dessert Bread
23	Veggie Hash with Eggs	Garlic Roasted Broccoli	Crispy Eggplant Rounds	Minty Watermelon Salad
24	Turkish Egg Bowl	Crispy Garlic Oven Potatoes	Freekeh, Chickpea, and Herb Salad	Light and Lemony Olive Oil Cupcakes
25	Egg Baked in Avocado	Parmesan Mushrooms	Fava Bean Purée with Chicory	Fresh Figs with Chocolate Sauce
26	Greek Yogurt Parfait with Granola	Zesty Fried Asparagus	Cauliflower Steak with Gremolata	Mediterranean Orange Yogurt Cake
27	Greek Egg and Tomato Scramble	Corn on the Cob	Broccoli-Cheese Fritters	Dried Fruit Compote
28	Oat and Fruit Parfait	Sautéed Garlic Spinach	Crustless Spinach Cheese Pie	Tortilla Fried Pies
29	Oatmeal with Apple and Cardamom	Puréed Cauliflower Soup	Tortellini in Red Pepper Sauce	Golden Coconut Cream Pops
30	Whole Wheat Blueberry Muffins	Asparagus Fries	Kate's Warm Mediterranean Farro Bowl	Almond Cookies

Chapter 2 Breakfasts

Greek Yogurt and Berries

Prep time: 5 minutes | Cook time: 30 minutes | Serves 4

4 cups plain full-fat Greek yogurt
1 cup granola
½ cup blackberries
2 bananas, sliced and frozen
1 teaspoon chia seeds, for

topping
1 teaspoon chopped fresh mint leaves, for topping
4 teaspoons honey, for topping (optional)

1. Evenly divide the yogurt among four bowls. Top with the granola, blackberries, bananas, chia seeds, mint, and honey (if desired), dividing evenly among the bowls. Serve.

Per Serving:
calories: 283 | fat: 9g | protein: 12g | carbs: 42g | fiber: 5g | sodium: 115mg

Spinach Pie

Prep time: 10 minutes | Cook time: 25 minutes | Serves 8

Nonstick cooking spray
2 tablespoons extra-virgin olive oil
1 onion, chopped
1 pound (454 g) frozen spinach, thawed
¼ teaspoon garlic salt
¼ teaspoon freshly ground black pepper

¼ teaspoon ground nutmeg
4 large eggs, divided
1 cup grated Parmesan cheese, divided
2 puff pastry doughs, (organic, if available), at room temperature
4 hard-boiled eggs, halved

1. Preheat the oven to 350°F(180°C). Spray a baking sheet with nonstick cooking spray and set aside. 2. Heat a large sauté pan or skillet over medium-high heat. Put in the oil and onion and cook for about 5 minutes, until translucent. 3. Squeeze the excess water from the spinach, then add to the pan and cook, uncovered, so that any excess water from the spinach can evaporate. Add the garlic salt, pepper, and nutmeg. Remove from heat and set aside to cool. 4. In a small bowl, crack 3 eggs and mix well. Add the eggs and ½ cup Parmesan cheese to the cooled spinach mix. 5. On the prepared baking sheet, roll out the pastry dough. Layer the spinach mix on top of dough, leaving 2 inches around each edge. 6. Once the spinach is spread onto the pastry dough, place hard-boiled egg halves evenly throughout the pie, then cover with the second pastry dough. Pinch the edges closed. 7. Crack the remaining egg in a small bowl and mix well. Brush the egg wash over the pastry dough. 8. Bake for 15 to 20 minutes, until golden brown and warmed through.

Per Serving:
calories: 417 | fat: 28g | protein: 17g | carbs: 25g | fiber: 3g | sodium: 490mg

Polenta with Sautéed Chard and Fried Eggs

Prep time: 5 minutes | Cook time: 20 minutes | Serves 4

For the Polenta:

2½ cups water
½ teaspoon kosher salt
¾ cups whole-grain cornmeal
¼ teaspoon freshly ground

black pepper
2 tablespoons grated Parmesan cheese

For the Chard:

1 tablespoon extra-virgin olive oil
1 bunch (about 6 ounces / 170 g) Swiss chard, leaves and stems chopped and separated

2 garlic cloves, sliced
¼ teaspoon kosher salt
⅛ teaspoon freshly ground black pepper
Lemon juice (optional)

For the Eggs:

1 tablespoon extra-virgin olive oil

4 large eggs

Make the Polenta: 1. Bring the water and salt to a boil in a medium saucepan over high heat. Slowly add the cornmeal, whisking constantly. 2. Decrease the heat to low, cover, and cook for 10 to 15 minutes, stirring often to avoid lumps. Stir in the pepper and Parmesan, and divide among 4 bowls. Make the Chard: 3. Heat the oil in a large skillet over medium heat. Add the chard stems, garlic, salt, and pepper; sauté for 2 minutes. Add the chard leaves and cook until wilted, about 3 to 5 minutes. 4. Add a spritz of lemon juice (if desired), toss together, and divide evenly on top of the polenta. Make the Eggs: 5. Heat the oil in the same large skillet over medium-high heat. Crack each egg into the skillet, taking care not to crowd the skillet and leaving space between the eggs. Cook until the whites are set and golden around the edges, about 2 to 3 minutes. 6. Serve sunny-side up or flip the eggs over carefully and cook 1 minute longer for over easy. Place one egg on top of the polenta and chard in each bowl.

Per Serving:
calories: 310 | fat: 18g | protein: 17g | carbs: 21g | fiber: 1g | sodium: 500mg

Broccoli-Mushroom Frittata

Prep time: 10 minutes | Cook time: 20 minutes | Serves 2

1 tablespoon olive oil
1½ cups broccoli florets, finely chopped
½ cup sliced brown mushrooms
¼ cup finely chopped onion
½ teaspoon salt
¼ teaspoon freshly ground black pepper
6 eggs
¼ cup Parmesan cheese

1. In a nonstick cake pan, combine the olive oil, broccoli, mushrooms, onion, salt, and pepper. Stir until the vegetables are thoroughly coated with oil. Place the cake pan in the air fryer basket and set the air fryer to 400ºF (204ºC). Air fry for 5 minutes until the vegetables soften. 2. Meanwhile, in a medium bowl, whisk the eggs and Parmesan until thoroughly combined. Pour the egg mixture into the pan and shake gently to distribute the vegetables. Air fry for another 15 minutes until the eggs are set. 3. Remove from the air fryer and let sit for 5 minutes to cool slightly. Use a silicone spatula to gently lift the frittata onto a plate before serving.

Per Serving:

calories: 329 | fat: 23g | protein: 24g | carbs: 6g | fiber: 0g | sodium: 793mg

Enjoy-Your-Veggies Breakfast

Prep time: 20 minutes | Cook time: 10 minutes | Serves 4

1 tablespoon olive oil
1 small sweet onion, peeled and diced
2 large carrots, peeled and diced
2 medium potatoes, peeled and diced
1 stalk celery, diced
1 large red bell pepper, seeded and diced
1 tablespoon low-sodium soy
sauce
¼ cup water
1 cup diced peeled zucchini or summer squash
2 medium tomatoes, peeled and diced
2 cups cooked brown rice
½ teaspoon ground black pepper

1. Press the Sauté button on the Instant Pot® and heat oil. Add onion and cook until just tender, about 2 minutes. 2. Stir in carrots, potatoes, celery, and bell pepper and cook until just tender, about 2 minutes. Add soy sauce and water. Press the Cancel button. 3. Close lid, set steam release to Sealing, press the Manual button, and set time to 2 minutes. When the timer beeps, quick-release the pressure until the float valve drops. Press the Cancel button. 4. Open lid and add squash and tomatoes, and stir. Close lid, set steam release to Sealing, press the Manual button, and set time to 1 minute. When the timer beeps, quick-release the pressure until the float valve drops. Press the Cancel button and open lid. 5. Serve over rice and sprinkle with black pepper.

Per Serving:

calories: 224 | fat: 5g | protein: 6g | carbs: 41g | fiber: 5g | sodium: 159mg

Herb & Cheese Fritters

Prep time: 10 minutes | Cook time: 15 minutes | Serves 5

3 medium zucchini
8 ounces (227 g) frozen spinach, thawed and squeezed dry (weight excludes water squeezed out)
4 large eggs
½ teaspoon salt
¼ teaspoon black pepper
3 tablespoons flax meal or
coconut flour
¼ cup grated Pecorino Romano
2 cloves garlic, minced
¼ cup chopped fresh herbs, such as parsley, basil, oregano, mint, chives, and/or thyme
¼ cup extra-virgin avocado oil or ghee

1. Grate the zucchini and place in a bowl lined with cheesecloth. Set aside for 5 minutes, then twist the cheesecloth around the zucchini and squeeze out as much liquid as you can. You should end up with about 13 ounces (370 g) of drained zucchini. 2. In a mixing bowl, combine the zucchini, spinach, eggs, salt, and pepper. Add the flax meal and Pecorino and stir again. Add the garlic and herbs and mix through. 3. Heat a large pan greased with 1 tablespoon of ghee over medium heat. Once hot, use a ¼-cup measuring cup to make the fritters (about 57 g/2 ounces each). Place in the hot pan and shape with a spatula. Cook in batches for 3 to 4 minutes per side, until crisp and golden. Grease the pan between each batch until all the ghee has been used. 4. Eat warm or cold, as a breakfast, side, or snack. Store in the fridge for up to 4 days or freeze for up to 3 months.

Per Serving:

calories: 239 | fat: 20g | protein: 10g | carbs: 8g | fiber: 3g | sodium: 426mg

Grilled Halloumi with Whole-Wheat Pita Bread

Prep time: 5 minutes | Cook time: 10 minutes | Serves 4

2 teaspoons olive oil
8 (½-inch-thick) slices of halloumi cheese
4 whole-wheat pita rounds
1 Persian cucumber, thinly sliced
1 large tomato, sliced
½ cup pitted Kalamata olives

1. Brush a bit of olive oil on a grill pan and heat it over medium-high heat. 2. Brush the cheese slices all over with olive oil. Add the cheese slices in a single layer and cook until grill marks appear on the bottom, about 3 minutes. Flip the slices over and grill until grill marks appear on the second side, about 2 to 3 minutes more. 3. While the cheese is cooking, heat the pita bread, either in a skillet or in a toaster. 4. Serve the cheese inside of the pita pockets with the sliced cucumber, tomato, and olives.

Per Serving:

calories: 358 | fat: 24g | protein: 17g | carbs: 21g | fiber: 4g | sodium: 612mg

Savory Feta, Spinach, and Red Pepper Muffins

Prep time: 10 minutes | Cook time: 22 minutes | Serves 12

2 cups all-purpose flour
¾ cup whole-wheat flour
¼ cup granulated sugar
2 teaspoons baking powder
1 teaspoon paprika
¾ teaspoonp salt
½ cup extra virgin olive oil
2 eggs
¾ cup low-fat 2% milk
¾ cup crumbled feta
1¼ cups fresh baby leaf spinach, thinly sliced
⅓ cup jarred red peppers, drained, patted dry, and chopped

1. Preheat the oven to 375°F (190°C) and line a large muffin pan with 12 muffin liners. 2. In a large bowl, combine the all-purpose flour, whole-wheat flour, sugar, baking powder, paprika, and salt. Mix well.3.In a medium bowl, whisk the olive oil, eggs, and milk. 4. Add the wet ingredients to the dry ingredients, and use a wooden spoon to stir until the ingredients are just blended and form a thick dough. 5. Add the feta, spinach, and peppers, and mix gently until all the ingredients are incorporated. Evenly divide the mixture among the muffin liners. 6. Transfer to the oven, and bake for 25 minutes or until a toothpick inserted into the middle of a muffin comes out clean. 7. Set the muffins aside to cool for 10 minutes, and remove them from the pan. Store in an airtight container in the refrigerator for up to 3 days. (Remove from the refrigerator 10 minutes before consuming.)

Per Serving:

calories: 243 | fat: 12g | protein: 6g | carbs: 27g | fiber: 2g | sodium: 306mg

Egg Baked in Avocado

Prep time: 5 minutes | Cook time: 15 minutes | Serves 2

1 ripe large avocado
2 large eggs
Salt
Freshly ground black pepper
4 tablespoons jarred pesto, for
serving
2 tablespoons chopped tomato, for serving
2 tablespoons crumbled feta, for serving (optional)

1. Preheat the oven to 425°F(220ºC). 2. Slice the avocado in half and remove the pit. Scoop out about 1 to 2 tablespoons from each half to create a hole large enough to fit an egg. Place the avocado halves on a baking sheet, cut-side up. 3. Crack 1 egg in each avocado half and season with salt and pepper. 4. Bake until the eggs are set and cooked to desired level of doneness, 10 to 15 minutes. 5. Remove from oven and top each avocado with 2 tablespoons pesto, 1 tablespoon chopped tomato, and 1 tablespoon crumbled feta (if using).

Per Serving:

calories: 248 | fat: 23g | protein: 10g | carbs: 2g | fiber: 1g | sodium: 377mg

Peachy Green Smoothie

Prep time: 10 minutes | Cook time: 0 minutes | Serves 2

1 cup almond milk
3 cups kale or spinach
1 banana, peeled
1 orange, peeled
1 small green apple
1 cup frozen peaches
¼ cup vanilla Greek yogurt

1. Put the ingredients in a blender in the order listed and blend on high until smooth. 2. Serve and enjoy.

Per Serving:

calories: 257 | fat: 5g | protein: 9g | carbs: 50g | fiber: 7g | sodium: 87mg

Honey-Vanilla Greek Yogurt with Blueberries

Prep time: 2 minutes| Cook time: 0 minutes | Serves 2 to3

2 cups plain Greek yogurt
¼ to ½ cup honey
¾ teaspoon vanilla extract
1 cup blueberries

1. In a medium bowl, stir together the yogurt, honey (start with the smaller amount; you can always add more later), and vanilla. Taste and add additional honey, if needed. 2. To serve, spoon the sweetened yogurt mixture into bowls and top with the blueberries.

Per Serving:

calories: 295 | fat: 0g | protein: 23g | carbs: 55g | fiber: 2g | sodium: 82mg

Mediterranean-Inspired White Smoothie

Prep time: 5 minutes | Cook time: 0 minutes | Serves

½ medium apple (any variety), peeled, halved, and seeded
5 roasted almonds
½ medium frozen banana, sliced (be sure to peel the
banana before freezing)
¼ cup full-fat Greek yogurt
½ cup low-fat 1% milk
¼ teaspoon ground cinnamon
½ teaspoon honey

1. Combine all the ingredients in a blender. Process until smooth. 2. Pour into a glass and serve promptly. (This recipe is best consumed fresh.)

Per Serving:

calories: 236 | fat: 7g | protein: 8g | carbs: 40g | fiber: 5g | sodium: 84mg

Breakfast Panini with Eggs, Olives, and Tomatoes

Prep time: 5 minutes | Cook time: 0 minutes | Serves 4

1 (12-ounce / 340-g) round whole-wheat pagnotta foggiana or other round, crusty bread
2 tablespoons olive oil
½ cup sliced pitted cured olives, such as Kalamata
8 hard-boiled eggs, peeled and sliced into rounds
2 medium tomatoes, thinly sliced into rounds
12 large leaves fresh basil

1. Split the bread horizontally and brush the cut sides with the olive oil. 2. Arrange the sliced olives on the bottom half of the bread in a single layer. Top with a layer of the egg slices, then the tomato slices, and finally the basil leaves. Cut the sandwich into quarters and serve immediately.

Per Serving:

calories: 427 | fat: 21g | protein: 23g | carbs: 39g | fiber: 7g | sodium: 674mg

Breakfast Pita

Prep time: 5 minutes | Cook time: 6 minutes | Serves 2

1 whole wheat pita
2 teaspoons olive oil
½ shallot, diced
¼ teaspoon garlic, minced
1 large egg
¼ teaspoon dried oregano
¼ teaspoon dried thyme
⅛ teaspoon salt
2 tablespoons shredded Parmesan cheese

1. Preheat the air fryer to 380°F(193ºC). 2. Brush the top of the pita with olive oil, then spread the diced shallot and minced garlic over the pita. 3. Crack the egg into a small bowl or ramekin, and season it with oregano, thyme, and salt. 4. Place the pita into the air fryer basket, and gently pour the egg onto the top of the pita. Sprinkle with cheese over the top. 5. Bake for 6 minutes. 6. Allow to cool for 5 minutes before cutting into pieces for serving.

Per Serving:

calories: 191 | fat: 10g | protein: 8g | carbs: 19g | fiber: 3g | sodium: 312mg

Buffalo Egg Cups

Prep time: 10 minutes | Cook time: 15 minutes | Serves 2

4 large eggs
2 ounces (57 g) full-fat cream cheese
2 tablespoons buffalo sauce
½ cup shredded sharp Cheddar cheese

1. Crack eggs into two ramekins. 2. In a small microwave-safe bowl, mix cream cheese, buffalo sauce, and Cheddar. Microwave for 20 seconds and then stir. Place a spoonful into each ramekin on top of the eggs. 3. Place ramekins into the air fryer basket. 4. Adjust the temperature to 320ºF (160ºC) and bake for 15 minutes. 5. Serve warm.

Per Serving:

calories: 354 | fat: 29g | protein: 21g | carbs: 3g | fiber: 0g | sodium: 343mg

Morning Buzz Iced Coffee

Prep time: 10 minutes | Cook time: 0 minutes | Serves 1

1 cup freshly brewed strong black coffee, cooled slightly
1 tablespoon extra-virgin olive oil
1 tablespoon half-and-half or
heavy cream (optional)
1 teaspoon MCT oil (optional)
⅛ teaspoon almond extract
⅛ teaspoon ground cinnamon

1. Pour the slightly cooled coffee into a blender or large glass (if using an immersion blender). 2. Add the olive oil, half-and-half (if using), MCT oil (if using), almond extract, and cinnamon. 3. Blend well until smooth and creamy. Drink warm and enjoy.

Per Serving:

calories: 124 | fat: 14g | protein: 0g | carbs: 0g | fiber: 0g | sodium: 5mg

Cauliflower Avocado Toast

Prep time: 15 minutes | Cook time: 8 minutes | Serves 2

1 (12-ounce / 340-g) steamer bag cauliflower
1 large egg
½ cup shredded Mozzarella cheese
1 ripe medium avocado
½ teaspoon garlic powder
¼ teaspoon ground black pepper

1. Cook cauliflower according to package instructions. Remove from bag and place into cheesecloth or clean towel to remove excess moisture. 2. Place cauliflower into a large bowl and mix in egg and Mozzarella. Cut a piece of parchment to fit your air fryer basket. Separate the cauliflower mixture into two, and place it on the parchment in two mounds. Press out the cauliflower mounds into a ¼-inch-thick rectangle. Place the parchment into the air fryer basket. 3. Adjust the temperature to 400ºF (204ºC) and set the timer for 8 minutes. 4. Flip the cauliflower halfway through the cooking time. 5. When the timer beeps, remove the parchment and allow the cauliflower to cool 5 minutes. 6. Cut open the avocado and remove the pit. Scoop out the inside, place it in a medium bowl, and mash it with garlic powder and pepper. Spread onto the cauliflower. Serve immediately.

Per Serving:

calories: 321 | fat: 22g | protein: 16g | carbs: 19g | fiber: 10g | sodium: 99mg

Strawberry Collagen Smoothie

Prep time: 5 minutes | Cook time: 0 minutes | Serves 1

3 ounces (85 g) fresh or frozen strawberries
¾ cup unsweetened almond milk
¼ cup coconut cream or goat's cream
1 large egg
1 tablespoon chia seeds or flax meal

2 tablespoons grass-fed collagen powder
¼ teaspoon vanilla powder or 1 teaspoon unsweetened vanilla extract
Zest from ½ lemon
1 tablespoon macadamia oil
Optional: ice cubes, to taste

1. Place all of the ingredients in a blender and pulse until smooth and frothy. Serve immediately.

Per Serving:

calories: 515 | fat: 42g | protein: 10g | carbs: 30g | fiber: 4g | sodium: 202mg

Spinach, Sun-Dried Tomato, and Feta Egg Wraps

Prep time: 10 minutes | Cook time: 7 minutes | Serves 2

1 tablespoon olive oil
¼ cup minced onion
3 to 4 tablespoons minced sun-dried tomatoes in olive oil and herbs
3 large eggs, beaten

1½ cups packed baby spinach
1 ounce (28 g) crumbled feta cheese
Salt
2 (8-inch) whole-wheat tortillas

1. In a large skillet, heat the olive oil over medium-high heat. Add the onion and tomatoes and sauté for about 3 minutes. 2. Turn the heat down to medium. Add the beaten eggs and stir to scramble them. 3. Add the spinach and stir to combine. Sprinkle the feta cheese over the eggs. Add salt to taste. 4. Warm the tortillas in the microwave for about 20 seconds each. 5. Fill each tortilla with half of the egg mixture. Fold in half or roll them up and serve.

Per Serving:

calories: 435 | fat: 28g | protein: 17g | carbs: 31g | fiber: 6g | sodium: 552mg

Red Pepper and Feta Egg Bites

Prep time: 5 minutes | Cook time: 8 minutes | Serves 6

1 tablespoon olive oil
½ cup crumbled feta cheese
¼ cup chopped roasted red peppers

6 large eggs, beaten
¼ teaspoon ground black pepper
1 cup water

1. Brush silicone muffin or poaching cups with oil. Divide feta and roasted red peppers among prepared cups. In a bowl with a pour spout, beat eggs with black pepper. 2. Place rack in the Instant Pot® and add water. Place cups on rack. Pour egg mixture into cups. Close lid, set steam release to Sealing, press the Manual button, and set time to 8 minutes. 3. When the timer beeps, quick-release the pressure until the float valve drops and open lid. Remove silicone cups carefully and slide eggs from cups onto plates. Serve warm.

Per Serving:

calories: 145 | fat: 11g | protein: 10g | carbs: 3g | fiber: 1g | sodium: 294mg

Whole-Wheat Toast with Apricots, Blue Cheese, and Honey

Prep time: 5 minutes | Cook time: 5 minutes | Serves 2

2 thick slices crusty whole-wheat bread
1 tablespoon olive oil
2 apricots, halved and cut into ¼-inch-thick slices

2 ounces (57 g) blue cheese
2 tablespoons honey
2 tablespoons toasted slivered almonds

1. Preheat the broiler to high. 2. Brush the bread on both sides with the olive oil. Arrange the slices on a baking sheet and broil until lightly browned, about 2 minutes per side. 3. Arrange the apricot slices on the toasted bread, dividing equally. Sprinkle the cheese over the top, dividing equally. Return the baking sheet to the broiler and broil for 1 to 2 minutes until the cheese melts and just begins to brown. Remove from the oven and serve drizzled with honey and garnished with the toasted almonds.

Per Serving:

calories: 379 | fat: 20g | protein: 13g | carbs: 40g | fiber: 4g | sodium: 595mg

Ricotta and Fruit Bruschetta

Prep time: 5 minutes | Cook time: 0 minutes | Serves 2

¼ cup full-fat ricotta cheese
1½ teaspoons honey, divided
3 drops almond extract
2 slices whole-grain bread, toasted
½ medium banana, peeled and

cut into ¼-inch slices
½ medium pear (any variety), thinly sliced
2 teaspoons chopped walnuts
2 pinches of ground cinnamon

1. In a small bowl, combine the ricotta, ¼ teaspoon honey, and the almond extract. Stir well. 2. Spread 1½ tablespoons of the ricotta mixture over each slice of toast. 3. Divide the pear slices and banana slices equally on top of each slice of toast. 4. Drizzle equal amounts of the remaining honey over each slice, and sprinkle 1 teaspoon of the walnuts over each slice. Top each serving with a pinch of cinnamon.

Per Serving:

calories: 207 | fat: 7g | protein: 8g | carbs: 30g | fiber: 4g | sodium: 162mg

Veggie Hash with Eggs

Prep time: 20 minutes | Cook time: 6¼ hours |
Serves 2

Nonstick cooking spray
1 onion, chopped
2 garlic cloves, minced
1 red bell pepper, chopped
1 yellow summer squash, chopped
2 carrots, chopped
2 Yukon Gold potatoes, peeled and chopped
2 large tomatoes, seeded and

chopped
¼ cup vegetable broth
½ teaspoon salt
⅛ teaspoon freshly ground black pepper
½ teaspoon dried thyme leaves
3 or 4 eggs
½ teaspoon ground sweet paprika

1. Spray the slow cooker with the nonstick cooking spray. 2. In the slow cooker, combine all the ingredients except the eggs and paprika, and stir. 3. Cover and cook on low for 6 hours. 4. Uncover and make 1 indentation in the vegetable mixture for each egg. Break 1 egg into a small cup and slip the egg into an indentation. Repeat with the remaining eggs. Sprinkle with the paprika. 5. Cover and cook on low for 10 to 15 minutes, or until the eggs are just set, and serve.

Per Serving:

calories: 381 | fat: 8g | protein: 17g | carbs: 64g | fiber: 12g | sodium: 747mg

Mediterranean Muesli and Breakfast Bowl

Prep time: 10 minutes | Cook time: 0 minutes |
Serves 12

Muesli:

3 cups old-fashioned rolled oats
1 cup wheat or rye flakes
1 cup pistachios or almonds, coarsely chopped

½ cup oat bran
8 dried apricots, chopped
8 dates, chopped
8 dried figs, chopped

Breakfast Bowl:

½ cup Mediterranean Muesli (above)
1 cup low-fat plain Greek yogurt or milk

2 tablespoons pomegranate seeds (optional)
½ teaspoon black or white sesame seeds

1. To make the muesli: In a medium bowl, combine the oats, wheat or rye flakes, pistachios or almonds, oat bran, apricots, dates, and figs. Transfer to an airtight container and store for up to 1 month. 2. To make the breakfast bowl: In a bowl, combine the muesli with the yogurt or milk. Top with the pomegranate seeds, if using, and the sesame seeds.

Per Serving:

calories: 234 | fat: 6g | protein: 8g | carbs: 40g | fiber: 6g | sodium: 54mg

Butternut Squash and Ricotta Frittata

Prep time: 10 minutes | Cook time: 33 minutes |
Serves 2 to 3

1 cup cubed (½-inch) butternut squash (5½ ounces / 156 g)
2 tablespoons olive oil
Kosher salt and freshly ground black pepper, to taste

4 fresh sage leaves, thinly sliced
6 large eggs, lightly beaten
½ cup ricotta cheese
Cayenne pepper

1. In a bowl, toss the squash with the olive oil and season with salt and black pepper until evenly coated. Sprinkle the sage on the bottom of a cake pan and place the squash on top. Place the pan in the air fryer and bake at 400ºF (204ºC) for 10 minutes. Stir to incorporate the sage, then cook until the squash is tender and lightly caramelized at the edges, about 3 minutes more. 2. Pour the eggs over the squash, dollop the ricotta all over, and sprinkle with cayenne. Bake at 300ºF (149ºC) until the eggs are set and the frittata is golden brown on top, about 20 minutes. Remove the pan from the air fryer and cut the frittata into wedges to serve.

Per Serving:

calories: 289 | fat: 22g | protein: 18g | carbs: 5g | fiber: 1g | sodium: 184mg

Mushroom-and-Tomato Stuffed Hash Browns

Prep time: 10 minutes | Cook time: 20 minutes |
Serves 4

Olive oil cooking spray
1 tablespoon plus 2 teaspoons olive oil, divided
4 ounces (113 g) baby bella mushrooms, diced
1 scallion, white parts and green parts, diced

1 garlic clove, minced
2 cups shredded potatoes
½ teaspoon salt
¼ teaspoon black pepper
1 Roma tomato, diced
½ cup shredded mozzarella

1. Preheat the air fryer to 380°F(193ºC). Lightly coat the inside of a 6-inch cake pan with olive oil cooking spray. 2. In a small skillet, heat 2 teaspoons olive oil over medium heat. Add the mushrooms, scallion, and garlic, and cook for 4 to 5 minutes, or until they have softened and are beginning to show some color. Remove from heat. 3. Meanwhile, in a large bowl, combine the potatoes, salt, pepper, and the remaining tablespoon olive oil. Toss until all potatoes are well coated. 4. Pour half of the potatoes into the bottom of the cake pan. Top with the mushroom mixture, tomato, and mozzarella. Spread the remaining potatoes over the top. 5. Bake in the air fryer for 12 to 15 minutes, or until the top is golden brown. 6. Remove from the air fryer and allow to cool for 5 minutes before slicing and serving.

Per Serving:

calories: 165 | fat: 9g | protein: 6g | carbs: 16g | fiber: 3g | sodium: 403mg

Quinoa and Yogurt Breakfast Bowls

Prep time: 10 minutes | Cook time: 12 minutes |
Serves 8

2 cups quinoa, rinsed and drained
4 cups water
1 teaspoon vanilla extract
¼ teaspoon salt

2 cups low-fat plain Greek yogurt
2 cups blueberries
1 cup toasted almonds
½ cup pure maple syrup

1. Place quinoa, water, vanilla, and salt in the Instant Pot®. Close lid and set steam release to Sealing. Press the Rice button and set time to 12 minutes. 2. When the timer beeps, let pressure release naturally, about 20 minutes. Open lid and fluff quinoa with a fork. 3. Stir in yogurt. Serve warm, topped with berries, almonds, and maple syrup.

Per Serving:

calories: 376 | fat: 13g | protein: 16g | carbs: 52g | fiber: 6g | sodium: 105mg

Oatmeal with Apple and Cardamom

Prep time: 10 minutes | Cook time: 7 minutes |
Serves 4

1 tablespoon light olive oil
1 large Granny Smith, Honeycrisp, or Pink Lady apple, peeled, cored, and diced
½ teaspoon ground cardamom

1 cup steel-cut oats
3 cups water
¼ cup maple syrup
½ teaspoon salt

1. Press the Sauté button on the Instant Pot® and heat oil. Add apple and cardamom and cook until apple is just softened, about 2 minutes. Press the Cancel button. 2. Add oats, water, maple syrup, and salt to pot, and stir well. Close lid, set steam release to Sealing, press the Manual button, and set time to 5 minutes. 3. When the timer beeps, let pressure release naturally for 10 minutes, then quick-release the remaining pressure until the float valve drops. Press the Cancel button, open lid, and stir well. Serve hot.

Per Serving:

calories: 249 | fat: 6g | protein: 6g | carbs: 48g | fiber: 5g | sodium: 298mg

Oat and Fruit Parfait

Prep time: 5 minutes | Cook time: 12 minutes |
Serves 2

½ cup whole-grain rolled or quickcooking oats (not instant)
½ cup walnut pieces
1 teaspoon honey

1 cup sliced fresh strawberries
1½ cups vanilla low-fat Greek yogurt
Fresh mint leaves for garnish

1. Preheat the oven to 300°F(150°C). 2. Spread the oats and walnuts in a single layer on a baking sheet. 3. Toast the oats and nuts just until you begin to smell the nuts, 10 to 12 minutes. Remove the pan from the oven and set aside. 4. In a small microwave-safe bowl, heat the honey just until warm, about 30 seconds. Add the strawberries and stir to coat. 5. Place 1 tablespoon of the strawberries in the bottom of each of 2 dessert dishes or 8-ounce glasses. Add a portion of yogurt and then a portion of oats and repeat the layers until the containers are full, ending with the berries. Serve immediately or chill until ready to eat.

Per Serving:

calories: 541 | fat: 25g | protein: 21g | carbs: 66g | fiber: 8g | sodium: 124mg

Breakfast Hash

Prep time: 10 minutes | Cook time: 30 minutes |
Serves 6

Oil, for spraying
3 medium russet potatoes, diced
½ yellow onion, diced
1 green bell pepper, seeded and diced

2 tablespoons olive oil
2 teaspoons granulated garlic
1 teaspoon salt
½ teaspoon freshly ground black pepper

1. Line the air fryer basket with parchment and spray lightly with oil. 2. In a large bowl, mix together the potatoes, onion, bell pepper, and olive oil. 3. Add the garlic, salt, and black pepper and stir until evenly coated. 4. Transfer the mixture to the prepared basket. 5. Air fry at 400°F (204°C) for 20 to 30 minutes, shaking or stirring every 10 minutes, until browned and crispy. If you spray the potatoes with a little oil each time you stir, they will get even crispier.

Per Serving:

calories: 133 | fat: 5g | protein: 3g | carbs: 21g | fiber: 2g | sodium: 395mg

Chapter 3 Beans and Grains

Greek Yogurt Corn Bread

Prep time: 15 minutes | Cook time: 25 minutes | Serves 4 to 6

⅓ cup olive oil, plus extra for greasing
1 cup cornmeal
1 cup all-purpose flour
¼ cup sugar
½ teaspoon baking soda
½ teaspoon baking powder
1 teaspoon sea salt
1 cup plain full-fat Greek yogurt
1 large egg
¼ cup crumbled feta cheese

1. Preheat the oven to 375°F(190°C). Lightly grease an 8-inch square baking dish with olive oil. 2. In a large bowl, stir together the cornmeal, flour, sugar, baking soda, baking powder, and salt until well mixed. Add the yogurt, olive oil, and egg and stir until smooth. Stir in the feta. 3. Pour the batter into the prepared baking dish and bake until a toothpick inserted into the center of the corn bread comes out clean, about 30 minutes. 4. Remove the corn bread from the oven, cut it into 9 squares, and serve.

Per Serving:

calories: 546 | fat: 24g | protein: 11g | carbs: 71g | fiber: 2g | sodium: 584mg

Three-Grain Pilaf

Prep time: 10 minutes | Cook time: 10 minutes | Serves 6

2 tablespoons extra-virgin olive oil
½ cup sliced scallions
1 cup jasmine rice
½ cup millet
½ cup quinoa, rinsed and drained
2½ cups vegetable stock
¼ teaspoon salt
¼ teaspoon ground black pepper

1. Press the Sauté button on the Instant Pot® and heat oil. Add scallions and cook until just tender, 2 minutes. Add rice, millet, and quinoa and cook for 3 minutes to toast. Add stock and stir well. Press the Cancel button. 2. Close lid, set steam release to Sealing, press the Manual button, and set time to 4 minutes. When the timer beeps, quick-release the pressure until the float valve drops and open the lid. Fluff pilaf with a fork and stir in salt and pepper. Serve warm.

Per Serving:

calories: 346 | fat: 7g | protein: 8g | carbs: 61g | fiber: 4g | sodium: 341mg

Brown Rice with Dried Fruit

Prep time: 15 minutes | Cook time: 20 minutes | Serves 6

2 tablespoons olive oil
2 stalks celery, thinly sliced
2 large carrots, peeled and diced
1 large sweet potato, peeled and diced
1½ cups brown rice
⅓ cup chopped prunes
⅓ cup chopped dried apricots
½ teaspoon ground cinnamon
2 teaspoons grated orange zest
3 cups water
1 bay leaf
½ teaspoon salt

1. Press the Sauté button on the Instant Pot® and heat oil. Add celery, carrots, sweet potato, and rice. Cook until vegetables are just tender, about 3 minutes. Stir in prunes, apricots, cinnamon, and orange zest. Cook until cinnamon is fragrant, about 30 seconds. Add water, bay leaf, and salt. 2. Press the Cancel button, close lid, set steam release to Sealing, press the Manual button, and set time to 16 minutes. When the timer beeps, let pressure release naturally for 10 minutes. Quick-release any remaining pressure until the float valve drops and open the lid. Fluff rice with a fork. 3. Remove and discard bay leaf. Transfer to a serving bowl. Serve hot.

Per Serving:

calories: 192 | fat: 5g | protein: 3g | carbs: 34g | fiber: 4g | sodium: 272mg

Skillet Bulgur with Kale and Tomatoes

Prep time: 15 minutes | Cook time: 8 minutes | Serves 2

2 tablespoons olive oil
2 cloves garlic, minced
1 bunch kale, trimmed and cut into bite-sized pieces
Juice of 1 lemon
2 cups cooked bulgur wheat
1 pint cherry tomatoes, halved
Sea salt and freshly ground pepper, to taste

1. Heat the olive oil in a large skillet over medium heat. Add the garlic and sauté for 1 minute. 2. Add the kale leaves and stir to coat. Cook for 5 minutes until leaves are cooked through and thoroughly wilted. 3. Add the lemon juice, then the bulgur and tomatoes. Season with sea salt and freshly ground pepper.

Per Serving:

calories: 311 | fat: 14g | protein: 8g | carbs: 43g | fiber: 10g | sodium: 21mg

Barley Risotto

Prep time: 10 minutes | Cook time: 30 minutes | Serves 6

2 tablespoons olive oil
1 large onion, peeled and diced
1 clove garlic, peeled and minced
1 stalk celery, finely minced
1½ cups pearl barley, rinsed and drained
⅓ cup dried mushrooms
4 cups low-sodium chicken broth
2¼ cups water
1 cup grated Parmesan cheese
2 tablespoons minced fresh parsley
¼ teaspoon salt

1. Press the Sauté button on the Instant Pot® and heat oil. Add onion and sauté 5 minutes. Add garlic and cook 30 seconds. Stir in celery, barley, mushrooms, broth, and water. Press the Cancel button. 2. Close lid, set steam release to Sealing, press the Manual button, and set time to 18 minutes. When the timer beeps, quick-release the pressure until the float valve drops and open the lid. 3. Drain off excess liquid, leaving enough to leave the risotto slightly soupy. Press the Cancel button, then press the Sauté button and cook until thickened, about 5 minutes. Stir in cheese, parsley, and salt. Serve immediately.

Per Serving:

calories: 175 | fat: 9g | protein: 10g | carbs: 13g | fiber: 2g | sodium: 447mg

White Bean Soup with Kale and Lemon

Prep time: 15 minutes | Cook time: 27 minutes | Serves 8

1 tablespoon light olive oil
2 stalks celery, chopped
1 medium yellow onion, peeled and chopped
2 cloves garlic, peeled and minced
1 tablespoon chopped fresh oregano
4 cups chopped kale
1 pound (454 g) dried Great Northern beans, soaked overnight and drained
8 cups vegetable broth
¼ cup lemon juice
1 tablespoon extra-virgin olive oil
1 teaspoon ground black pepper

1. Press the Sauté button on the Instant Pot® and heat light olive oil. Add celery and onion and cook 5 minutes. Add garlic and oregano and sauté 30 seconds. Add kale and turn to coat, then cook until just starting to wilt, about 1 minute. Press the Cancel button. 2. Add beans, broth, lemon juice, extra-virgin olive oil, and pepper to the Instant Pot® and stir well. Close lid, set steam release to Sealing, press the Manual button, and set time to 20 minutes. When the timer beeps, let pressure release naturally, about 20 minutes. Open lid and stir well. Serve hot.

Per Serving:

calories: 129 | fat: 3g | protein: 7g | carbs: 22g | fiber: 6g | sodium: 501mg

Chili-Spiced Beans

Prep time: 10 minutes | Cook time: 30 minutes | Serves 8

1 pound (454 g) dried pinto beans, soaked overnight and drained
1 medium onion, peeled and chopped
¼ cup chopped fresh cilantro
1 (15-ounce / 425-g) can tomato sauce
¼ cup chili powder
2 tablespoons smoked paprika
1 teaspoon ground cumin
1 teaspoon ground coriander
½ teaspoon ground black pepper
2 cups vegetable broth
1 cup water

1. Place all ingredients in the Instant Pot® and stir to combine. 2. Close lid, set steam release to Sealing, press the Chili button, and cook for the default time of 30 minutes. When the timer beeps, quick-release the pressure until the float valve drops, open lid, and stir well. If beans are too thin, press the Cancel button, then press the Sauté button and let beans simmer, uncovered, until desired thickness is reached. Serve warm.

Per Serving:

calories: 86 | fat: 0g | protein: 5g | carbs: 17g | fiber: 4g | sodium: 323mg

Black Lentil Dhal

Prep time: 10 minutes | Cook time: 8 to 10 hours | Serves 6

2 cups dry whole black lentils
1 medium onion, finely chopped
1 heaped tablespoon freshly grated ginger
3 garlic cloves, chopped
3 fresh tomatoes, puréed, or 7 to 8 ounces (198 to 227 g) canned tomatoes, blended
2 fresh green chiles, chopped
2 tablespoons ghee
½ teaspoon turmeric
1 teaspoon chili powder
2 teaspoons coriander seeds, ground
1 teaspoon cumin seeds, ground
1 teaspoon sea salt
6⅓ cups water
1 to 2 tablespoons butter (optional)
1 teaspoon garam masala
1 teaspoon dried fenugreek leaves
Handful fresh coriander leaves, chopped

1. Preheat the slow cooker on high. 2. Clean and wash the black lentils. 3. Put the lentils, onion, ginger, garlic, tomatoes, chiles, ghee, turmeric, chili powder, coriander seeds, cumin seeds, salt, and water into the slow cooker. Cover and cook for 10 hours on low or for 8 hours on high. 4. When the lentils are cooked and creamy, stir in the butter (if using), garam masala, and fenugreek leaves to make the dhal rich and delicious. Garnish with a sprinkle of fresh coriander leaves and serve.

Per Serving:

calories: 271 | fat: 3g | protein: 17g | carbs: 47g | fiber: 9g | sodium: 415mg

Puréed Red Lentil Soup

Prep time: 15 minutes | Cook time: 21 minutes | Serves 6

2 tablespoons olive oil
1 medium yellow onion, peeled and chopped
1 medium carrot, peeled and chopped
1 medium red bell pepper, seeded and chopped
1 clove garlic, peeled and minced
1 bay leaf
½ teaspoon ground black pepper
¼ teaspoon salt
1 (15-ounce / 425-g) can diced tomatoes, drained
2 cups dried red lentils, rinsed and drained
6 cups low-sodium chicken broth

1. Press the Sauté button on the Instant Pot® and heat oil. Add onion, carrot, and bell pepper. Cook until just tender, about 5 minutes. Add garlic, bay leaf, black pepper, and salt, and cook until fragrant, about 30 seconds. Press the Cancel button. 2. Add tomatoes, lentils, and broth, then close lid, set steam release to Sealing, press the Manual button, and set time to 15 minutes. When the timer beeps, let pressure release naturally, about 15 minutes. Open lid, remove and discard bay leaf, and purée with an immersion blender or in batches in a blender. Serve warm.

Per Serving:

calories: 289 | fat: 6g | protein: 18g | carbs: 39g | fiber: 8g | sodium: 438mg

Mediterranean Bulgur Medley

Prep time: 15 minutes | Cook time: 20 minutes | Serves 6

2 tablespoons extra-virgin olive oil
1 medium onion, peeled and diced
½ cup chopped button mushrooms
½ cup golden raisins (sultanas)
¼ cup pine nuts
2 cups vegetable stock
1 teaspoon ground cumin
½ teaspoon salt
½ teaspoon ground black pepper
1 cup medium bulgur wheat
1 tablespoon petimezi or honey
12 chestnuts, roasted, peeled, and halved
1 teaspoon sesame seeds

1. Press the Sauté button on the Instant Pot® and heat oil. Add onion and sauté 3 minutes. Add mushrooms, raisins, and pine nuts and cook 2 minutes. 2. Add stock, cumin, salt, pepper, bulgur, and petimezi. Cook, stirring, for 3 minutes. Add chestnuts, then press the Cancel button. 3. Close lid, set steam release to Sealing, press the Rice button, and set time to 12 minutes. When the timer beeps, quick-release the pressure until the float valve drops and open lid. Stir well, then let stand, uncovered, on the Keep Warm setting for 10 minutes. Sprinkle with sesame seeds and serve.

Per Serving:

calories: 129 | fat: 1g | protein: 3g | carbs: 28g | fiber: 2g | sodium: 219mg

Brown Rice Vegetable Bowl with Roasted Red Pepper Dressing

Prep time: 10 minutes | Cook time: 22 minutes | Serves 2

¼ cup chopped roasted red bell pepper
2 tablespoons extra-virgin olive oil
1 tablespoon red wine vinegar
1 teaspoon honey
2 tablespoons light olive oil
2 cloves garlic, peeled and minced
½ teaspoon ground black pepper
¼ teaspoon salt
1 cup brown rice
1 cup vegetable broth
¼ cup chopped fresh flat-leaf parsley
2 tablespoons chopped fresh chives
2 tablespoons chopped fresh dill
½ cup diced tomato
½ cup chopped red onion
½ cup diced cucumber
½ cup chopped green bell pepper

1. Place roasted red pepper, extra-virgin olive oil, red wine vinegar, and honey in a blender. Purée until smooth, about 1 minute. Refrigerate until ready to serve. 2. Press the Sauté button on the Instant Pot® and heat light olive oil. Add garlic and cook until fragrant, about 30 seconds. Add black pepper, salt, and rice and stir well. Press the Cancel button. 3. Stir in broth. Close lid, set steam release to Sealing, press the Manual button, and set time to 22 minutes.

Per Serving:

calories: 561 | fat: 23g | protein: 10g | carbs: 86g | fiber: 5g | sodium: 505mg

Lentil Bowl

Prep time: 10 minutes | Cook time: 6 to 8 hours | Serves 6

1 cup dried lentils, any color, rinsed well under cold water and picked over to remove debris
3 cups low-sodium vegetable broth
1 (15-ounce/ 425-g) can no-salt-added diced tomatoes
1 small onion, chopped
3 celery stalks, chopped
3 carrots, chopped
3 garlic cloves, minced
2 tablespoons Italian seasoning
1 teaspoon sea salt
½ teaspoon freshly ground black pepper
2 bay leaves
1 tablespoon freshly squeezed lemon juice

1. In a slow cooker, combine the lentils, vegetable broth, tomatoes, onion, celery, carrots, garlic, Italian seasoning, salt, pepper, and bay leaves. Stir to mix well. 2. Cover the cooker and cook for 6 to 8 hours on Low heat. 3. Stir in the lemon juice before serving.

Per Serving:

calories: 152 | fat: 1g | protein: 10g | carbs: 29g | fiber: 13g | sodium: 529mg

Sweet Potato and Chickpea Moroccan Stew

Prep time: 10 minutes | Cook time: 40 minutes |

Serves 4

6 tablespoons extra virgin olive oil
2 medium red or white onions, finely chopped
6 garlic cloves, minced
3 medium carrots (about 8 ounces /227 g), peeled and cubed
1 teaspoon ground cumin
1 teaspoon ground coriander
½ teaspoon smoked paprika
½ teaspoon ground turmeric
1 cinnamon stick
½ pound (227 g) butternut squash, peeled and cut into

½-inch cubes
2 medium sweet potatoes, peeled and cut into ½-inch cubes
4 ounces (113 g) prunes, pitted
4 tomatoes (any variety), chopped, or 20 ounces (567g) canned chopped tomatoes
14 ounces (397 g) vegetable broth
14 ounces (397 g) canned chickpeas
½ cup chopped fresh parsley, for serving

1. Place a deep pan over medium heat and add the olive oil. When the oil is shimmering, add the onions and sauté for 5 minutes, then add the garlic and carrots, and sauté for 1 more minute. 2. Add the cumin, coriander, paprika, turmeric, and cinnamon stick. Continue cooking, stirring continuously, for 1 minute, then add the squash, sweet potatoes, prunes, tomatoes, and vegetable broth. Stir, cover, then reduce the heat to low and simmer for 20 minutes, stirring occasionally and checking the water levels, until the vegetables are cooked through. (If the stew appears to be drying out, add small amounts of hot water until the stew is thick.) 3. Add the chickpeas to the pan, stir, and continue simmering for 10 more minutes, adding more water if necessary. Remove the pan from the heat, discard the cinnamon stick, and set the stew aside to cool for 10 minutes. 4. When ready to serve, sprinkle the chopped parsley over the top of the stew. Store covered in the refrigerator for up to 4 days.

Per Serving:

calories: 471 | fat: 23g | protein: 9g | carbs: 63g | fiber: 12g | sodium: 651mg

Mediterranean Lentils and Rice

Prep time: 5 minutes |Cook time: 25 minutes|

Serves: 4

2¼ cups low-sodium or no-salt-added vegetable broth
½ cup uncooked brown or green lentils
½ cup uncooked instant brown rice
½ cup diced carrots (about 1 carrot)

½ cup diced celery (about 1 stalk)
1 (2¼-ounce / 64-g) can sliced olives, drained (about ½ cup)
¼ cup diced red onion (about ⅛ onion)
¼ cup chopped fresh curly-leaf parsley

1½ tablespoons extra-virgin olive oil
1 tablespoon freshly squeezed lemon juice (from about ½ small lemon)

1 garlic clove, minced (about ½ teaspoon)
¼ teaspoon kosher or sea salt
¼ teaspoon freshly ground black pepper

1. In a medium saucepan over high heat, bring the broth and lentils to a boil, cover, and lower the heat to medium-low. Cook for 8 minutes. 2. Raise the heat to medium, and stir in the rice. Cover the pot and cook the mixture for 15 minutes, or until the liquid is absorbed. Remove the pot from the heat and let it sit, covered, for 1 minute, then stir. 3. While the lentils and rice are cooking, mix together the carrots, celery, olives, onion, and parsley in a large serving bowl. 4. In a small bowl, whisk together the oil, lemon juice, garlic, salt, and pepper. Set aside. 5. When the lentils and rice are cooked, add them to the serving bowl. Pour the dressing on top, and mix everything together. Serve warm or cold, or store in a sealed container in the refrigerator for up to 7 days.

Per Serving:

calories: 183 | fat: 6g | protein: 4.9g | carbs: 29.5g | fiber: 3.3g | sodium: 552mg

No-Stir Polenta with Arugula, Figs, and Blue Cheese

Prep time: 15 minutes | Cook time: 40 minutes |

Serves 4

1 cup coarse-ground cornmeal
½ cup oil-packed sun-dried tomatoes, chopped
1 teaspoon minced fresh thyme or ¼ teaspoon dried
½ teaspoon table salt
¼ teaspoon pepper
3 tablespoons extra-virgin olive

oil, divided
2 ounces (57 g) baby arugula
4 figs, cut into ½-inch-thick wedges
1 tablespoon balsamic vinegar
2 ounces (57 g) blue cheese, crumbled (½ cup)
2 tablespoons pine nuts, toasted

1. Arrange trivet included with Instant Pot in base of insert and add 1 cup water. Fold sheet of aluminum foil into 16 by 6-inch sling, then rest 1½-quart round soufflé dish in center of sling. Whisk 4 cups water, cornmeal, tomatoes, thyme, salt, and pepper together in bowl, then transfer mixture to soufflé dish. Using sling, lower soufflé dish into pot and onto trivet; allow narrow edges of sling to rest along sides of insert. 2. Lock lid in place and close pressure release valve. Select high pressure cook function and cook for 40 minutes. Turn off Instant Pot and quick-release pressure. Carefully remove lid, allowing steam to escape away from you. 3. Using sling, transfer soufflé dish to wire rack. Whisk 1 tablespoon oil into polenta, smoothing out any lumps. Let sit until thickened slightly, about 10 minutes. Season with salt and pepper to taste. 4. Toss arugula and figs with vinegar and remaining 2 tablespoons oil in bowl, and season with salt and pepper to taste. Divide polenta among individual serving plates and top with arugula mixture, blue cheese, and pine nuts. Serve.

Per Serving:

calories: 360 | fat: 21g | protein: 7g | carbs: 38g | fiber: 8g | sodium: 510mg

Lemon and Garlic Rice Pilaf

Prep time: 10 minutes | Cook time: 34 minutes |
Serves 8

2 tablespoons olive oil
1 medium yellow onion, peeled and chopped
4 cloves garlic, peeled and minced
1 tablespoon grated lemon zest
½ teaspoon ground black pepper

1 teaspoon dried thyme
1 teaspoon dried oregano
¼ teaspoon salt
2 tablespoons white wine
2 tablespoons lemon juice
2 cups brown rice
2 cups vegetable broth

1. Press the Sauté button on the Instant Pot® and heat oil. Add onion and cook until soft, about 6 minutes. Add garlic and cook until fragrant, about 30 seconds. Add lemon zest, pepper, thyme, oregano, and salt. Cook until fragrant, about 1 minute. 2. Add wine and lemon juice and cook, stirring well, until liquid has almost evaporated, about 1 minute. Add rice and cook, stirring constantly, until coated and starting to toast, about 3 minutes. Press the Cancel button. 3. Stir in broth. Close lid, set steam release to Sealing, press the Manual button, and set time to 22 minutes. 4. When the timer beeps, let pressure release naturally for 10 minutes, then quick-release the remaining pressure until the float valve drops. Open lid and fluff rice with a fork. Serve warm.

Per Serving:
calories: 202 | fat: 5g | protein: 4g | carbs: 37g | fiber: 1g | sodium: 274mg

Lentil and Zucchini Boats

Prep time: 15 minutes | Cook time: 50 minutes |
Serves 4

1 cup dried green lentils, rinsed and drained
¼ teaspoon salt
2 cups water
1 tablespoon olive oil
½ medium red onion, peeled and diced
1 clove garlic, peeled and minced

1 cup marinara sauce
¼ teaspoon crushed red pepper flakes
4 medium zucchini, trimmed and cut lengthwise
½ cup shredded part-skim mozzarella cheese
¼ cup chopped fresh flat-leaf parsley

1. Add lentils, salt, and water to the Instant Pot®. Close lid, set steam release to Sealing, press the Manual button, and set time to 12 minutes. When the timer beeps, quick-release the pressure until the float valve drops. Press the Cancel button. Open lid and drain off any excess liquid. Transfer lentils to a medium bowl. Set aside. 2. Press the Sauté button and heat oil. Add onion and cook until tender, about 3 minutes. Add garlic and cook until fragrant, about 30 seconds. Add marinara sauce and crushed red pepper flakes and stir to combine. Press the Cancel button. Stir in lentils. 3. Preheat oven to 350°F (180°C) and spray a 9" × 13" baking dish with nonstick cooking spray. 4. Using a teaspoon, hollow out each zucchini half. Lay zucchini in prepared baking dish. Divide lentil

mixture among prepared zucchini. Top with cheese. Bake for 30–35 minutes, or until zucchini are tender and cheese is melted and browned. Top with parsley and serve hot.

Per Serving:
calories: 326 | fat: 10g | protein: 22g | carbs: 39g | fiber: 16g | sodium: 568mg

Rice with Pork Chops

Prep time: 10 minutes | Cook time: 3 to 5 hours |
Serves 4

1 cup raw long-grain brown rice, rinsed
2½ cups low-sodium chicken broth
1 cup sliced tomato
8 ounces (227 g) fresh spinach, chopped
1 small onion, chopped

2 garlic cloves, minced
2 teaspoons dried oregano
2 teaspoons dried basil
1 teaspoon sea salt
½ teaspoon freshly ground black pepper
4 thick-cut pork chops
¼ cup grated Parmesan cheese

1. In a slow cooker, combine the rice, chicken broth, tomato, spinach, onion, garlic, oregano, basil, salt, and pepper. Stir to mix well. 2. Place the pork chops on top of the rice mixture. 3. Cover the cooker and cook for 3 to 5 hours on Low heat. 4. Top with the Parmesan cheese for serving.

Per Serving:
calories: 482 | fat: 11g | protein: 51g | carbs: 44g | fiber: 4g | sodium: 785mg

Fava and Garbanzo Bean Fūl

Prep time: 10 minutes | Cook time: 10 minutes |
Serves 6

1 (16-ounce/ 454-g) can garbanzo beans, rinsed and drained
1 (15-ounce/ 425-g) can fava beans, rinsed and drained
3 cups water

½ cup lemon juice
3 cloves garlic, peeled and minced
1 teaspoon salt
3 tablespoons extra-virgin olive oil

1. In a 3-quart pot over medium heat, cook the garbanzo beans, fava beans, and water for 10 minutes. 2. Reserving 1 cup of the liquid from the cooked beans, drain the beans and put them in a bowl. 3. Mix the reserved liquid, lemon juice, minced garlic, and salt together and add to the beans in the bowl. Using a potato masher, mash up about half the beans in the bowl. 4. After mashing half the beans, give the mixture one more stir to make sure the beans are evenly mixed. 5. Drizzle the olive oil over the top. 6. Serve warm or cold with pita bread.

Per Serving:
calories: 199 | fat: 9g | protein: 10g | carbs: 25g | fiber: 9g | sodium: 395mg

Mediterranean Creamed Green Peas

Prep time: 5 minutes | Cook time: 25 minutes | Serves 4

1 cup cauliflower florets, fresh or frozen
½ white onion, roughly chopped
2 tablespoons olive oil
½ cup unsweetened almond milk
3 cups green peas, fresh or frozen
3 garlic cloves, minced
2 tablespoons fresh thyme leaves, chopped
1 teaspoon fresh rosemary leaves, chopped
½ teaspoon salt
½ teaspoon black pepper
Shredded Parmesan cheese, for garnish
Fresh parsley, for garnish

1. Preheat the air fryer to 380°F(193°C). 2. In a large bowl, combine the cauliflower florets and onion with the olive oil and toss well to coat. 3. Put the cauliflower-and-onion mixture into the air fryer basket in an even layer and bake for 15 minutes. 4. Transfer the cauliflower and onion to a food processor. Add the almond milk and pulse until smooth. 5. In a medium saucepan, combine the cauliflower purée, peas, garlic, thyme, rosemary, salt, and pepper and mix well. Cook over medium heat for an additional 10 minutes, stirring regularly. 6. Serve with a sprinkle of Parmesan cheese and chopped fresh parsley.

Per Serving:

calories: 313 | fat: 16.4g | protein: 14.7g | carbs: 28.8g | fiber: 8.3g | sodium: 898mg

Lentil and Spinach Curry

Prep time: 10 minutes | Cook time: 17 minutes | Serves 4

1 tablespoon olive oil
½ cup diced onion
1 clove garlic, peeled and minced
1 cup dried yellow lentils, rinsed and drained
4 cups water
½ teaspoon ground coriander
½ teaspoon ground turmeric
½ teaspoon curry powder
½ cup diced tomatoes
5 ounces (142 g) baby spinach leaves

1. Press the Sauté button on the Instant Pot® and heat oil. Add onion and cook until translucent, about 5 minutes. Add garlic and cook for 30 seconds. Add lentils and toss to combine. Press the Cancel button. 2. Pour in water. Close lid, set steam release to Sealing, press the Manual button, and set time to 6 minutes. When the timer beeps, quick-release the pressure until the float valve drops and open lid. Press the Cancel button. Drain any residual liquid. Stir in coriander, turmeric, curry powder, tomatoes, and spinach. 3. Press the Sauté button, press the Adjust button to change the heat to Less, and simmer uncovered until tomatoes are heated through and spinach has wilted, about 5 minutes. 4. Transfer to a dish and serve.

Per Serving:

calories: 195 | fat: 4g | protein: 13g | carbs: 26g | fiber: 8g | sodium: 111mg

Wheat Berry Salad

Prep time: 20 minutes | Cook time: 50 minutes | Serves 12

1½ tablespoons vegetable oil
6¾ cups water
1½ cups wheat berries
1½ teaspoons Dijon mustard
1 teaspoon sugar
1 teaspoon salt
½ teaspoon ground black pepper
¼ cup white wine vinegar
½ cup extra-virgin olive oil
½ small red onion, peeled and
diced
1⅓ cups frozen corn, thawed
1 medium zucchini, trimmed, grated, and drained
2 stalks celery, finely diced
1 medium red bell pepper, seeded and diced
4 scallions, diced
¼ cup diced sun-dried tomatoes
¼ cup chopped fresh parsley

1. Add vegetable oil, water, and wheat berries to the Instant Pot®. Close lid, set steam release to Sealing, press the Manual button, and set time to 50 minutes. When the timer beeps, quick-release the pressure until the float valve drops and open lid. Fluff wheat berries with a fork. Drain any excess liquid, transfer to a large bowl, and set aside to cool. 2. Purée mustard, sugar, salt, black pepper, vinegar, olive oil, and onion in a blender. Stir dressing into wheat berries. Stir in rest of ingredients. Serve.

Per Serving:

calories: 158 | fat: 10g | protein: 2g | carbs: 16g | fiber: 2g | sodium: 268mg

Fasolakia (Greek Green Beans)

Prep time: 5 minutes | Cook time: 45 minutes | Serves 2

⅓ cup olive oil (any variety)
1 medium onion (red or white), chopped
1 medium russet or white potato, sliced into ¼-inch (.5cm) thick slices
1 pound (454 g) green beans (fresh or frozen)
3 medium tomatoes, grated, or 1 (15-ounce / 425-g) can crushed tomatoes
¼ cup chopped fresh parsley
1 teaspoon granulated sugar
½ teaspoon salt
¼ teaspoon freshly ground black pepper

1. Add the olive oil a medium pot over medium-low heat. When the oil begins to shimmer, add the onions and sauté until soft, about 5 minutes. 2. Add the potatoes to the pot, and sauté for an additional 2–3 minutes. 3. Add the green beans and stir until the beans are thoroughly coated with the olive oil. Add the tomatoes, parsley, sugar, salt, and black pepper. Stir to combine. 4. Add just enough hot water to the pot to cover half the beans. Cover and simmer for 40 minutes or until there is no water left in the pot and the beans are soft. (Do not allow the beans to boil.) 5. Allow the beans to cool until they're warm or until they reach room temperature, but do not serve hot. Store in refrigerator for up to 3 days.

Per Serving:

calories: 536 | fat: 37g | protein: 9g | carbs: 50g | fiber: 11g | sodium: 617mg

Spiced Quinoa Salad

Prep time: 15 minutes | Cook time: 17 minutes | Serves 6

2 tablespoons vegetable oil
1 medium white onion, peeled and chopped
2 cloves garlic, peeled and minced
½ teaspoon ground cumin
½ teaspoon ground coriander
½ teaspoon smoked paprika
½ teaspoon salt

¼ teaspoon ground black pepper
1½ cups quinoa, rinsed and drained
2 cups vegetable broth
1⅓ cups water
2 cups fresh baby spinach leaves
2 plum tomatoes, seeded and chopped

1. Press the Sauté button on the Instant Pot® and heat oil. Add onion and cook until tender, about 3 minutes. Add garlic, cumin, coriander, paprika, salt, and pepper, and cook 30 seconds until garlic and spices are fragrant. 2. Add quinoa and toss to coat in spice mixture. Cook 2 minutes to lightly toast quinoa. Add broth and water, making sure to scrape bottom and sides of pot to loosen any brown bits. Press the Cancel button. 3. Close lid and set steam release to Sealing. Press the Rice button and set time to 12 minutes. 4. When the timer beeps, let pressure release naturally, about 20 minutes. Open lid, add spinach and tomatoes, and fluff quinoa with a fork. Serve warm, at room temperature, or cold.

Per Serving:
calories: 215 | fat: 7g | protein: 7g | carbs: 32g | fiber: 4g | sodium: 486mg

Kale with Chickpeas

Prep time: 10 minutes | Cook time: 4 to 6 hours | Serves 6

1 to 2 tablespoons rapeseed oil
½ teaspoon mustard seeds
1 teaspoon cumin seeds
1 large onion, diced
4 garlic cloves, crushed
4 plum tomatoes, finely chopped
1 heaped teaspoon coriander seeds, ground
1 fresh green chile, chopped

1 teaspoon chili powder
1 teaspoon turmeric
1 teaspoon salt
2 (16-ounce / 454-g) cans cooked chickpeas, drained and rinsed
¾ cup water
7 to 8 ounces (198 to 227 g) kale, chopped
1 fresh green chile, sliced, for garnish

1. Heat the oil in a frying pan (or in the slow cooker if you have a sear setting). When it's hot add the mustard seeds and then the cumin seeds until they pop and become fragrant. 2. Add the diced onion and cook, stirring, for 10 minutes. Add the garlic and cook for a few minutes. Then add the tomatoes. Add the ground coriander seeds, green chile, chili powder, turmeric, and salt. 3. Add the chickpeas and water. Cover and cook on low for 6 hours, or on high for 4 hours. 4. Add the chopped kale, a handful at a time, stirring between. Leave this to cook for another 10 to 15 minutes, until the kale is soft and tender. 5. Top with the sliced chile.

Per Serving:
calories: 202 | fat: 6g | protein: 10g | carbs: 30g | fiber: 10g | sodium: 619mg

Chapter 4 Poultry

Chicken Chili Verde over Rice

Prep time: 15 minutes | Cook time: 6 hours | Serves 2

1 cup diced tomatillos
1 onion, halved and sliced thin
2 garlic cloves, minced
1 jalapeño pepper, seeds and membranes removed, minced
1 teaspoon ground cumin
1 teaspoon ground coriander
1 teaspoon extra-virgin olive oil

½ cup long-grain brown rice
1 cup low-sodium chicken broth
2 boneless, skinless chicken breasts, about 8 ounces (227 g) each, cut into 4-inch tenders
¼ cup fresh cilantro

1. Combine the tomatillos, onion, garlic, jalapeño, cumin, and coriander in a food processor. Pulse until it has a sauce-like consistency but is still slightly chunky. 2. Grease the inside of the slow cooker with the olive oil. 3. Add the rice to the slow cooker and pour in the chicken broth. Gently stir to make sure the rice grains are fully submerged. 4. Place the chicken on top of the rice and pour the tomatillo salsa over the top. 5. Cover and cook on low for 6 hours.

Per Serving:

calories: 536 | fat: 11g | protein: 59g | carbs: 48g | fiber: 4g | sodium: 148mg

Blackened Chicken

Prep time: 10 minutes | Cook time: 20 minutes | Serves 4

1 large egg, beaten
¾ cup Blackened seasoning
2 whole boneless, skinless

chicken breasts (about 1 pound / 454 g each), halved
1 to 2 tablespoons oil

1. Place the beaten egg in one shallow bowl and the Blackened seasoning in another shallow bowl. 2. One at a time, dip the chicken pieces in the beaten egg and the Blackened seasoning, coating thoroughly. 3. Preheat the air fryer to 360ºF (182ºC). Line the air fryer basket with parchment paper. 4. Place the chicken pieces on the parchment and spritz with oil. 5. Cook for 10 minutes. Flip the chicken, spritz it with oil, and cook for 10 minutes more until the internal temperature reaches 165ºF (74ºC) and the chicken is no longer pink inside. Let sit for 5 minutes before serving.

Per Serving:

calories: 225 | fat: 10g | protein: 28g | carbs: 8g | fiber: 6g | sodium: 512mg

Chicken in Cream Sauce

Prep time: 10 minutes | Cook time: 35 minutes | Serves 6

3 tablespoons olive oil
6 (4-ounce / 113-g) boneless, skinless chicken breasts
½ zucchini, chopped into 2-inch pieces
1 celery stalk, chopped
1 red bell pepper, thinly sliced
2 tomatoes on the vine, chopped

3 garlic cloves, minced
½ teaspoon dried thyme
½ teaspoon dried marjoram
½ teaspoon dried basil
½ cup baby spinach
1 cup heavy (whipping) cream
¼ cup chopped fresh Italian parsley (optional)

1. In a large skillet, heat the olive oil over medium-high heat. Add the chicken and cook for 8 to 10 minutes on each side, until cooked through. Transfer the chicken to a plate and set aside. 2. Add the zucchini, celery, bell pepper, tomatoes, and garlic and sauté for 8 to 10 minutes, until the vegetables are softened. Add the thyme, marjoram, and basil and cook for 1 minute. Add the spinach and cook until wilted, about 3 minutes. 3. Add the cream and mix well. Return the chicken to the skillet and cook until warmed through, about 4 minutes. 4. Garnish with the parsley, if desired, and serve.

Per Serving:

calories: 341 | fat: 24g | protein: 27g | carbs: 4g | fiber: 1g | sodium: 83mg

Crispy Mediterranean Chicken Thighs

Prep time: 5 minutes | Cook time: 30 to 35 minutes | Serves 6

2 tablespoons extra-virgin olive oil
2 teaspoons dried rosemary
1½ teaspoons ground cumin
1½ teaspoons ground coriander

¾ teaspoon dried oregano
⅛ teaspoon salt
6 bone-in, skin-on chicken thighs (about 3 pounds / 1.4 kg)

1. Preheat the oven to 450ºF (235ºC). Line a baking sheet with parchment paper. 2. Place the olive oil and spices into a large bowl and mix together, making a paste. Add the chicken and mix together until evenly coated. Place on the prepared baking sheet. 3. Bake for 30 to 35 minutes, or until golden brown and the chicken registers an internal temperature of 165ºF (74ºC).

Per Serving:

calories: 440 | fat: 34g | protein: 30g | carbs: 1g | fiber: 0g | sodium: 180mg

Taco Chicken

Prep time: 10 minutes | Cook time: 23 minutes | Serves 4

2 large eggs
1 tablespoon water
Fine sea salt and ground black pepper, to taste
1 cup pork dust
1 teaspoon ground cumin
1 teaspoon smoked paprika
4 (5-ounce / 142-g) boneless,

skinless chicken breasts or thighs, pounded to ¼ inch thick
1 cup salsa
1 cup shredded Monterey Jack cheese (about 4 ounces / 113 g) (omit for dairy-free)
Sprig of fresh cilantro, for garnish (optional)

1. Spray the air fryer basket with avocado oil. Preheat the air fryer to 400ºF (204ºC). 2. Crack the eggs into a shallow baking dish, add the water and a pinch each of salt and pepper, and whisk to combine. In another shallow baking dish, stir together the pork dust, cumin, and paprika until well combined. 3. Season the chicken breasts well on both sides with salt and pepper. Dip 1 chicken breast in the eggs and let any excess drip off, then dredge both sides of the chicken breast in the pork dust mixture. Spray the breast with avocado oil and place it in the air fryer basket. Repeat with the remaining 3 chicken breasts. 4. Air fry the chicken in the air fryer for 20 minutes, or until the internal temperature reaches 165ºF (74ºC) and the breading is golden brown, flipping halfway through. 5. Dollop each chicken breast with ¼ cup of the salsa and top with ¼ cup of the cheese. Return the breasts to the air fryer and cook for 3 minutes, or until the cheese is melted. Garnish with cilantro before serving, if desired. 6. Store leftovers in an airtight container in the refrigerator for up to 4 days. Reheat in a preheated 400ºF (204ºC) air fryer for 5 minutes, or until warmed through.

Per Serving:

calories: 360 | fat: 15g | protein: 20g | carbs: 4g | fiber: 1g | sodium: 490mg

Harissa Yogurt Chicken Thighs

Prep time: 5 minutes | Cook time: 25 minutes | Serves 4

½ cup plain Greek yogurt
2 tablespoons harissa
1 tablespoon lemon juice
½ teaspoon kosher salt

¼ teaspoon freshly ground black pepper
1½ pounds (680 g) boneless, skinless chicken thighs

1. In a bowl, combine the yogurt, harissa, lemon juice, salt, and black pepper. Add the chicken and mix together. Marinate for at least 15 minutes, and up to 4 hours in the refrigerator. 2. Preheat the oven to 425ºF (220ºC). Line a baking sheet with parchment paper or foil. Remove the chicken thighs from the marinade and arrange in a single layer on the baking sheet. Roast for 20 minutes, turning the chicken over halfway. 3. Change the oven temperature to broil. Broil the chicken until golden brown in spots, 2 to 3 minutes.

Per Serving:

calories: 190 | fat: 10g | protein: 24g | carbs: 1g | fiber: 0g | sodium: 230mg

Crunchy Chicken Tenders

Prep time: 5 minutes | Cook time: 12 minutes | Serves 4

1 egg
¼ cup unsweetened almond milk
¼ cup whole wheat flour
¼ cup whole wheat bread crumbs
½ teaspoon salt

½ teaspoon black pepper
½ teaspoon dried thyme
½ teaspoon dried sage
½ teaspoon garlic powder
1 pound (454 g) chicken tenderloins
1 lemon, quartered

1. Preheat the air fryer to 360°F(182ºC). 2. In a shallow bowl, beat together the egg and almond milk until frothy. 3. In a separate shallow bowl, whisk together the flour, bread crumbs, salt, pepper, thyme, sage, and garlic powder. 4. Dip each chicken tenderloin into the egg mixture, then into the bread crumb mixture, coating the outside with the crumbs. Place the breaded chicken tenderloins into the bottom of the air fryer basket in an even layer, making sure that they don't touch each other. 5. Cook for 6 minutes, then turn and cook for an additional 5 to 6 minutes. Serve with lemon slices.

Per Serving:

calories: 224 | fat: 7g | protein: 26g | carbs: 14g | fiber: 2g | sodium: 464mg

Mediterranean Roasted Turkey Breast

Prep time: 15 minutes | Cook time: 6 to 8 hours | Serves 4

3 garlic cloves, minced
1 teaspoon sea salt
1 teaspoon dried oregano
½ teaspoon freshly ground black pepper
½ teaspoon dried basil
½ teaspoon dried parsley
½ teaspoon dried rosemary
½ teaspoon dried thyme
¼ teaspoon dried dill
¼ teaspoon ground nutmeg
2 tablespoons extra-virgin olive oil

2 tablespoons freshly squeezed lemon juice
1 (4- to 6-pound / 1.8- to 2.7-kg) boneless or bone-in turkey breast
1 onion, chopped
½ cup low-sodium chicken broth
4 ounces (113 g) whole Kalamata olives, pitted
1 cup sun-dried tomatoes (packaged, not packed in oil), chopped

1. In a small bowl, stir together the garlic, salt, oregano, pepper, basil, parsley, rosemary, thyme, dill, and nutmeg. 2. Drizzle the olive oil and lemon juice all over the turkey breast and generously season it with the garlic-spice mix. 3. In a slow cooker, combine the onion and chicken broth. Place the seasoned turkey breast on top of the onion. Top the turkey with the olives and sun-dried tomatoes. 4. Cover the cooker and cook for 6 to 8 hours on Low heat. 5. Slice or shred the turkey for serving.

Per Serving:

calories: 676 | fat: 19g | protein: 111g | carbs: 14g | fiber: 3g | sodium: 626mg

Pomegranate-Glazed Chicken

Prep time: 10 minutes | Cook time: 30 minutes | Serves 6

1 teaspoon cumin
1 clove garlic, minced
Sea salt and freshly ground
pepper, to taste
6 tablespoons olive oil, divided
6 boneless, skinless chicken
breasts

1 cup pomegranate juice (no
sugar added)
2 tablespoons honey
1 tablespoon Dijon mustard
½ teaspoon dried thyme
1 fresh pomegranate, seeds
removed

1. Mix the cumin, garlic, sea salt, and freshly ground pepper with 2 tablespoons of olive oil, and rub into the chicken. 2. Heat the remaining olive oil in a large skillet over medium heat. 3. Add the chicken breasts and sauté for 10 minutes, turning halfway through the cooking time, so the chicken breasts are golden brown on each side. 4. Add the pomegranate juice, honey, Dijon mustard, and thyme. 5. Lower the heat and simmer for 20 minutes, or until the chicken is cooked through and the sauce reduces by half. 6. Transfer the chicken and sauce to a serving platter, and top with fresh pomegranate seeds.

Per Serving:

calories: 532 | fat: 21g | protein: 62g | carbs: 20g | fiber: 2g | sodium: 157mg

Catalonian Chicken with Spiced Lemon Rice

Prep time: 10 minutes | Cook time: 4 hours 10 minutes | Serves 4

3 tablespoons all-purpose flour
2 tablespoons paprika
1 tablespoon garlic powder
Sea salt
Black pepper
6 chicken thighs
¼ cup olive oil
1 (15-ounce / 425-g) can diced
tomatoes, with the juice
2 green bell peppers, diced into

2-inch pieces
1 large yellow onion, sliced into
thick pieces
2 tablespoons tomato paste
4 cups chicken stock
1 cup uncooked brown rice
½ teaspoon red pepper flakes
Zest and juice from 1 lemon
½ cup pitted green olives

1. In a large resealable bag, mix together the flour, paprika, and garlic powder and season with salt and pepper. Add the chicken, reseal the bag, and toss to coat. 2. In a large skillet over medium heat, heat the olive oil. Add the chicken and brown on both sides, 3 to 4 minutes per side. 3. While the chicken is cooking, add the tomatoes, bell peppers, and onion to the slow cooker. 4. Place the browned chicken thighs in the slow cooker. 5. In same skillet used to brown the chicken, add the tomato paste and cook for 1 minute, stirring constantly. 6. Add 2 cups of the chicken stock to the skillet and bring to a simmer, stirring with a wooden spoon to scrape up the flavorful browned bits off the bottom of the pan. Pour over the top of the chicken in the slow cooker. 7. Cook on low for 4 hours, or until the chicken is extremely tender. 8. In a heavy medium saucepan over medium-high heat, combine the remaining 2 cups stock, the rice, red pepper flakes, lemon zest, and juice of one-half of the lemon, and season with salt. Bring to a boil, reduce the heat to low, and simmer, covered, until the rice is tender and has absorbed all the liquid, about 25 minutes. 9. To serve, spoon the rice onto plates and ladle the Catalonian chicken and vegetables over the top. Garnish with the olives and squeeze the juice from the remaining one-half lemon over the dish.

Per Serving:

calories: 791 | fat: 31g | protein: 69g | carbs: 60g | fiber: 8g | sodium: 497mg

Marinated Chicken

Prep time: 5 minutes | Cook time: 16 minutes | Serves 4

½ cup olive oil
2 tablespoon fresh rosemary
1 teaspoon minced garlic
Juice and zest of 1 lemon
¼ cup chopped flat-leaf parsley

Sea salt and freshly ground
pepper, to taste
4 boneless, skinless chicken
breasts

1. Mix all ingredients except the chicken together in a plastic bag or bowl. 2. Place the chicken in the container and shake/stir so the marinade thoroughly coats the chicken. 3. Refrigerate up to 24 hours. 4. Heat a grill to medium heat and cook the chicken for 6–8 minutes a side. Turn only once during the cooking process. 5. Serve with a Greek salad and brown rice.

Per Serving:

calories: 571 | fat: 34g | protein: 61g | carbs: 1g | fiber: 0g | sodium: 126mg

Garlic Dill Wings

Prep time: 5 minutes | Cook time: 25 minutes | Serves 4

2 pounds (907 g) bone-in
chicken wings, separated at
joints
½ teaspoon salt
½ teaspoon ground black

pepper
½ teaspoon onion powder
½ teaspoon garlic powder
1 teaspoon dried dill

1. In a large bowl, toss wings with salt, pepper, onion powder, garlic powder, and dill until evenly coated. Place wings into ungreased air fryer basket in a single layer, working in batches if needed. 2. Adjust the temperature to 400ºF (204ºC) and air fry for 25 minutes, shaking the basket every 7 minutes during cooking. Wings should have an internal temperature of at least 165ºF (74ºC) and be golden brown when done. Serve warm.

Per Serving:

calories: 290 | fat: 8g | protein: 50g | carbs: 1g | fiber: 0g | sodium: 475mg

Chicken Marinara and Zucchini

Prep time: 10 minutes | Cook time: 15 minutes | Serves 4

2 large zucchini, trimmed and chopped
4 (6-ounce / 170-g) chicken breast halves
3 cups marinara sauce
1 tablespoon Italian seasoning
½ teaspoon salt
1 cup shredded mozzarella cheese

1. Place zucchini on the bottom of the Instant Pot®. Place chicken on zucchini. Pour marinara sauce over chicken. Sprinkle with Italian seasoning and salt. 2. Close lid, set steam release to Sealing, press the Poultry button, and cook for the default time of 15 minutes. When the timer beeps, let pressure release naturally for 10 minutes. Quick-release any remaining pressure until the float valve drops and then open lid. Check chicken using a meat thermometer to ensure the internal temperature is at least 165ºF (74ºC). 3. Sprinkle chicken with cheese. Close lid and let stand on the Keep Warm setting for 5 minutes to allow the cheese to melt. 4. Transfer chicken and zucchini to a serving platter. Serve hot.

Per Serving:

calories: 21 | fat: 13g | protein: 51g | carbs: 21g | fiber: 5g | sodium: 442mg

Za'atar Chicken Tenders

Prep time: 5 minutes | Cook time: 15 minutes | Serves 4

Olive oil cooking spray
1 pound (454 g) chicken tenders
1½ tablespoons za'atar
½ teaspoon kosher salt
¼ teaspoon freshly ground black pepper

1. Preheat the oven to 450ºF (235ºC). Line a baking sheet with parchment paper or foil and lightly spray with olive oil cooking spray. 2. In a large bowl, combine the chicken, za'atar, salt, and black pepper. Mix together well, covering the chicken tenders fully. Arrange in a single layer on the baking sheet and bake for 15 minutes, turning the chicken over once halfway through the cooking time.

Per Serving:

calories: 145 | fat: 4g | protein: 26g | carbs: 0g | fiber: 0g | sodium: 190mg

Fenugreek Chicken

Prep time: 15 minutes | Cook time: 6½ hours | Serves 6

1 tablespoon vegetable oil
2 teaspoons cumin seeds
2 onions, finely diced
2 tablespoons freshly grated
ginger
3 garlic cloves, finely chopped
1 teaspoon turmeric
2 tomatoes, puréed
1 teaspoon chili powder
1 teaspoon coriander seeds, ground
1 teaspoon salt
1 or 2 fresh green chiles, chopped
8 boneless chicken thighs, skinned, trimmed, and cut into
chunks
2 bunches fresh fenugreek leaves, washed and finely chopped (or 3 tablespoons dried fenugreek leaves)
2 tablespoons yogurt
2 teaspoons garam masala

1. Heat the oil in a frying pan (or in the slow cooker if you have a sear setting). Add the cumin seeds. Once fragrant, add the onions and cook until they begin to brown, about 10 minutes. Add the ginger, garlic, and turmeric, and cook for a few minutes. 2. Stir in the puréed tomatoes, chili powder, ground coriander seeds, salt, and green chiles. Put everything in the slow cooker and set the cooker to high. 3. Stir in the chicken pieces. Cover and cook on high for 4 hours, or on low for 6 hours. 4. Add the fenugreek leaves and stir into the sauce. Leave the cover off and cook for another half hour on high. This will also reduce the sauce and thicken it slightly. 5. Turn the cooker to low and stir in the yogurt, 1 tablespoon at a time, until it's fully incorporated into the sauce. 6. Turn off the heat, stir in the garam masala, and serve.

Per Serving:

calories: 405 | fat: 14g | protein: 54g | carbs: 15g | fiber: 3g | sodium: 664mg

Lemon-Rosemary Spatchcock Chicken

Prep time: 20 minutes | Cook time: 45 minutes | Serves 6 to 8

½ cup extra-virgin olive oil, divided
1 (3- to 4-pound/ 1.4- to 1.8-kg) roasting chicken
8 garlic cloves, roughly chopped
2 to 4 tablespoons chopped fresh rosemary
2 teaspoons salt, divided
1 teaspoon freshly ground black pepper, divided
2 lemons, thinly sliced

1. Preheat the oven to 425°F(220ºC). 2. Pour 2 tablespoons olive oil in the bottom of a 9-by-13-inch baking dish or rimmed baking sheet and swirl to coat the bottom. 3. To spatchcock the bird, place the whole chicken breast-side down on a large work surface. Using a very sharp knife, cut along the backbone, starting at the tail end and working your way up to the neck. Pull apart the two sides, opening up the chicken. Flip it over, breast-side up, pressing down with your hands to flatten the bird. Transfer to the prepared baking dish. 4. Loosen the skin over the breasts and thighs by cutting a small incision and sticking one or two fingers inside to pull the skin away from the meat without removing it. 5. To prepare the filling, in a small bowl, combine ¼ cup olive oil, garlic, rosemary, 1 teaspoon salt, and ½ teaspoon pepper and whisk together. 6. Rub the garlic-herb oil evenly under the skin of each breast and each thigh. Add the lemon slices evenly to the same areas. 7. Whisk together the remaining 2 tablespoons olive oil, 1 teaspoon salt, and ½ teaspoon pepper and rub over the outside of the chicken. 8. Place in the oven, uncovered, and roast for 45 minutes, or until cooked through and golden brown. Allow to rest 5 minutes before carving to serve.

Per Serving:

calories: 317 | fat: 18g | protein: 35g | carbs: 2g | fiber: 1g | sodium: 710mg

Chicken Jalfrezi

Prep time: 15 minutes | Cook time: 15 minutes | Serves 4

Chicken:

1 pound (454 g) boneless, skinless chicken thighs, cut into 2 or 3 pieces each
1 medium onion, chopped
1 large green bell pepper, stemmed, seeded, and chopped
2 tablespoons olive oil
1 teaspoon ground turmeric
1 teaspoon garam masala
1 teaspoon kosher salt
½ to 1 teaspoon cayenne pepper

Sauce:

¼ cup tomato sauce
1 tablespoon water
1 teaspoon garam masala
½ teaspoon kosher salt
½ teaspoon cayenne pepper
Side salad, rice, or naan bread, for serving

1. For the chicken: In a large bowl, combine the chicken, onion, bell pepper, oil, turmeric, garam masala, salt, and cayenne. Stir and toss until well combined. 2. Place the chicken and vegetables in the air fryer basket. Set the air fryer to 350ºF (177ºC) for 15 minutes, stirring and tossing halfway through the cooking time. Use a meat thermometer to ensure the chicken has reached an internal temperature of 165ºF (74ºC). 3. Meanwhile, for the sauce: In a small microwave-safe bowl, combine the tomato sauce, water, garam masala, salt, and cayenne. Microwave on high for 1 minute. Remove and stir. Microwave for another minute; set aside. 4. When the chicken is cooked, remove and place chicken and vegetables in a large bowl. Pour the sauce over all. Stir and toss to coat the chicken and vegetables evenly. 5. Serve with rice, naan, or a side salad.

Per Serving:

calories: 224 | fat: 12g | protein: 23g | carbs: 6g | fiber: 2g | sodium: 827mg

Tuscan Turkey

Prep time: 15 minutes | Cook time: 6 to 8 hours | Serves 4

1 pound (454 g) new potatoes, halved
1 red bell pepper, seeded and sliced
1 small onion, sliced
4 boneless, skinless turkey breast fillets (about 2 pounds / 907 g)
1 cup low-sodium chicken broth
½ cup grated Parmesan cheese
3 garlic cloves, minced
1 teaspoon dried oregano
1 teaspoon dried rosemary
½ teaspoon sea salt
½ teaspoon freshly ground black pepper
½ teaspoon dried thyme
¼ cup chopped fresh basil

1. In a slow cooker, combine the potatoes, bell pepper, and onion. Stir to mix well. 2. Place the turkey on top of the vegetables. 3. In a small bowl, whisk together the chicken broth, Parmesan cheese, garlic, oregano, rosemary, salt, black pepper, and thyme until blended. Pour the sauce over the turkey. 4. Cover the cooker and cook for 6 to 8 hours on Low heat. 5. Garnish with fresh basil for serving.

Per Serving:

calories: 402 | fat: 5g | protein: 65g | carbs: 24g | fiber: 3g | sodium: 673mg

Simply Terrific Turkey Meatballs

Prep time: 10 minutes | Cook time: 7 to 10 minutes | Serves 4

1 red bell pepper, seeded and coarsely chopped
2 cloves garlic, coarsely chopped
¼ cup chopped fresh parsley
1½ pounds (680 g) 85% lean
ground turkey
1 egg, lightly beaten
½ cup grated Parmesan cheese
1 teaspoon salt
½ teaspoon freshly ground black pepper

1. Preheat the air fryer to 400ºF (204ºC). 2. In a food processor fitted with a metal blade, combine the bell pepper, garlic, and parsley. Pulse until finely chopped. Transfer the vegetables to a large mixing bowl. 3. Add the turkey, egg, Parmesan, salt, and black pepper. Mix gently until thoroughly combined. Shape the mixture into 1¼-inch meatballs. 4. Working in batches if necessary, arrange the meatballs in a single layer in the air fryer basket; coat lightly with olive oil spray. Pausing halfway through the cooking time to shake the basket, air fry for 7 to 10 minutes, until lightly browned and a thermometer inserted into the center of a meatball registers 165ºF (74ºC).

Per Serving:

calories: 388 | fat: 25g | protein: 34g | carbs: 5g | fiber: 1g | sodium: 527mg

Chipotle Drumsticks

Prep time: 5 minutes | Cook time: 25 minutes | Serves 4

1 tablespoon tomato paste
½ teaspoon chipotle powder
¼ teaspoon apple cider vinegar
¼ teaspoon garlic powder
8 chicken drumsticks
½ teaspoon salt
⅛ teaspoon ground black pepper

1. In a small bowl, combine tomato paste, chipotle powder, vinegar, and garlic powder. 2. Sprinkle drumsticks with salt and pepper, then place into a large bowl and pour in tomato paste mixture. Toss or stir to evenly coat all drumsticks in mixture. 3. Place drumsticks into ungreased air fryer basket. Adjust the temperature to 400ºF (204ºC) and air fry for 25 minutes, turning drumsticks halfway through cooking. Drumsticks will be dark red with an internal temperature of at least 165ºF (74ºC) when done. Serve warm.

Per Serving:

calories: 306 | fat: 10g | protein: 51g | carbs: 1g | fiber: 0g | sodium: 590mg

Rosemary Baked Chicken Thighs

Prep time: 20 minutes | Cook time: 20 minutes | Serves 4 to 6

5 tablespoons extra-virgin olive oil, divided
3 medium shallots, diced
4 garlic cloves, peeled and crushed
1 rosemary sprig
2 to 2½ pounds (907 g to 1.1 kg) bone-in, skin-on chicken

thighs (about 6 pieces)
2 teaspoons kosher salt
¼ teaspoon freshly ground black pepper
1 lemon, juiced and zested
⅓ cup low-sodium chicken broth

1. In a large sauté pan or skillet, heat 3 tablespoons of olive oil over medium heat. Add the shallots and garlic and cook for about a minute, until fragrant. Add the rosemary sprig. 2. Season the chicken with salt and pepper. Place it in the skillet, skin-side down, and brown for 3 to 5 minutes. 3. Once it's cooked halfway through, turn the chicken over and add lemon juice and zest. 4. Add the chicken broth, cover the pan, and continue to cook for 10 to 15 more minutes, until cooked through and juices run clear. Serve.

Per Serving:

calories: 294 | fat: 18g | protein: 30g | carbs: 3g | fiber: 1g | sodium: 780mg

Grilled Chicken and Vegetables with Lemon-Walnut Sauce

Prep time: 20 minutes | Cook time: 16 minutes | Serves 4

1 cup chopped walnuts, toasted
1 small shallot, very finely chopped
½ cup olive oil, plus more for brushing
Juice and zest of 1 lemon
4 boneless, skinless chicken breasts

Sea salt and freshly ground pepper, to taste
2 zucchini, sliced diagonally ¼-inch thick
½ pound (227 g) asparagus
1 red onion, sliced ⅓-inch thick
1 teaspoon Italian seasoning

1. Preheat a grill to medium-high. 2. Put the walnuts, shallots, olive oil, lemon juice, and zest in a food processor and process until smooth and creamy. 3. Season the chicken with sea salt and freshly ground pepper, and grill on an oiled grate until cooked through, about 7–8 minutes a side or until an instant-read thermometer reaches 180ºF (82ºC) in the thickest part. 4. When the chicken is halfway done, put the vegetables on the grill. Sprinkle Italian seasoning over the chicken and vegetables to taste. 5. To serve, lay the grilled veggies on a plate, place the chicken breast on the grilled vegetables, and spoon the lemon-walnut sauce over the chicken and vegetables.

Per Serving:

calories: 800 | fat: 54g | protein: 68g | carbs: 13g | fiber: 5g | sodium: 134mg

Chicken and Shrimp Paella

Prep time: 20 minutes | Cook time: 40 minutes | Serves 6

3 tablespoons olive oil
1 onion, chopped (about 2 cups)
5 garlic cloves, minced
1 pound (454 g) chicken breasts, cut into 1-inch pieces
1 cup Arborio rice
1 teaspoon ground cumin
1 teaspoon smoked paprika
½ teaspoon ground turmeric
1½ cups low-sodium chicken broth
1 (14½-ounce / 411-g) can

diced tomatoes, with their juices
Zest and juice of 1 lemon
½ teaspoon salt
1 cup thawed frozen peas
1 medium zucchini, cut into cubes (about 2 cups)
8 ounces (227 g) uncooked shrimp, thawed, peeled, and deveined
2 tablespoons chopped fresh parsley

1. In a large saucepan, heat 2 tablespoons of the olive oil over medium heat. Add the onion and cook, occasionally stirring, for 5 minutes, or until softened. Add the garlic, chicken, rice, and remaining 1 tablespoon olive oil. Stir until the rice is coated with the oil. 2. Add the cumin, smoked paprika, turmeric, broth, tomatoes with their juices, lemon zest, lemon juice, and salt. Spread the rice mixture evenly in the pan. Bring to a boil. Reduce the heat to medium-low, cover, and cook for 25 minutes—do not stir. 3. Remove the lid and stir in the peas and zucchini. Add the shrimp, nestling them into the rice. Cover and cook for 8 to 10 minutes. Remove from the heat and let stand for 10 minutes. 4. Top with the parsley and serve.

Per Serving:

calories: 310 | fat: 18g | protein: 26g | carbs: 18g | fiber: 7g | sodium: 314mg

Cashew Chicken and Snap Peas

Prep time: 15 minutes | Cook time: 6 hours | Serves 2

16 ounces (454 g) boneless, skinless chicken breasts, cut into 2-inch pieces
2 cups sugar snap peas, strings removed
1 teaspoon grated fresh ginger
1 teaspoon minced garlic
2 tablespoons low-sodium soy

sauce
1 tablespoon ketchup
1 tablespoon rice vinegar
1 teaspoon honey
Pinch red pepper flakes
¼ cup toasted cashews
1 scallion, white and green parts, sliced thin

1. Put the chicken and sugar snap peas into the slow cooker. 2. In a measuring cup or small bowl, whisk together the ginger, garlic, soy sauce, ketchup, vinegar, honey, and red pepper flakes. Pour the mixture over the chicken and snap peas. 3. Cover and cook on low for 6 hours. The chicken should be cooked through, and the snap peas should be tender, but not mushy. 4. Just before serving, stir in the cashews and scallions.

Per Serving:

calories: 463 | fat: 14g | protein: 59g | carbs: 23g | sugars: 6g | fiber: 5g | sodium: 699mg

Chicken with Dates and Almonds

Prep time: 15 minutes | Cook time: 6 to 8 hours | Serves 4

1 onion, sliced
1 (15-ounce / 425-g) can reduced-sodium chickpeas, drained and rinsed
2½ pounds (1.1 kg) bone-in, skin-on chicken thighs
½ cup low-sodium chicken broth
2 garlic cloves, minced
1 teaspoon sea salt

1 teaspoon ground cumin
½ teaspoon ground ginger
½ teaspoon ground coriander
¼ teaspoon ground cinnamon
¼ teaspoon freshly ground black pepper
½ cup dried dates
¼ cup sliced almonds

1. In a slow cooker, gently toss together the onion and chickpeas. 2. Place the chicken on top of the chickpea mixture and pour the chicken broth over the chicken. 3. In a small bowl, stir together the garlic, salt, cumin, ginger, coriander, cinnamon, and pepper. Sprinkle the spice mix over everything. 4. Top with the dates and almonds. 5. Cover the cooker and cook for 6 to 8 hours on Low heat.

Per Serving:

calories: 841 | fat: 48g | protein: 57g | carbs: 41g | fiber: 9g | sodium: 812mg

Chapter 5 Beef, Pork, and Lamb

Balsamic Pork Chops with Figs and Pears

Prep time: 15 minutes | Cook time: 13 minutes | Serves 2

2 (8-ounce/ 227-g) bone-in pork chops	2 tablespoons olive oil
½ teaspoon salt	1 medium sweet onion, peeled and sliced
1 teaspoon ground black pepper	3 medium pears, peeled, cored, and chopped
¼ cup balsamic vinegar	5 dried figs, stems removed and halved
¼ cup low-sodium chicken broth	
1 tablespoon dried mint	

1. Pat pork chops dry with a paper towel and season both sides with salt and pepper. Set aside. 2. In a small bowl, whisk together vinegar, broth, and mint. Set aside. 3. Press the Sauté button on the Instant Pot® and heat oil. Brown pork chops for 5 minutes per side. Remove chops and set aside. 4. Add vinegar mixture and scrape any brown bits from sides and bottom of pot. Layer onion slices in the pot, then scatter pears and figs over slices. Place pork chops on top. Press the Cancel button. 5. Close lid, set steam release to Sealing, press the Steam button, and set time to 3 minutes. When the timer beeps, let pressure release naturally for 10 minutes. Quick-release any remaining pressure until the float valve drops and then open lid. 6. Using a slotted spoon, transfer pork, onion, figs, and pears to a serving platter. Serve warm.

Per Serving:
calories: 672 | fat: 32g | protein: 27g | carbs: 68g | fiber: 13g | sodium: 773mg

Beef and Mushroom Stroganoff

Prep time: 15 minutes | Cook time: 31 minutes | Serves 6

2 tablespoons olive oil	¼ teaspoon ground black pepper
1 medium onion, peeled and chopped	2 cups beef broth
2 cloves garlic, peeled and minced	1 pound (454 g) sliced button mushrooms
1 pound (454 g) beef stew meat, cut into 1" pieces	1 pound (454 g) wide egg noodles
3 tablespoons all-purpose flour	½ cup low-fat plain Greek yogurt
¼ teaspoon salt	

1. Press the Sauté button on the Instant Pot®. and heat oil. Add onion and cook until soft, about 5 minutes. Add garlic and cook until fragrant, about 30 seconds. 2. Combine beef, flour, salt, and pepper in a medium bowl and toss to coat beef completely. Add beef to the pot and cook, stirring often, until browned, about 10 minutes. Stir in beef broth and scrape any brown bits from bottom of pot. Stir in mushrooms and press the Cancel button. 3. Close lid, set steam release to Sealing, press the Manual button, and set time to 10 minutes. When the timer beeps, quick-release the pressure until the float valve drops, open lid, and stir well. Press the Cancel button. 4. Add noodles and stir, making sure noodles are submerged in liquid. Close lid, set steam release to Sealing, press the Manual button, and set time to 5 minutes. 5. When the timer beeps, quick-release the pressure until the float valve drops. Open lid and stir well. Press the Cancel button and cool for 5 minutes, then stir in yogurt. Serve hot.

Per Serving:
calories: 446 | fat: 13g | protein: 19g | carbs: 63g | fiber: 4g | sodium: 721mg

Stuffed Flank Steak

Prep time: 20 minutes | Cook time: 6 hours | Serves 6

2 pounds (907 g) flank steak	½ cup dried tomatoes, chopped
Sea salt and freshly ground pepper, to taste	½ cup roasted red peppers, diced
1 tablespoon olive oil	½ cup almonds, toasted and chopped
¼ cup onion, diced	Kitchen twine
1 clove garlic, minced	½ cup chicken stock
2 cups baby spinach, chopped	

1. Lay the flank steak out on a cutting board, and generously season with sea salt and freshly ground pepper 2. Heat the olive oil in a medium saucepan. Add the onion and garlic. 3. Cook 5 minutes on medium heat, or until onion is tender and translucent, stirring frequently. 4. Add the spinach, tomatoes, peppers, and chopped almonds, and cook an additional 3 minutes, or until the spinach wilts slightly. 5. Let the tomato and spinach mixture cool to room temperature. Spread the tomato and spinach mixture evenly over the flank steak. 6. Roll the flank steak up slowly, and tie it securely with kitchen twine on both ends and in the middle. 7. Brown the flank steak in the same pan for 5 minutes, turning it carefully to brown all sides. 8. Place steak in a slow cooker with the chicken stock. Cover and cook on low for 4–6 hours. 9. Cut into rounds, discarding the twine, and serve.

Per Serving:
calories: 287 | fat: 14g | protein: 35g | carbs: 4g | fiber: 2g | sodium: 95mg

Braised Lamb Shanks with Bell Pepper and Harissa

Prep time: 10 minutes | Cook time: 1 hour 20 minutes | Serves 4

4 (10- to 12-ounce/ 283- to 340-g) lamb shanks, trimmed
¾ teaspoon salt, divided
1 tablespoon extra-virgin olive oil
1 onion, chopped
1 red bell pepper, stemmed, seeded, and cut into 1-inch pieces
¼ cup harissa, divided
4 garlic cloves, minced
1 tablespoon tomato paste
½ cup chicken broth
1 bay leaf
2 tablespoons chopped fresh mint

1. Pat lamb shanks dry with paper towels and sprinkle with ½ teaspoon salt. Using highest sauté function, heat oil in Instant Pot for 5 minutes (or until just smoking). Brown 2 shanks on all sides, 8 to 10 minutes; transfer to plate. Repeat with remaining shanks; transfer to plate. 2. Add onion, bell pepper, and remaining ¼ teaspoon salt to fat left in pot and cook, using highest sauté function, until vegetables are softened, about 5 minutes. Stir in 2 tablespoons harissa, garlic, and tomato paste and cook until fragrant, about 30 seconds. Stir in broth and bay leaf, scraping up any browned bits. Nestle shanks into pot and add any accumulated juices. Lock lid in place and close pressure release valve. Select high pressure cook function and cook for 60 minutes. 3. Turn off Instant Pot and let pressure release naturally for 15 minutes. Quick-release any remaining pressure, then carefully remove lid, allowing steam to escape away from you. Transfer shanks to serving dish, tent with aluminum foil, and let rest while finishing sauce. 4. Strain braising liquid through fine-mesh strainer into fat separator. Discard bay leaf and transfer solids to blender. Let braising liquid settle for 5 minutes, then pour ¾ cup defatted liquid into blender with solids; discard remaining liquid. Add remaining 2 tablespoons harissa and process until smooth, about 1 minute. Season with salt and pepper to taste. Pour portion of sauce over shanks and sprinkle with mint. Serve, passing remaining sauce separately.

Per Serving:

calories: 450 | fat: 33g | protein: 28g | carbs: 9g | fiber: 3g | sodium: 780mg

Pork Loin Roast

Prep time: 30 minutes | Cook time: 55 minutes | Serves 6

1½ pounds (680 g) boneless pork loin roast, washed
1 teaspoon mustard seeds
1 teaspoon garlic powder
1 teaspoon porcini powder
1 teaspoon shallot powder
¾ teaspoon sea salt flakes
1 teaspoon red pepper flakes, crushed
2 dried sprigs thyme, crushed
2 tablespoons lime juice

1. Firstly, score the meat using a small knife; make sure to not cut too deep. 2. In a small-sized mixing dish, combine all seasonings in the order listed above; mix to combine well. 3. Massage the spice mix into the pork meat to evenly distribute. Drizzle with lemon juice. 4. Set the air fryer to 360°F (182°C). Place the pork in the air fryer basket; roast for 25 to 30 minutes. Pause the machine, check for doneness and cook for 25 minutes more.

Per Serving:

calories: 157 | fat: 5g | protein: 26g | carbs: 1g | fiber: 0g | sodium: 347mg

Mustard Lamb Chops

Prep time: 5 minutes | Cook time: 14 minutes | Serves 4

Oil, for spraying
1 tablespoon Dijon mustard
2 teaspoons lemon juice
½ teaspoon dried tarragon
¼ teaspoon salt
¼ teaspoon freshly ground black pepper
4 (1¼-inch-thick) loin lamb chops

1. Preheat the air fryer to 390°F (199°C). Line the air fryer basket with parchment and spray lightly with oil. 2. In a small bowl, mix together the mustard, lemon juice, tarragon, salt, and black pepper. 3. Pat dry the lamb chops with a paper towel. Brush the chops on both sides with the mustard mixture. 4. Place the chops in the prepared basket. You may need to work in batches, depending on the size of your air fryer. 5. Cook for 8 minutes, flip, and cook for another 6 minutes, or until the internal temperature reaches 125°F (52°C) for rare, 145°F (63°C) for medium-rare, or 155°F (68°C) for medium.

Per Serving:

calories: 96 | fat: 4g | protein: 14g | carbs: 0g | fiber: 0g | sodium: 233mg

Pork Souvlaki

Prep time: 1 hour 15 minutes | Cook time: 10 minutes | Serves 4

1 (1½-pound / 680-g) pork loin
2 tablespoons garlic, minced
⅓ cup extra-virgin olive oil
⅓ cup lemon juice
1 tablespoon dried oregano
1 teaspoon salt
Pita bread and tzatziki, for serving (optional)

1. Cut the pork into 1-inch cubes and put them into a bowl or plastic zip-top bag. 2. In a large bowl, mix together the garlic, olive oil, lemon juice, oregano, and salt. 3. Pour the marinade over the pork and let it marinate for at least 1 hour. 4. Preheat a grill, grill pan, or lightly oiled skillet to high heat. Using wood or metal skewers, thread the pork onto the skewers. 5. Cook the skewers for 3 minutes on each side, for 12 minutes in total. 6. Serve with pita bread and tzatziki sauce, if desired.

Per Serving:

calories: 393 | fat: 25g | protein: 38g | carbs: 3g | fiber: 0g | sodium: 666mg

Southern Chili

1 pound (454 g) ground beef (85% lean)	tomatoes with green chilies
1 cup minced onion	1 (15-ounce / 425-g) can light red kidney beans, rinsed and drained
1 (28-ounce / 794-g) can tomato purée	¼ cup Chili seasoning
1 (15-ounce / 425-g) can diced	

1. Preheat the air fryer to 400°F (204°C). 2. In a baking pan, mix the ground beef and onion. Place the pan in the air fryer. 3. Cook for 4 minutes. Stir and cook for 4 minutes more until browned. Remove the pan from the fryer. Drain the meat and transfer to a large bowl. 4. Reduce the air fryer temperature to 350°F (177°C). 5. To the bowl with the meat, add in the tomato purée, diced tomatoes and green chilies, kidney beans, and Chili seasoning. Mix well. Pour the mixture into the baking pan. 6. Cook for 25 minutes, stirring every 10 minutes, until thickened.

Per Serving:
calories: 455 | fat: 18g | protein: 32g | carbs: 44g | fiber: 11g | sodium: 815mg

Spiced Beef on Whole-Wheat Flatbread

6 ounces (170 g) lean ground beef	⅛ teaspoon ground cinnamon
2 garlic cloves, minced	4 whole-wheat flatbread rounds
1 small onion, grated	½ cup plain Greek yogurt, for garnish
3 tablespoons tomato paste	
1 tablespoon minced flat-leaf parsley	2 tablespoons cilantro leaves, for garnish
½ teaspoon salt	1 Persian cucumber, cut lengthwise into thin sheets
¼ teaspoon cayenne pepper	
¼ teaspoon ground cumin	½ small red onion, thinly sliced
¼ teaspoon sweet paprika	Lemon wedges, for serving

1. Preheat the oven to 475°F(245°C). 2 In medium skillet, brown the meat over medium-high heat, breaking up with a spatula, about 4 minutes. When the meat is browned, drain off the excess fat. Add the garlic and grated onion and cook, stirring, 1 minute. Add the tomato paste, parsley, salt, cayenne, cumin, paprika, and cinnamon and cook, stirring, for 1 more minute. 3. Place 2 flatbread rounds onto each of 2 large baking sheets and spoon the meat on top of them, dividing equally. Bake in the preheated oven, rotating the pans halfway through, for 6 to 8 minutes, until the edges of the flatbread are beginning to brown. 4. Remove from the oven and serve with a dollop of yogurt, a sprinkling of cilantro, a few strips of cucumber, and a few slices of red onion on top. Serve lemon wedges on the side for squeezing over the meat.

Per Serving:
calories: 293 | fat: 8g | protein: 21g | carbs: 37g | fiber: 5g | sodium: 793mg

Pork and Cannellini Bean Stew

1 cup dried cannellini beans	1 (8-ounce/ 227-g) can tomato paste
¼ cup olive oil	
1 medium onion, diced	¼ cup flat-leaf parsley, chopped
2 pounds (907 g) pork roast, cut into 1-inch chunks	½ teaspoon dried thyme
3 cups water	Sea salt and freshly ground pepper, to taste

1. Rinse and sort the beans. 2. Cover beans with water, and allow to soak overnight. Heat the olive oil in a large stew pot. 3. Add the onion, stirring occasionally, until golden brown. 4. Add the pork chunks and cook 5–8 minutes, stirring frequently, until the pork is browned. Drain and rinse the beans, and add to the pot. 5. Add the water, and bring to a boil. Reduce heat and simmer for 45 minutes, until beans are tender. 6. Add the tomato paste, parsley, and thyme, and simmer an additional 15 minutes, or until the sauce thickens slightly. Season to taste.

Per Serving:
calories: 373 | fat: 16g | protein: 39g | carbs: 19g | fiber: 4g | sodium: 107mg

Italian Braised Pork

2½ pounds (1.1 kg) boneless pork shoulder	1 stalk celery, finely diced
Coarse sea salt	¾ teaspoon fennel seeds
Black pepper	½ cup dry red wine
2 tablespoons olive oil	1 (28-ounce / 794-g) can crushed tomatoes
1 large yellow onion, finely diced	4 cups prepared hot couscous, for serving
3 cloves garlic, minced	

1. Season the pork with salt and pepper. 2. In a large skillet, heat the olive oil over medium-high heat. Cook the pork, turning occasionally, until browned on all sides, about 8 minutes. Transfer the pork to the slow cooker. 3. Reduce the heat under the skillet to medium, and add the onion, garlic, celery, and fennel seeds. Cook, stirring often, until the onion is softened, about 4 minutes. 4. Add the wine and cook, stirring with a wooden spoon and scraping up the flavorful browned bits from the bottom of the pan, until the liquid is reduced by half, about 2 minutes. Add the wine mixture to the slow cooker, and stir in the tomatoes. 5. Cover and cook on high for 4 hours, or until the pork is very tender, or on low for 8 hours. 6. Transfer the pork to a cutting board. Shred the meat into bite-size pieces. Discard any pieces of fat. 7. Skim the fat off the sauce in the slow cooker and discard. Return the shredded pork to the slow cooker and stir to combine. Cook the pork and sauce for 5 minutes to reheat. 8. Serve hot over the couscous.

Per Serving:
calories: 669 | fat: 17g | protein: 72g | carbs: 49g | fiber: 7g | sodium: 187mg

Roast Pork Loin with Juniper Berries and Honey

Prep time: 5 minutes | Cook time: 1 hour | Serves 6

2 cloves garlic, chopped
3 or 4 leaves fresh sage, chopped
1 tablespoon chopped fresh rosemary
1 tablespoon juniper berries, crushed
2 tablespoons olive oil, divided

1 bone-in pork loin roast (3–4 pounds/ 1.4 to 1.8 kg), trimmed
1 cup low-sodium chicken broth
2 teaspoons honey
½ teaspoon kosher salt
¼ teaspoon ground black pepper

1. Preheat the oven to 400°F(205°C) . 2. In a small bowl, stir together the garlic, sage, rosemary, juniper berries, and 1 tablespoon of the oil. Rub this mixture all over the pork loin and place in a large baking dish. 3. Roast the pork loin, turning the meat over once, until a thermometer placed in the center reads 150°F(66°C), about 50 minutes. Remove the pork from the baking dish and set aside to rest. 4. Strain the juices from the baking dish into a small saucepan. Add the broth, honey, salt, and pepper and bring to a boil. Reduce the heat to a simmer and cook until thickened, about 8 minutes. 5. To serve, slice the pork and drizzle the sauce over top.

Per Serving:

calories: 366 | fat: 16g | protein: 50g | carbs: 4g | fiber: 0g | sodium: 342mg

Kofta with Vegetables in Tomato Sauce

Prep time: 15 minutes | Cook time: 6 to 8 hours | Serves 4

1 pound (454 g) raw ground beef
1 small white or yellow onion, finely diced
2 garlic cloves, minced
1 tablespoon dried parsley
2 teaspoons ground coriander
1 teaspoon ground cumin
½ teaspoon sea salt
½ teaspoon freshly ground black pepper

¼ teaspoon ground nutmeg
¼ teaspoon dried mint
¼ teaspoon paprika
1 (28-ounce/ 794-g) can no-salt-added diced tomatoes
2 or 3 zucchini, cut into 1½-inch-thick rounds
4 ounces (113 g) mushrooms
1 large red onion, chopped
1 green bell pepper, seeded and chopped

1. In large bowl, mix together the ground beef, white or yellow onion, garlic, parsley, coriander, cumin, salt, pepper, nutmeg, mint, and paprika until well combined and all of the spices and onion are well blended into the meat. Form the meat mixture into 10 to 12 oval patties. Set aside. 2. In a slow cooker, combine the tomatoes, zucchini, mushrooms, red onion, and bell pepper. Stir to mix well. 3. Place the kofta patties on top of the tomato mixture. 4. Cover the cooker and cook for 6 to 8 hours on Low heat.

Per Serving:

calories: 263 | fat: 9g | protein: 27g | carbs: 23g | fiber: 7g | sodium: 480mg

Poblano Pepper Cheeseburgers

Prep time: 5 minutes | Cook time: 30 minutes | Serves 4

2 poblano chile peppers
1½ pounds (680 g) 85% lean ground beef
1 clove garlic, minced
1 teaspoon salt

½ teaspoon freshly ground black pepper
4 slices Cheddar cheese (about 3 ounces / 85 g)
4 large lettuce leaves

1. Preheat the air fryer to 400ºF (204ºC). 2. Arrange the poblano peppers in the basket of the air fryer. Pausing halfway through the cooking time to turn the peppers, air fry for 20 minutes, or until they are softened and beginning to char. Transfer the peppers to a large bowl and cover with a plate. When cool enough to handle, peel off the skin, remove the seeds and stems, and slice into strips. Set aside. 3. Meanwhile, in a large bowl, combine the ground beef with the garlic, salt, and pepper. Shape the beef into 4 patties. 4. Lower the heat on the air fryer to 360ºF (182ºC). Arrange the burgers in a single layer in the basket of the air fryer. Pausing halfway through the cooking time to turn the burgers, air fry for 10 minutes, or until a thermometer inserted into the thickest part registers 160ºF (71ºC). 5. Top the burgers with the cheese slices and continue baking for a minute or two, just until the cheese has melted. Serve the burgers on a lettuce leaf topped with the roasted poblano peppers.

Per Serving:

calories: 489 | fat: 35g | protein: 39g | carbs: 3g | fiber: 1g | sodium: 703mg

Rosemary Roast Beef

Prep time: 30 minutes | Cook time: 30 to 35 minutes | Serves 8

1 (2-pound / 907-g) top round beef roast, tied with kitchen string
Sea salt and freshly ground black pepper, to taste

2 teaspoons minced garlic
2 tablespoons finely chopped fresh rosemary
¼ cup avocado oil

1. Season the roast generously with salt and pepper. 2. In a small bowl, whisk together the garlic, rosemary, and avocado oil. Rub this all over the roast. Cover loosely with aluminum foil or plastic wrap and refrigerate for at least 12 hours or up to 2 days. 3. Remove the roast from the refrigerator and allow to sit at room temperature for about 1 hour. 4. Set the air fryer to 325ºF (163ºC). Place the roast in the air fryer basket and roast for 15 minutes. Flip the roast and cook for 15 to 20 minutes more, until the meat is browned and an instant-read thermometer reads 120ºF (49ºC) at the thickest part (for medium-rare). 5. Transfer the meat to a cutting board, and let it rest for 15 minutes before thinly slicing and serving.

Per Serving:

calories: 208 | fat: 12g | protein: 25g | carbs: 0g | fiber: 0g | sodium: 68mg

Goat Cheese-Stuffed Flank Steak

Prep time: 10 minutes | Cook time: 14 minutes | Serves 6

1 pound (454 g) flank steak	black pepper
1 tablespoon avocado oil	2 ounces (57 g) goat cheese, crumbled
½ teaspoon sea salt	
½ teaspoon garlic powder	1 cup baby spinach, chopped
¼ teaspoon freshly ground	

1. Place the steak in a large zip-top bag or between two pieces of plastic wrap. Using a meat mallet or heavy-bottomed skillet, pound the steak to an even ¼-inch thickness. 2. Brush both sides of the steak with the avocado oil. 3. Mix the salt, garlic powder, and pepper in a small dish. Sprinkle this mixture over both sides of the steak. 4. Sprinkle the goat cheese over top, and top that with the spinach. 5. Starting at one of the long sides, roll the steak up tightly. Tie the rolled steak with kitchen string at 3-inch intervals. 6. Set the air fryer to 400°F (204°C). Place the steak roll-up in the air fryer basket. Air fry for 7 minutes. Flip the steak and cook for an additional 7 minutes, until an instant-read thermometer reads 120°F (49°C) for medium-rare (adjust the cooking time for your desired doneness).

Per Serving:

calories: 151 | fat: 8g | protein: 18g | carbs: 0g | fiber: 0g | sodium: 281mg

Cube Steak Roll-Ups

Prep time: 30 minutes | Cook time: 8 to 10 minutes | Serves 4

4 cube steaks (6 ounces / 170 g each)	½ cup finely chopped yellow onion
1 (16-ounce / 454-g) bottle Italian dressing	½ cup finely chopped green bell pepper
1 teaspoon salt	½ cup finely chopped mushrooms
½ teaspoon freshly ground black pepper	1 to 2 tablespoons oil

1. In a large resealable bag or airtight storage container, combine the steaks and Italian dressing. Seal the bag and refrigerate to marinate for 2 hours. 2. Remove the steaks from the marinade and place them on a cutting board. Discard the marinade. Evenly season the steaks with salt and pepper. 3. In a small bowl, stir together the onion, bell pepper, and mushrooms. Sprinkle the onion mixture evenly over the steaks. Roll up the steaks, jelly roll-style, and secure with toothpicks. 4. Preheat the air fryer to 400°F (204°C). 5. Place the steaks in the air fryer basket. 6. Cook for 4 minutes. Flip the steaks and spritz them with oil. Cook for 4 to 6 minutes more until the internal temperature reaches 145°F (63°C). Let rest for 5 minutes before serving.

Per Serving:

calories: 364 | fat: 20g | protein: 37g | carbs: 7g | fiber: 1g | sodium: 715mg

Braised Lamb Shanks

Prep time: 10 minutes | Cook time: 2 hours | Serves 4 to 6

3 tablespoons extra-virgin olive oil	1 (15-ounce/ 425-g) can diced tomatoes
6 lamb shanks	6 cups water
1 large onion, chopped	3 bay leaves
3 carrots, chopped	1 teaspoon salt

1. Place a large pot with a lid or Dutch oven over high heat and add the olive oil and lamb shanks. Brown on each side, about 8 minutes total. 2. Put the shanks onto a plate and add the onion and carrots to the same pot; cook for 5 minutes. 3. Add the tomatoes, water, bay leaves, and salt. Stir to combine. Add the lamb shanks back to the pot and bring to a simmer. 4. Turn the heat down to low and cover the pot. Let the shanks cook for 1 hour and 30 minutes. Remove the cover and let cook for another 20 minutes. 5. Remove the bay leaves from the pot and spoon the lamb shanks and sauce onto a serving dish. Serve warm with rice or couscous.

Per Serving:

calories: 462 | fat: 18g | protein: 69g | carbs: 8g | fiber: 3g | sodium: 670mg

Ground Pork and Eggplant Casserole

Prep time: 20 minutes | Cook time: 18 minutes | Serves 8

2 pounds (907 g) lean ground pork	1 tablespoon freeze-dried parsley
1 large yellow onion, peeled and diced	3 tablespoons tomato paste
1 stalk celery, diced	½ teaspoon hot sauce
1 medium green bell pepper, seeded and diced	2 teaspoons Worcestershire sauce
2 medium eggplants, cut into ½" pieces	1 teaspoon salt
4 cloves garlic, peeled and minced	½ teaspoon ground black pepper
⅛ teaspoon dried thyme	1 large egg, beaten
	½ cup low-sodium chicken broth

1. Press the Sauté button on the Instant Pot® and add pork, onion, celery, and bell pepper to the pot. Cook until pork is no longer pink, breaking it apart as it cooks, about 8 minutes. 2. Drain and discard any fat rendered from pork. Add eggplant, garlic, thyme, parsley, tomato paste, hot sauce, Worcestershire sauce, salt, pepper, and egg. Stir well, then press the Cancel button. 3. Pour in chicken broth. Close lid, set steam release to Sealing, press the Manual button, and set time to 10 minutes. When the timer beeps, let pressure release naturally, about 25 minutes. Open lid and serve hot.

Per Serving:

calories: 292 | fat: 18g | protein: 22g | carbs: 10g | fiber: 4g | sodium: 392mg

Indian Mint and Chile Kebabs

Prep time: 30 minutes | Cook time: 15 minutes | Serves 4

1 pound (454 g) ground lamb
½ cup finely minced onion
¼ cup chopped fresh mint
¼ cup chopped fresh cilantro
1 tablespoon minced garlic
½ teaspoon ground turmeric
½ teaspoon cayenne pepper
¼ teaspoon ground cardamom
¼ teaspoon ground cinnamon
1 teaspoon kosher salt

1. In the bowl of a stand mixer fitted with the paddle attachment, combine the lamb, onion, mint, cilantro, garlic, turmeric, cayenne, cardamom, cinnamon, and salt. Mix on low speed until you have a sticky mess of spiced meat. If you have time, let the mixture stand at room temperature for 30 minutes (or cover and refrigerate for up to a day or two, until you're ready to make the kebabs). 2. Divide the meat into eight equal portions. Form each into a long sausage shape. Place the kebabs in a single layer in the air fryer basket. Set the air fryer to 350ºF (177ºC) for 10 minutes. Increase the air fryer temperature to 400ºF (204ºC) and cook for 3 to 4 minutes more to brown the kebabs. Use a meat thermometer to ensure the kebabs have reached an internal temperature of 160ºF / 71ºC (medium).

Per Serving:
calories: 231 | fat: 14g | protein: 23g | carbs: 3g | fiber: 1g | sodium: 648mg

Lamb Stew

Prep time: 20 minutes | Cook time: 2 hours 20 minutes | Serves 6

3 carrots, peeled and sliced
2 onions, minced
2 cups white wine
½ cup flat-leaf parsley, chopped
2 garlic cloves, minced
3 bay leaves
1 teaspoon dried rosemary leaves
¼ teaspoon nutmeg
¼ teaspoon ground cloves
2 pounds (907 g) boneless lamb, cut into 1-inch pieces
¼ cup olive oil
1 package frozen artichoke hearts
Sea salt and freshly ground pepper, to taste

1. Combine the carrots, onion, white wine, parsley, garlic, bay leaves, and seasonings in a plastic bag or shallow dish. 2. Add the lamb and marinate overnight. 3. Drain the lamb, reserving the marinade, and pat dry. 4. Heat the olive oil in a large stew pot. Brown the lamb meat, turning frequently. 5. Pour the marinade into the stew pot, cover, and simmer on low for 2 hours. 6. Add the artichoke hearts and simmer an additional 20 minutes. Season with sea salt and freshly ground pepper.

Per Serving:
calories: 399 | fat: 18g | protein: 33g | carbs: 13g | fiber: 3g | sodium: 167mg

Greek Lamb Chops

Prep time: 10 minutes | Cook time: 6 to 8 hours | Serves 6

3 pounds (1.4 kg) lamb chops
½ cup low-sodium beef broth
Juice of 1 lemon
1 tablespoon extra-virgin olive oil
2 garlic cloves, minced
1 teaspoon dried oregano
1 teaspoon sea salt
½ teaspoon freshly ground black pepper

1. Put the lamb chops in a slow cooker. 2. In a small bowl, whisk together the beef broth, lemon juice, olive oil, garlic, oregano, salt, and pepper until blended. Pour the sauce over the lamb chops. 3. Cover the cooker and cook for 6 to 8 hours on Low heat.

Per Serving:
calories: 325 | fat: 13g | protein: 47g | carbs: 1g | fiber: 0g | sodium: 551mg

Lebanese Malfouf (Stuffed Cabbage Rolls)

Prep time: 15 minutes | Cook time: 33 minutes | Serves 4

1 head green cabbage
1 pound (454 g) lean ground beef
½ cup long-grain brown rice
4 garlic cloves, minced
1 teaspoon salt
½ teaspoon black pepper
1 teaspoon ground cinnamon
2 tablespoons chopped fresh mint
Juice of 1 lemon
Olive oil cooking spray
½ cup beef broth
1 tablespoon olive oil

1. Cut the cabbage in half and remove the core. Remove 12 of the larger leaves to use for the cabbage rolls. 2. Bring a large pot of salted water to a boil, then drop the cabbage leaves into the water, boiling them for 3 minutes. Remove from the water and set aside. 3. In a large bowl, combine the ground beef, rice, garlic, salt, pepper, cinnamon, mint, and lemon juice, and mix together until combined. Divide this mixture into 12 equal portions. 4. Preheat the air fryer to 360°F(182ºC). Lightly coat a small casserole dish with olive oil cooking spray. 5. Place a cabbage leaf on a clean work surface. Place a spoonful of the beef mixture on one side of the leaf, leaving space on all other sides. Fold the two perpendicular sides inward and then roll forward, tucking tightly as rolled (similar to a burrito roll). Place the finished rolls into the baking dish, stacking them on top of each other if needed. 6. Pour the beef broth over the top of the cabbage rolls so that it soaks down between them, and then brush the tops with the olive oil. 7. Place the casserole dish into the air fryer basket and bake for 30 minutes.

Per Serving:
calories: 329 | fat: 10g | protein: 29g | carbs: 33g | fiber: 7g | sodium: 700mg

Smoky Herb Lamb Chops and Lemon-Rosemary Dressing

Prep time: 1 hour 35 minutes | Cook time: 10 minutes | Serves 6

4 large cloves garlic
1 cup lemon juice
⅓ cup fresh rosemary
1 cup extra-virgin olive oil

1½ teaspoons salt
1 teaspoon freshly ground black pepper
6 (1-inch-thick) lamb chops

1. In a food processor or blender, blend the garlic, lemon juice, rosemary, olive oil, salt, and black pepper for 15 seconds. Set aside. 2. Put the lamb chops in a large plastic zip-top bag or container. Cover the lamb with two-thirds of the rosemary dressing, making sure that all of the lamb chops are coated with the dressing. Let the lamb marinate in the fridge for 1 hour. 3. When you are almost ready to eat, take the lamb chops out of the fridge and let them sit on the counter-top for 20 minutes. Preheat a grill, grill pan, or lightly oiled skillet to high heat. 4. Cook the lamb chops for 3 minutes on each side. To serve, drizzle the lamb with the remaining dressing.

Per Serving:

calories: 484 | fat: 42g | protein: 24g | carbs: 5g | fiber: 1g | sodium: 655mg

Chapter 6 Fish and Seafood

Shrimp in Creamy Pesto over Zoodles

Prep time: 10 minutes | Cook time: 10 minutes |
Serves 4

1 pound (454 g) peeled and deveined fresh shrimp	jarred pesto
Salt	¾ cup crumbled goat or feta cheese, plus more for serving
Freshly ground black pepper	6 cups zucchini noodles (from about 2 large zucchini), for serving
2 tablespoons extra-virgin olive oil	
½ small onion, slivered	¼ cup chopped flat-leaf Italian parsley, for garnish
8 ounces (227 g) store-bought	

1. In a bowl, season the shrimp with salt and pepper and set aside. 2. In a large skillet, heat the olive oil over medium-high heat. Sauté the onion until just golden, 5 to 6 minutes. 3. Reduce the heat to low and add the pesto and cheese, whisking to combine and melt the cheese. Bring to a low simmer and add the shrimp. Reduce the heat back to low and cover. Cook until the shrimp is cooked through and pink, another 3 to 4 minutes. 4. Serve warm over zucchini noodles, garnishing with chopped parsley and additional crumbled cheese, if desired.

Per Serving:

calories: 608 | fat: 49g | protein: 37g | carbs: 9g | fiber: 3g | sodium: 564mg

Shrimp with White Beans and Feta

Prep time: 15 minutes | Cook time: 15 minutes |
Serves 4

3 tablespoons lemon juice, divided	salt-added or low-sodium cannellini beans, rinsed and drained
2 tablespoons extra-virgin olive oil, divided	¼ cup fresh mint, chopped
½ teaspoon kosher salt, divided	1 teaspoon lemon zest
1 pound (454 g) shrimp, peeled and deveined	1 tablespoon white wine vinegar
1 large shallot, diced	¼ teaspoon freshly ground black pepper
¼ cup no-salt-added vegetable stock	¼ cup crumbled feta cheese, for garnish
1 (15-ounce / 425-g) can no-	

1. In a small bowl, whisk together 1 tablespoon of the lemon juice, 1 tablespoon of the olive oil, and ¼ teaspoon of the salt. Add the shrimp and set aside. 2. Heat the remaining 1 tablespoon olive oil in a large skillet or sauté pan over medium heat. Add the shallot and sauté until translucent, about 2 to 3 minutes. Add the vegetable stock and deglaze the pan, scraping up any brown bits, and bring to a boil. Add the beans and shrimp. Reduce the heat to low, cover, and simmer until the shrimp are cooked through, about 3 to 4 minutes. 3. Turn off the heat and add the mint, lemon zest, vinegar, and black pepper. Stir gently to combine. Garnish with the feta.

Per Serving:

calories: 340 | fat: 11g | protein: 32g | carbs: 28g | fiber: 6g | sodium: 415mg

Chili Tilapia

Prep time: 5 minutes | Cook time: 20 minutes |
Serves 4

4 tilapia fillets, boneless	1 tablespoon avocado oil
1 teaspoon chili flakes	1 teaspoon mustard
1 teaspoon dried oregano	

1. Rub the tilapia fillets with chili flakes, dried oregano, avocado oil, and mustard and put in the air fryer. 2. Cook it for 10 minutes per side at 360°F (182°C).

Per Serving:

calories: 146 | fat: 6g | protein: 23g | carbs: 1g | fiber: 0g | sodium: 94mg

Shrimp Risotto

Prep time: 10 minutes | Cook time: 4 to 6 hours |
Serves 4

1½ cups raw arborio rice	¼ teaspoon freshly ground black pepper
4½ cups low-sodium chicken broth	1 pound (454 g) whole raw medium shrimp, peeled and deveined
½ cup diced onion	
2 garlic cloves, minced	
½ teaspoon sea salt	¼ cup grated Parmesan cheese
½ teaspoon dried parsley	

1. In a slow cooker, combine the rice, chicken broth, onion, garlic, salt, parsley, and pepper. Stir to mix well. 2. Cover the cooker and cook for 4 to 6 hours on Low heat. 3. Stir in the shrimp and Parmesan cheese. Replace the cover on the cooker and cook for 15 to 30 minutes on Low heat, or until the shrimp have turned pink and the cheese is melted.

Per Serving:

calories: 376 | fat: 3g | protein: 28g | carbs: 59g | fiber: 1g | sodium: 602mg

Italian Baccalà

Prep time: 2 to 3 hours | Cook time: 4 to 6 hours | Serves 4

1½ pounds (680 g) salt cod
1 (15-ounce / 425-g) can no-salt-added diced tomatoes
½ onion, chopped
2 garlic cloves, minced

½ teaspoon red pepper flakes
¼ cup chopped fresh parsley, plus more for garnish
Juice of ½ lemon

1. Wash the salt cod to remove any visible salt. Completely submerge the cod in a large bowl of water and let it soak for at least 2 to 3 hours. If you are soaking it for longer than 24 hours, change the water after 12 hours. 2. In a slow cooker, combine the tomatoes, onion, garlic, red pepper flakes, parsley, and lemon juice. Stir to mix well. Drain the cod and add it to the slow cooker, breaking it apart as necessary to make it fit. 3. Cover the cooker and cook for 4 to 6 hours on Low heat. 4. Garnish with the remaining fresh parsley for serving.

Per Serving:

calories: 211 | fat: 2g | protein: 39g | carbs: 8g | fiber: 2g | sodium: 179mg

Apple Cider Mussels

Prep time: 10 minutes | Cook time: 2 minutes | Serves 5

2 pounds (907 g) mussels, cleaned, peeled
1 teaspoon onion powder

1 teaspoon ground cumin
1 tablespoon avocado oil
¼ cup apple cider vinegar

1. Mix mussels with onion powder, ground cumin, avocado oil, and apple cider vinegar. 2. Put the mussels in the air fryer and cook at 395ºF (202ºC) for 2 minutes.

Per Serving:

calories: 187 | fat: 7g | protein: 22g | carbs: 7g | fiber: 0g | sodium: 521mg

Mediterranean-Style Cod

Prep time: 5 minutes | Cook time: 12 minutes | Serves 4

4 (6-ounce / 170-g) cod fillets
3 tablespoons fresh lemon juice
1 tablespoon olive oil
¼ teaspoon salt

6 cherry tomatoes, halved
¼ cup pitted and sliced kalamata olives

1. Place cod into an ungreased round nonstick baking dish. Pour lemon juice into dish and drizzle cod with olive oil. Sprinkle with salt. Place tomatoes and olives around baking dish in between fillets. 2. Place dish into air fryer basket. Adjust the temperature to 350ºF (177ºC) and bake for 12 minutes, carefully turning cod halfway through cooking. Fillets will be lightly browned, easily flake, and have an internal temperature of at least 145ºF (63ºC) when done. Serve warm.

Per Serving:

calories: 186 | fat: 5g | protein: 31g | carbs: 2g | fiber: 1g | sodium: 300mg

Mediterranean Grilled Shrimp

Prep time: 20 minutes | Cook time: 5 minutes | Serves 4 to 6

2 tablespoons garlic, minced
½ cup lemon juice
3 tablespoons fresh Italian parsley, finely chopped

¼ cup extra-virgin olive oil
1 teaspoon salt
2 pounds (907 g) jumbo shrimp (21-25), peeled and deveined

1. In a large bowl, mix the garlic, lemon juice, parsley, olive oil, and salt. 2. Add the shrimp to the bowl and toss to make sure all the pieces are coated with the marinade. Let the shrimp sit for 15 minutes. 3. Preheat a grill, grill pan, or lightly oiled skillet to high heat. While heating, thread about 5 to 6 pieces of shrimp onto each skewer. 4. Place the skewers on the grill, grill pan, or skillet and cook for 2 to 3 minutes on each side until cooked through. Serve warm.

Per Serving:

calories: 217 | fat: 10g | protein: 31g | carbs: 2g | fiber: 0g | sodium: 569mg

Steamed Cod with Garlic and Swiss Chard

Prep time: 5 minutes | Cook time: 12 minutes | Serves 4

1 teaspoon salt
½ teaspoon dried oregano
½ teaspoon dried thyme
½ teaspoon garlic powder
4 cod fillets

½ white onion, thinly sliced
2 cups Swiss chard, washed, stemmed, and torn into pieces
¼ cup olive oil
1 lemon, quartered

1. Preheat the air fryer to 380ºF(193ºC). 2. In a small bowl, whisk together the salt, oregano, thyme, and garlic powder. 3. Tear off four pieces of aluminum foil, with each sheet being large enough to envelop one cod fillet and a quarter of the vegetables. 4. Place a cod fillet in the middle of each sheet of foil, then sprinkle on all sides with the spice mixture. 5. In each foil packet, place a quarter of the onion slices and ½ cup Swiss chard, then drizzle 1 tablespoon olive oil and squeeze ¼ lemon over the contents of each foil packet. 6. Fold and seal the sides of the foil packets and then place them into the air fryer basket. Steam for 12 minutes. 7. Remove from the basket, and carefully open each packet to avoid a steam burn.

Per Serving:

calories: 324 | fat: 15g | protein: 42g | carbs: 4g | fiber: 1g | sodium: 746mg

Breaded Shrimp Tacos

Prep time: 10 minutes | Cook time: 9 minutes |
Makes 8 tacos

2 large eggs
1 teaspoon prepared yellow mustard
1 pound (454 g) small shrimp, peeled, deveined, and tails removed
½ cup finely shredded Gouda or Parmesan cheese

½ cup pork dust
For Serving:
8 large Boston lettuce leaves
¼ cup pico de gallo
¼ cup shredded purple cabbage
1 lemon, sliced
Guacamole (optional)

1. Preheat the air fryer to 400°F (204°C). 2. Crack the eggs into a large bowl, add the mustard, and whisk until well combined. Add the shrimp and stir well to coat. 3. In a medium-sized bowl, mix together the cheese and pork dust until well combined. 4. One at a time, roll the coated shrimp in the pork dust mixture and use your hands to press it onto each shrimp. Spray the coated shrimp with avocado oil and place them in the air fryer basket, leaving space between them. 5. Air fry the shrimp for 9 minutes, or until cooked through and no longer translucent, flipping after 4 minutes. 6. To serve, place a lettuce leaf on a serving plate, place several shrimp on top, and top with 1½ teaspoons each of pico de gallo and purple cabbage. Squeeze some lemon juice on top and serve with guacamole, if desired. 7. Store leftover shrimp in an airtight container in the refrigerator for up to 3 days. Reheat in a preheated 400°F (204°C) air fryer for 5 minutes, or until warmed through.

Per Serving:
calories: 115 | fat: 4g | protein: 18g | carbs: 2g | fiber: 1g | sodium: 253mg

Sesame-Ginger Cod

Prep time: 10 minutes | Cook time: 4 to 6 hours |
Serves 4

¼ cup low-sodium soy sauce
2 tablespoons balsamic vinegar
1 tablespoon freshly squeezed lemon juice
2 teaspoons extra-virgin olive oil
1 tablespoon ground ginger
½ teaspoon sea salt

¼ teaspoon freshly ground black pepper
Nonstick cooking spray
2 pounds (907 g) fresh cod fillets
½ teaspoon sesame seeds
4 scallions, green parts only, cut into 3-inch lengths

1. In a small bowl, whisk together the soy sauce, vinegar, lemon juice, olive oil, ginger, salt, and pepper until combined. Set aside. 2. Coat a slow-cooker insert with cooking spray and place the cod in the prepared slow cooker. Pour the soy sauce mixture over the cod. 3. Cover the cooker and cook for 4 to 6 hours on Low heat. 4. Garnish with sesame seeds and scallions for serving.

Per Serving:
calories: 282 | fat: 4g | protein: 52g | carbs: 4g | fiber: 1g | sodium: 869mg

Seafood Fideo

Prep time: 15 minutes | Cook time: 20 minutes |
Serves 6 to 8

2 tablespoons extra-virgin olive oil, plus ½ cup, divided
6 cups zucchini noodles, roughly chopped (2 to 3 medium zucchini)
1 pound (454 g) shrimp, peeled, deveined and roughly chopped
6 to 8 ounces (170 to 227 g) canned chopped clams, drained
4 ounces (113 g) crabmeat
½ cup crumbled goat cheese

½ cup crumbled feta cheese
1 (28-ounce / 794-g) can chopped tomatoes, with their juices
1 teaspoon salt
1 teaspoon garlic powder
½ teaspoon smoked paprika
½ cup shredded Parmesan cheese
¼ cup chopped fresh flat-leaf Italian parsley, for garnish

1. Preheat the oven to 375°F(190°C). 2. Pour 2 tablespoons olive oil in the bottom of a 9-by-13-inch baking dish and swirl to coat the bottom. 3. In a large bowl, combine the zucchini noodles, shrimp, clams, and crabmeat. 4. In another bowl, combine the goat cheese, feta, and ¼ cup olive oil and stir to combine well. Add the canned tomatoes and their juices, salt, garlic powder, and paprika and combine well. Add the mixture to the zucchini and seafood mixture and stir to combine. 5. Pour the mixture into the prepared baking dish, spreading evenly. Spread shredded Parmesan over top and drizzle with the remaining ¼ cup olive oil. Bake until bubbly, 20 to 25 minutes. Serve warm, garnished with chopped parsley.

Per Serving:
calories: 302 | fat: 21g | protein: 22g | carbs: 9g | fiber: 3g | sodium: 535mg

Poached Salmon

Prep time: 10 minutes | Cook time: 5 minutes |
Serves 4

1 lemon, sliced ¼ inch thick
4 (6-ounce / 170-g) skinless salmon fillets, 1½ inches thick

½ teaspoon table salt
¼ teaspoon pepper

1. Add ½ cup water to Instant Pot. Fold sheet of aluminum foil into 16 by 6-inch sling. Arrange lemon slices widthwise in 2 rows across center of sling. Sprinkle flesh side of salmon with salt and pepper, then arrange skinned side down on top of lemon slices. 2. Using sling, lower salmon into Instant Pot; allow narrow edges of sling to rest along sides of insert. Lock lid in place and close pressure release valve. Select high pressure cook function and cook for 3 minutes. 3. Turn off Instant Pot and quick-release pressure. Carefully remove lid, allowing steam to escape away from you. Using sling, transfer salmon to large plate. Gently lift and tilt fillets with spatula to remove lemon slices. Serve.

Per Serving:
calories: 350 | fat: 23g | protein: 35g | carbs: 0g | fiber: 0g | sodium: 390mg

Crispy Herbed Salmon

Prep time: 5 minutes | Cook time: 9 to 12 minutes | Serves 4

4 (6-ounce / 170-g) skinless salmon fillets	½ teaspoon dried basil
3 tablespoons honey mustard	¼ cup panko bread crumbs
½ teaspoon dried thyme	⅓ cup crushed potato chips
	2 tablespoons olive oil

1. Place the salmon on a plate. In a small bowl, combine the mustard, thyme, and basil, and spread evenly over the salmon. 2. In another small bowl, combine the bread crumbs and potato chips and mix well. Drizzle in the olive oil and mix until combined. 3. Place the salmon in the air fryer basket and gently but firmly press the bread crumb mixture onto the top of each fillet. 4. Bake at 320°F (160°C) for 9 to 12 minutes or until the salmon reaches at least 145°F (63°C) on a meat thermometer and the topping is browned and crisp.

Per Serving:

calories: 322 | fat: 16g | protein: 36g | carbs: 7g | fiber: 1g | sodium: 306mg

Fried Fresh Sardines

Prep time: 5 minutes | Cook time: 5 minutes | Serves 4

Avocado oil	1 teaspoon freshly ground black pepper
1½ pounds (680 g) whole fresh sardines, scales removed	2 cups flour
1 teaspoon salt	

1. Preheat a deep skillet over medium heat. Pour in enough oil so there is about 1 inch of it in the pan. 2. Season the fish with the salt and pepper. 3. Dredge the fish in the flour so it is completely covered. 4. Slowly drop in 1 fish at a time, making sure not to overcrowd the pan. 5. Cook for about 3 minutes on each side or just until the fish begins to brown on all sides. Serve warm.

Per Serving:

calories: 581 | fat: 20g | protein: 48g | carbs: 48g | fiber: 2g | sodium: 583mg

Halibut in Parchment with Zucchini, Shallots, and Herbs

Prep time: 15 minutes | Cook time: 15 minutes | Serves 4

½ cup zucchini, diced small	¼ teaspoon kosher salt
1 shallot, minced	⅛ teaspoon freshly ground black pepper
4 (5-ounce / 142-g) halibut fillets (about 1 inch thick)	1 lemon, sliced into ⅛-inch-thick rounds
4 teaspoons extra-virgin olive oil	8 sprigs of thyme

1. Preheat the oven to 450°F (235°C). Combine the zucchini and shallots in a medium bowl. 2. Cut 4 (15-by-24-inch) pieces of parchment paper. Fold each sheet in half horizontally. Draw a large half heart on one side of each folded sheet, with the fold along the center of the heart. Cut out the heart, open the parchment, and lay it flat. 3. Place a fillet near the center of each parchment heart. Drizzle 1 teaspoon olive oil on each fillet. Sprinkle with salt and pepper. Top each fillet with lemon slices and 2 sprigs of thyme. Sprinkle each fillet with one-quarter of the zucchini and shallot mixture. Fold the parchment over. 4. Starting at the top, fold the edges of the parchment over, and continue all the way around to make a packet. Twist the end tightly to secure. 5. Arrange the 4 packets on a baking sheet. Bake for about 15 minutes. Place on plates; cut open. Serve immediately.

Per Serving:

calories: 190 | fat: 7g | protein: 27g | carbs: 5g | fiber: 1g | sodium: 170mg

Oregano Tilapia Fingers

Prep time: 15 minutes | Cook time: 9 minutes | Serves 4

1 pound (454 g) tilapia fillet	½ teaspoon ground paprika
½ cup coconut flour	1 teaspoon dried oregano
2 eggs, beaten	1 teaspoon avocado oil

1. Cut the tilapia fillets into fingers and sprinkle with ground paprika and dried oregano. 2. Then dip the tilapia fingers in eggs and coat in the coconut flour. 3. Sprinkle fish fingers with avocado oil and cook in the air fryer at 370°F (188°C) for 9 minutes.

Per Serving:

calories: 187 | fat: 9g | protein: 26g | carbs: 2g | fiber: 1g | sodium: 92mg

Cayenne Flounder Cutlets

Prep time: 15 minutes | Cook time: 10 minutes | Serves 2

1 egg	taste
1 cup Pecorino Romano cheese, grated	½ teaspoon cayenne pepper
Sea salt and white pepper, to	1 teaspoon dried parsley flakes
	2 flounder fillets

1. To make a breading station, whisk the egg until frothy. 2. In another bowl, mix Pecorino Romano cheese, and spices. 3. Dip the fish in the egg mixture and turn to coat evenly; then, dredge in the cracker crumb mixture, turning a couple of times to coat evenly. 4. Cook in the preheated air fryer at 390°F (199°C) for 5 minutes; turn them over and cook another 5 minutes. Enjoy!

Per Serving:

calories: 280 | fat: 13g | protein: 36g | carbs: 3g | fiber: 1g | sodium: 257mg

Tuna Steak

Prep time: 10 minutes | Cook time: 12 minutes |
Serves 4

1 pound (454 g) tuna steaks, boneless and cubed
1 tablespoon mustard

1 tablespoon avocado oil
1 tablespoon apple cider vinegar

1. Mix avocado oil with mustard and apple cider vinegar. 2. Then brush tuna steaks with mustard mixture and put in the air fryer basket. 3. Cook the fish at 360°F (182°C) for 6 minutes per side.

Per Serving:
calories: 197 | fat: 9g | protein: 27g | carbs: 0g | fiber: 0g | sodium: 87mg

Cod with Jalapeño

Prep time: 5 minutes | Cook time: 14 minutes |
Serves 4

4 cod fillets, boneless
1 jalapeño, minced

1 tablespoon avocado oil
½ teaspoon minced garlic

1. In the shallow bowl, mix minced jalapeño, avocado oil, and minced garlic. 2. Put the cod fillets in the air fryer basket in one layer and top with minced jalapeño mixture. 3. Cook the fish at 365°F (185°C) for 7 minutes per side.

Per Serving:
calories: 222 | fat: 5g | protein: 41g | carbs: 0g | fiber: 0g | sodium: 125mg

Flounder with Tomatoes and Basil

Prep time: 10 minutes | Cook time: 20 minutes |
Serves 4

1 pound (454 g) cherry tomatoes
4 garlic cloves, sliced
2 tablespoons extra-virgin olive oil
2 tablespoons lemon juice
2 tablespoons basil, cut into

ribbons
½ teaspoon kosher salt
¼ teaspoon freshly ground black pepper
4 (5- to 6-ounce / 142- to 170-g) flounder fillets

1. Preheat the oven to 425°F (220°C). 2. In a baking dish, combine the tomatoes, garlic, olive oil, lemon juice, basil, salt, and black pepper; mix well. Bake for 5 minutes. 3. Remove the baking dish from the oven and arrange the flounder on top of the tomato mixture. Bake until the fish is opaque and begins to flake, about 10 to 15 minutes, depending on thickness.

Per Serving:
calories: 215 | fat: 9g | protein: 28g | carbs: 6g | fiber: 2g | sodium: 261mg

Citrus-Glazed Salmon with Zucchini Noodles

Prep time: 10 minutes | Cook time: 20 minutes |
Serves 4

4 (5- to 6-ounce / 142- to 170-g) pieces salmon
½ teaspoon kosher salt
¼ teaspoon freshly ground black pepper
1 tablespoon extra-virgin olive oil
1 cup freshly squeezed orange juice

1 teaspoon low-sodium soy sauce
2 zucchini (about 16 ounces / 454 g), spiralized
1 tablespoon fresh chives, chopped
1 tablespoon fresh parsley, chopped

1. Preheat the oven to 350°F (180°C). Season the salmon with salt and black pepper. 2. Heat the olive oil in a large oven-safe skillet or sauté pan over medium-high heat. Add the salmon, skin-side down, and sear for 5 minutes, or until the skin is golden brown and crispy. Turn the salmon over and transfer to the oven until your desired doneness is reached—about 5 minutes for medium-rare, 7 minutes for medium, and 9 minutes for medium-well. Place the salmon on a cutting board to rest. 3. Place the same pan on the stove over medium-high heat. Add the orange juice and soy sauce to deglaze the pan. Bring to a simmer, scraping up any brown bits, and continue to simmer 5 to 7 minutes, until the liquid is reduced by half to a syrup-like consistency. 4. Divide the zucchini noodles among 4 plates and place 1 piece of salmon on each. Pour the orange glaze over the salmon and zucchini noodles. Garnish with the chives and parsley.

Per Serving:
calories: 280 | fat: 13g | protein: 30g | carbs: 11g | fiber: 1g | sodium: 255mg

Ouzo Mussels

Prep time: 10 minutes | Cook time: 15 minutes |
Serves 4

1 tablespoon olive oil
2 shallots, chopped
4 cloves garlic, sliced
1 pound (454 g) mussels, scrubbed and debearded
1 cup low-sodium chicken

broth or water
½ cup ouzo
Grated peel of 1 lemon
2 tablespoons chopped fresh flat-leaf parsley

1. In a large pot over medium heat, warm the oil. Cook the shallots and garlic until softened, 5 minutes. Increase the heat and add the mussels, broth or water, and ouzo. Cover, bring to a boil, and cook until the mussels have opened, about 8 minutes. 2. Discard any unopened mussels. Sprinkle the lemon peel and parsley over the top. Serve the mussels with their broth.

Per Serving:
calories: 238 | fat: 6g | protein: 16g | carbs: 22g | fiber: 0g | sodium: 344mg

Steamed Shrimp and Asparagus

Prep time: 15 minutes | Cook time: 1 minute | Serves 4

1 cup water
1 bunch asparagus, trimmed
½ teaspoon salt, divided
1 pound (454 g) shrimp, peeled

and deveined
1½ tablespoons lemon juice
2 tablespoons olive oil

1. Pour water into the Instant Pot®. Insert rack and place steamer basket onto rack. 2. Spread asparagus on the bottom of the steamer basket. Sprinkle with ¼ teaspoon salt. Add shrimp. Drizzle with lemon juice and sprinkle with remaining ¼ teaspoon salt. Drizzle olive oil over shrimp. 3. Close lid, set steam release to Sealing, press the Manual button, and set time to 1 minute. When the timer beeps, quick-release the pressure until the float valve drops and open lid. 4. Transfer shrimp and asparagus to a platter and serve.

Per Serving:
calories: 145 | fat: 8g | protein: 19g | carbs: 1g | fiber: 0g | sodium: 295mg

Ahi Tuna Steaks

Prep time: 5 minutes | Cook time: 14 minutes | Serves 2

2 (6-ounce / 170-g) ahi tuna
steaks
2 tablespoons olive oil

3 tablespoons everything bagel
seasoning

1. Drizzle both sides of each steak with olive oil. Place seasoning on a medium plate and press each side of tuna steaks into seasoning to form a thick layer. 2. Place steaks into ungreased air fryer basket. Adjust the temperature to 400°F (204°C) and air fry for 14 minutes, turning steaks halfway through cooking. Steaks will be done when internal temperature is at least 145°F (63°C) for well-done. Serve warm.

Per Serving:
calories: 305 | fat: 14g | protein: 42g | carbs: 0g | fiber: 0g | sodium: 377mg

Poached Cod

Prep time: 10 minutes | Cook time: 20 minutes | Serves 4

1 tablespoon olive oil
½ cup onion, thinly sliced
1 cup fennel, thinly sliced
1 tablespoon garlic, minced
1 (15-ounce / 425-g) can diced
tomatoes

2 cups chicken broth
½ cup white wine
Juice and zest of 1 orange
1 pinch red pepper flakes
1 bay leaf
1 pound (454 g) cod

1. Heat the olive oil in a large skillet. Add the onion and fennel, and cook 10 minutes, or until translucent and soft. Add the garlic and

cook 1 minute. 2. Add the tomatoes, chicken broth, wine, orange juice and zest, red pepper flakes, and bay leaf, and simmer for 5 minutes to meld the flavors. 3. Carefully add the fish in a single layer. Cover and simmer 6–7 minutes. 4. Transfer fish to a serving dish, Ladle the remaining sauce over the fish.

Per Serving:
calories: 370 | fat: 13g | protein: 48g | carbs: 10g | fiber: 3g | sodium: 578mg

Honeyed Salmon

Prep time: 10 minutes | Cook time: 1 hour | Serves 6

6 (6-ounce / 170-g) salmon
fillets
½ cup honey
2 tablespoons lime juice
3 tablespoons worcestershire

sauce
1 tablespoon water
2 cloves garlic, minced
1 teaspoon ground ginger
½ teaspoon black pepper

1. Place the salmon fillets in the slow cooker. 2. In medium bowl, whisk the honey, lime juice, Worcestershire sauce, water, garlic, ginger, and pepper. Pour sauce over salmon. 3. Cover and cook on high for 1 hour.

Per Serving:
calories: 313 | fat: 8g | protein: 35g | carbs: 26g | fiber: 0g | sodium: 212mg

Shrimp Fra Diavolo

Prep time: 10 minutes | Cook time: 10 minutes | Serves 4

2 tablespoons extra-virgin olive
oil
1 onion, diced small
1 fennel bulb, cored and diced
small, plus ¼ cup fronds for
garnish
1 bell pepper, diced small
½ teaspoon dried oregano
½ teaspoon dried thyme
½ teaspoon kosher salt

¼ teaspoon red pepper flakes
1 (14½-ounce / 411-g) can no-
salt-added diced tomatoes
1 pound (454 g) shrimp, peeled
and deveined
Juice of 1 lemon
Zest of 1 lemon
2 tablespoons fresh parsley,
chopped, for garnish

1. Heat the olive oil in a large skillet or sauté pan over medium heat. Add the onion, fennel, bell pepper, oregano, thyme, salt, and red pepper flakes and sauté until translucent, about 5 minutes. 2. Deglaze the pan with the juice from the canned tomatoes, scraping up any brown bits, and bring to a boil. Add the diced tomatoes and the shrimp. Lower heat to a simmer, cover, and cook until the shrimp are cooked through, about 3 minutes. 3. Turn off the heat. Add the lemon juice and lemon zest, and toss well to combine. Garnish with the parsley and the fennel fronds.

Per Serving:
calories: 240 | fat: 9g | protein: 25g | carbs: 13g | fiber: 3g | sodium:335 mg

Steamed Cod with Capers and Lemon

Prep time: 10 minutes | Cook time: 3 minutes | Serves 4

1 cup water
4 (4-ounce / 113-g) cod fillets, rinsed and patted dry
½ teaspoon ground black pepper
1 small lemon, thinly sliced

2 tablespoons extra-virgin olive oil
¼ cup chopped fresh parsley
2 tablespoons capers
1 tablespoon chopped fresh chives

1. Add water to the Instant Pot® and place the rack inside. 2. Season fish fillets with pepper. Top each fillet with three slices of lemon. Place fillets on rack. Close lid, set steam release to Sealing, press the Steam button, and set time to 3 minutes. 3. While fish cooks, combine olive oil, parsley, capers, and chives in a small bowl and mix well. Set aside. 4. When the timer beeps, quick-release the pressure until the float valve drops. Press the Cancel button and open lid. Place cod fillets on a serving platter. Remove and discard lemon slices and drizzle fish with olive oil mixture, making sure each fillet has herbs and capers on top. Serve immediately.

Per Serving:
calories: 140 | fat: 10g | protein: 14g | carbs: 0g | fiber: 0g | sodium: 370mg

Baked Swordfish with Herbs

Prep time: 10 minutes | Cook time: 20 minutes | Serves 4

Olive oil spray
1 cup fresh Italian parsley
¼ cup fresh thyme
¼ cup lemon juice

2 cloves garlic
¼ cup extra-virgin olive oil
½ teaspoon salt
4 swordfish steaks (each 5 to 7 ounces / 142 to 198 g)

1. Preheat the oven to 450°F (235°C). Coat a large baking dish with olive oil spray. 2. In a food processor, pulse the parsley, thyme, lemon juice, garlic, olive oil, and salt 10 times. 3. Place the swordfish in the prepared baking dish. Spoon the parsley mixture over the steaks. 4. Put the fish in the oven to bake for 17 to 20 minutes.

Per Serving:
calories: 397 | fat: 22g | protein: 44g | carbs: 3g | fiber: 1g | sodium: 495mg

Chapter 7 Snacks and Appetizers

Charred Eggplant Dip with Feta and Mint

Prep time: 5 minutes | Cook time: 20 minutes | Makes about 1½ cups

1 medium eggplant (about 1 pound / 454 g)	3 tablespoons chopped fresh mint leaves
2 tablespoons lemon juice	1 tablespoon finely chopped flat-leaf parsley
¼ cup olive oil	¼ teaspoon cayenne pepper
½ cup crumbled feta cheese	¾ teaspoon salt
½ cup finely diced red onion	

1. Preheat the broiler to high. 2. Line a baking sheet with aluminum foil. 3. Put the whole eggplant on the prepared baking sheet and poke it in several places with the tines of a fork. Cook under the broiler, turning about every 5 minutes, until the eggplant is charred on all sides and very soft in the center, about 15 to 20 minutes total. Remove from the oven and set aside until cool enough to handle. 4. When the eggplant is cool enough to handle, cut it in half lengthwise and scoop out the flesh, discarding the charred skin. 5. Add the lemon juice and olive oil and mash to a chunky purée with a fork. Add the cheese, onion, mint, parsley, cayenne, and salt. 6. Serve at room temperature.

Per Serving:
½ cup: calories: 71 | fat: 6g | protein: 2g | carbs: 3g | fiber: 2g | sodium: 237mg

Turmeric-Spiced Crunchy Chickpeas

Prep time: 15 minutes | Cook time: 30 minutes | Serves 4

2 (15-ounce / 425-g) cans organic chickpeas, drained and rinsed	2 teaspoons turmeric
	½ teaspoon dried oregano
3 tablespoons extra-virgin olive oil	½ teaspoon salt
	¼ teaspoon ground ginger
2 teaspoons Turkish or smoked paprika	⅛ teaspoon ground white pepper (optional)

1. Preheat the oven to 400°F(205ºC). Line a baking sheet with parchment paper and set aside. 2. Completely dry the chickpeas. Lay the chickpeas out on a baking sheet, roll them around with paper towels, and allow them to air-dry. I usually let them dry for at least 2½ hours, but can also be left to dry overnight. 3. In a medium bowl, combine the olive oil, paprika, turmeric, oregano, salt, ginger, and white pepper (if using). 4. Add the dry chickpeas to the bowl and toss to combine. 5. Put the chickpeas on the prepared baking sheet and cook for 30 minutes, or until the chickpeas turn golden brown. At 15 minutes, move the chickpeas around on the baking sheet to avoid burning. Check every 10 minutes in case the chickpeas begin to crisp up before the full cooking time has elapsed. 6. Remove from the oven and set them aside to cool.

Per Serving:
½ cup: calories: 308 | fat: 13g | protein: 11g | carbs: 40g | fiber: 11g | sodium: 292mg

Grilled Halloumi with Watermelon, Cherry Tomatoes, Olives, and Herb Oil

Prep time: 5 minutes | Cook time: 5 minutes | Serves 4

½ cup coarsely chopped fresh basil	black pepper, plus a pinch
	¾ pound (340 g) cherry tomatoes
3 tablespoons coarsely chopped fresh mint leaves, plus thinly sliced mint for garnish	8 ounces (227 g) Halloumi cheese, cut crosswise into 8 slices
1 clove garlic, coarsely chopped	
½ cup olive oil, plus more for brushing	2 cups thinly sliced watermelon, rind removed
½ teaspoon salt, plus a pinch	¼ cup sliced, pitted Kalamata olives
½ teaspoon freshly ground	

1. Heat a grill or grill pan to high. 2. In a food processor or blender, combine the basil, chopped mint, and garlic and pulse to chop. While the machine is running, add the olive oil in a thin stream. Strain the oil through a fine-meshed sieve and discard the solids. Stir in ½ teaspoon of salt and ½ teaspoon of pepper. 3. Brush the grill rack with olive oil. Drizzle 2 tablespoons of the herb oil over the tomatoes and cheese and season them with pinches of salt and pepper. Place the tomatoes on the grill and cook, turning occasionally, until their skins become blistered and begin to burst, about 4 minutes. Place the cheese on the grill and cook until grill marks appear and the cheese begins to get melty, about 1 minute per side. 4. Arrange the watermelon on a serving platter. Arrange the grilled cheese and tomatoes on top of the melon. Drizzle the herb oil over the top and garnish with the olives and sliced mint. Serve immediately.

Per Serving:
calories: 535 | fat: 50g | protein: 14g | carbs: 12g | fiber: 2g | sodium: 663mg

Tirokafteri (Spicy Feta and Yogurt Dip)

Prep time: 10 minutes | Cook time: 0 minutes | Serves 8

1 teaspoon red wine vinegar
1 small green chili, seeded and sliced
2 teaspoons extra virgin olive

oil
9 ounces (255 g) full-fat feta
¾ cup full-fat Greek yogurt

1. Combine the vinegar, chili, and olive oil in a food processor. Blend until smooth. 2. In a small bowl, combine the feta and Greek yogurt, and use a fork to mash the ingredients until a paste is formed. Add the pepper mixture and stir until blended. 3. Cover and transfer to the refrigerator to chill for at least 1 hour before serving. Store covered in the refrigerator for up to 3 days.

Per Serving:
calories: 109 | fat: 8g | protein: 6g | carbs: 4g | fiber: 0g | sodium: 311mg

Crunchy Tex-Mex Tortilla Chips

Prep time: 5 minutes | Cook time: 5 minutes | Serves 4

Olive oil
½ teaspoon salt
½ teaspoon ground cumin
½ teaspoon chili powder

½ teaspoon paprika
Pinch cayenne pepper
8 (6-inch) corn tortillas, each cut into 6 wedges

1. Spray fryer basket lightly with olive oil. 2. In a small bowl, combine the salt, cumin, chili powder, paprika, and cayenne pepper. 3. Place the tortilla wedges in the air fryer basket in a single layer. Spray the tortillas lightly with oil and sprinkle with some of the seasoning mixture. You will need to cook the tortillas in batches. 4. Air fry at 375ºF (191ºC) for 2 to 3 minutes. Shake the basket and cook until the chips are light brown and crispy, an additional 2 to 3 minutes. Watch the chips closely so they do not burn.

Per Serving:
calories: 118 | fat: 1g | protein: 3g | carbs: 25g | fiber: 3g | sodium: 307mg

Lemon Shrimp with Garlic Olive Oil

Prep time: 5 minutes | Cook time: 6 minutes | Serves 4

1 pound (454 g) medium shrimp, cleaned and deveined
¼ cup plus 2 tablespoons olive oil, divided
Juice of ½ lemon
3 garlic cloves, minced and divided

½ teaspoon salt
¼ teaspoon red pepper flakes
Lemon wedges, for serving (optional)
Marinara sauce, for dipping (optional)

1. Preheat the air fryer to 380ºF(193ºC). 2. In a large bowl, combine the shrimp with 2 tablespoons of the olive oil, as well as the lemon juice, ⅓ of the minced garlic, salt, and red pepper flakes. Toss to

coat the shrimp well. 3. In a small ramekin, combine the remaining ¼ cup of olive oil and the remaining minced garlic. 4. Tear off a 12-by-12-inch sheet of aluminum foil. Pour the shrimp into the center of the foil, then fold the sides up and crimp the edges so that it forms an aluminum foil bowl that is open on top. Place this packet into the air fryer basket. 5. Roast the shrimp for 4 minutes, then open the air fryer and place the ramekin with oil and garlic in the basket beside the shrimp packet. Cook for 2 more minutes. 6. Transfer the shrimp on a serving plate or platter with the ramekin of garlic olive oil on the side for dipping. You may also serve with lemon wedges and marinara sauce, if desired.

Per Serving:
calories: 283 | fat: 21g | protein: 23g | carbs: 1g | fiber: 0g | sodium: 427mg

Seared Halloumi with Pesto and Tomato

Prep time: 2 minutes | Cook time: 5 minutes | Serves 2

3 ounces (85 g) Halloumi cheese, cut crosswise into 2 thinner, rectangular pieces
2 teaspoons prepared pesto

sauce, plus additional for drizzling if desired
1 medium tomato, sliced

1. Heat a nonstick skillet over medium-high heat and place the slices of Halloumi in the hot pan. After about 2 minutes, check to see if the cheese is golden on the bottom. If it is, flip the slices, top each with 1 teaspoon of pesto, and cook for another 2 minutes, or until the second side is golden. 2. Serve with slices of tomato and a drizzle of pesto, if desired, on the side.

Per Serving:
calories: 177 | fat: 14g | protein: 10g | carbs: 4g | fiber: 1g | sodium: 233mg

Kale Chips

Prep time: 5 minutes | Cook time: 30 minutes | Serves 2 to 4

2 large bunches kale, ribs removed
1 tablespoon extra-virgin olive

oil
1 teaspoon salt

1. Arrange the oven racks in the upper and middle positions. Preheat the oven to 250ºF(120ºC). Line 2 baking sheets with aluminum foil. 2. Rinse the kale and dry very well with a towel or salad spinner. Tear into large pieces. 3. Toss the kale with the olive oil and arrange in a single layer on the baking sheets. Sprinkle with salt. 4. Bake for 20 minutes and then use tongs to gently turn each leaf over. Bake until dry and crisp, another 10 to 15 minutes. Serve warm.

Per Serving:
calories: 141 | fat: 6g | protein: 10g | carbs: 20g | fiber: 8g | sodium: 668mg

Creamy Traditional Hummus

Prep time: 5 minutes | Cook time: 0 minutes | Serves 8

1 (15-ounce / 425-g) can garbanzo beans, rinsed and drained
2 cloves garlic, peeled
¼ cup lemon juice

1 teaspoon salt
¼ cup plain Greek yogurt
½ cup tahini paste
2 tablespoons extra-virgin olive oil, divided

1. Add the garbanzo beans, garlic cloves, lemon juice, and salt to a food processor fitted with a chopping blade. Blend for 1 minute, until smooth. 2. Scrape down the sides of the processor. Add the Greek yogurt, tahini paste, and 1 tablespoon of olive oil and blend for another minute, until creamy and well combined. 3. Spoon the hummus into a serving bowl. Drizzle the remaining tablespoon of olive oil on top.

Per Serving:

calories: 189 | fat: 13g | protein: 7g | carbs: 14g | fiber: 4g | sodium: 313mg

Tuna Croquettes

Prep time: 40 minutes | Cook time: 25 minutes | Makes 36 croquettes

6 tablespoons extra-virgin olive oil, plus 1 to 2 cups
5 tablespoons almond flour, plus 1 cup, divided
1¼ cups heavy cream
1 (4-ounce / 113-g) can olive oil-packed yellowfin tuna
1 tablespoon chopped red onion

2 teaspoons minced capers
½ teaspoon dried dill
¼ teaspoon freshly ground black pepper
2 large eggs
1 cup panko breadcrumbs (or a gluten-free version)

1. In a large skillet, heat 6 tablespoons olive oil over medium-low heat. Add 5 tablespoons almond flour and cook, stirring constantly, until a smooth paste forms and the flour browns slightly, 2 to 3 minutes. 2. Increase the heat to medium-high and gradually add the heavy cream, whisking constantly until completely smooth and thickened, another 4 to 5 minutes. 3. Remove from the heat and stir in the tuna, red onion, capers, dill, and pepper. 4. Transfer the mixture to an 8-inch square baking dish that is well coated with olive oil and allow to cool to room temperature. Cover and refrigerate until chilled, at least 4 hours or up to overnight. 5. To form the croquettes, set out three bowls. In one, beat together the eggs. In another, add the remaining almond flour. In the third, add the panko. Line a baking sheet with parchment paper. 6. Using a spoon, place about a tablespoon of cold prepared dough into the flour mixture and roll to coat. Shake off excess and, using your hands, roll into an oval. 7. Dip the croquette into the beaten egg, then lightly coat in panko. Set on lined baking sheet and repeat with the remaining dough. 8. In a small saucepan, heat the remaining 1 to 2 cups of olive oil, so that the oil is about 1 inch deep, over medium-high heat. The smaller the pan, the less oil you will need, but you will need more for each batch. 9. Test if the oil is ready by throwing a pinch of panko into pot. If it sizzles, the oil is ready

for frying. If it sinks, it's not quite ready. Once the oil is heated, fry the croquettes 3 or 4 at a time, depending on the size of your pan, removing with a slotted spoon when golden brown. You will need to adjust the temperature of the oil occasionally to prevent burning. If the croquettes get dark brown very quickly, lower the temperature.

Per Serving:

2 croquettes: calories: 271 | fat: 26g | protein: 5g | carbs: 6g | fiber: 1g | sodium: 89mg

Goat Cheese–Mackerel Pâté

Prep time: 10 minutes | Cook time: 0 minutes | Serves 4

4 ounces (113 g) olive oil-packed wild-caught mackerel
2 ounces (57 g) goat cheese
Zest and juice of 1 lemon
2 tablespoons chopped fresh parsley
2 tablespoons chopped fresh arugula

1 tablespoon extra-virgin olive oil
2 teaspoons chopped capers
1 to 2 teaspoons fresh horseradish (optional)
Crackers, cucumber rounds, endive spears, or celery, for serving (optional)

1. In a food processor, blender, or large bowl with immersion blender, combine the mackerel, goat cheese, lemon zest and juice, parsley, arugula, olive oil, capers, and horseradish (if using). Process or blend until smooth and creamy. 2. Serve with crackers, cucumber rounds, endive spears, or celery. 3. Store covered in the refrigerator for up to 1 week.

Per Serving:

calories: 142 | fat: 10g | protein: 11g | carbs: 1g | fiber: 0g | sodium: 203mg

Stuffed Figs with Goat Cheese and Honey

Prep time: 5 minutes | Cook time: 10 minutes | Serves 4

8 fresh figs
2 ounces (57 g) goat cheese
¼ teaspoon ground cinnamon

1 tablespoon honey, plus more for serving
1 tablespoon olive oil

1. Preheat the air fryer to 360°F (182°C). 2. Cut the stem off of each fig. 3. Cut an X into the top of each fig, cutting halfway down the fig. Leave the base intact. 4. In a small bowl, mix together the goat cheese, cinnamon, and honey. 5. Spoon the goat cheese mixture into the cavity of each fig. 6. Place the figs in a single layer in the air fryer basket. Drizzle the olive oil over top of the figs and roast for 10 minutes. 7. Serve with an additional drizzle of honey.

Per Serving:

calories: 152 | fat: 9g | protein: 5g | carbs: 16g | fiber: 2g | sodium: 62mg

Sfougato

Prep time: 10 minutes | Cook time: 8 minutes | Serves 4

½ cup crumbled feta cheese
¼ cup bread crumbs
1 medium onion, peeled and minced
4 tablespoons all-purpose flour
2 tablespoons minced fresh mint

½ teaspoon salt
½ teaspoon ground black pepper
1 tablespoon dried thyme
6 large eggs, beaten
1 cup water

1. In a medium bowl, mix cheese, bread crumbs, onion, flour, mint, salt, pepper, and thyme. Stir in eggs. 2. Spray an 8" round baking dish with nonstick cooking spray. Pour egg mixture into dish. 3. Place rack in the Instant Pot® and add water. Fold a long piece of foil in half lengthwise. Lay foil over rack to form a sling and top with dish. Cover loosely with foil. Close lid, set steam release to Sealing, press the Manual button, and set time to 8 minutes. 4. When the timer beeps, quick-release the pressure until the float valve drops. Open lid. Let stand 5 minutes, then remove dish from pot.

Per Serving:

calories: 226 | fat: 12g | protein: 14g | carbs: 15g | fiber: 1g | sodium: 621mg

Whole Wheat Pitas

Prep time: 5 minutes | Cook time: 30 minutes | Makes 8 pitas

2 cups whole wheat flour
1¼ cups all-purpose flour
1¼ teaspoons table salt
1¼ cup warm water (105°–

110°F)
1 (¼-ounce / 7-g) package active dry yeast (2½ teaspoons)
1 teaspoon olive oil

1. In the bowl of an electric stand mixer (or a large bowl), whisk together the flours and salt. In a small bowl or glass measuring cup, whisk together the water and yeast until the yeast is dissolved. Let sit until foamy, about 5 minutes. Add the yeast mixture to the flour mixture. Fit the mixer with the dough hook and mix on low (or stir) until it forms a shaggy dough. 2. Increase the speed to medium and knead until the dough is smooth and elastic, 2 to 3 minutes. If kneading by hand, turn the dough out onto a lightly floured work surface and knead about 10 minutes. 3. Form the dough into a ball and return it to the bowl. Pour in the oil, turning the dough to coat. Cover the bowl with a kitchen towel and let the dough rise until doubled in size, about 1 hour. 4. Preheat the oven to 475°F(245°C). Place a baking sheet on the lowest rack of the oven. 5. When the dough has risen, take it out of the bowl and give it a few gentle kneads. Divide the dough into 8 equal portions and shape into balls. Place on a lightly floured surface and cover with the kitchen towel. 6. Roll out each dough ball to form a 6" circle. Place on the heated baking sheet. Bake until puffed up and beginning to turn color, 6 to 7 minutes. Remove with a metal spatula or tongs and place in a bread basket or on a serving platter. Repeat with the remaining dough balls. 7. To make a pocket in the pita, allow it to cool. Slice

off ¼ of the pita from 1 edge, and then carefully insert the knife into the pita to cut the pocket. Gently pull the sides apart to make the pocket larger.

Per Serving:

calories: 181 | fat: 2g | protein: 6g | carbs: 37g | fiber: 4g | sodium: 366mg

Eggplant Fries

Prep time: 10 minutes | Cook time: 7 to 8 minutes per batch | Serves 4

1 medium eggplant
1 teaspoon ground coriander
1 teaspoon cumin
1 teaspoon garlic powder
½ teaspoon salt

1 cup crushed panko bread crumbs
1 large egg
2 tablespoons water
Oil for misting or cooking spray

1. Peel and cut the eggplant into fat fries, ⅜- to ½-inch thick. 2. Preheat the air fryer to 390°F (199°C). 3. In a small cup, mix together the coriander, cumin, garlic, and salt. 4. Combine 1 teaspoon of the seasoning mix and panko crumbs in a shallow dish. 5. Place eggplant fries in a large bowl, sprinkle with remaining seasoning, and stir well to combine. 6. Beat eggs and water together and pour over eggplant fries. Stir to coat. 7. Remove eggplant from egg wash, shaking off excess, and roll in panko crumbs. 8. Spray with oil. 9. Place half of the fries in air fryer basket. You should have only a single layer, but it's fine if they overlap a little. 10. Cook for 5 minutes. Shake basket, mist lightly with oil, and cook 2 to 3 minutes longer, until browned and crispy. 11. Repeat step 10 to cook remaining eggplant.

Per Serving:

calories: 163 | fat: 3g | protein: 7g | carbs: 28g | fiber: 6g | sodium: 510mg

Citrus-Marinated Olives

Prep time: 10 minutes | Cook time: 0 minutes | Makes 2 cups

2 cups mixed green olives with pits
¼ cup red wine vinegar
¼ cup extra-virgin olive oil
4 garlic cloves, finely minced
Zest and juice of 2 clementines

or 1 large orange
1 teaspoon red pepper flakes
2 bay leaves
½ teaspoon ground cumin
½ teaspoon ground allspice

1. In a large glass bowl or jar, combine the olives, vinegar, oil, garlic, orange zest and juice, red pepper flakes, bay leaves, cumin, and allspice and mix well. Cover and refrigerate for at least 4 hours or up to a week to allow the olives to marinate, tossing again before serving.

Per Serving:

¼ cup: calories: 112 | fat: 10g | protein: 1g | carbs: 5g | fiber: 2g | sodium: 248mg

Roasted Pepper Bruschetta with Capers and Basil

Prep time: 10 minutes | Cook time: 15 minutes |
Serves 6 to 8

2 red bell peppers
2 yellow bell peppers
2 orange bell peppers
2 tablespoons olive oil, plus ¼ cup
¾ teaspoon salt, divided
½ teaspoon freshly ground black pepper, divided

3 tablespoons red wine vinegar
1 teaspoon Dijon mustard
1 clove garlic, minced
2 tablespoons capers, drained
¼ cup chopped fresh basil leaves, divided
1 whole-wheat baguette or other crusty bread, thinly sliced

1. Preheat the broiler to high and line a large baking sheet with aluminum foil. 2. Brush the peppers all over with 2 tablespoons of the olive oil and sprinkle with ½ teaspoon of the salt and ¼ teaspoon of the pepper. 3. Broil the peppers, turning every 3 minutes or so, until the skin is charred on all sides. Place them in a bowl, cover with plastic wrap, and let steam for 10 minutes. Slip the skins off and discard them. Seed and dice the peppers. 4. In a large bowl, whisk together the vinegar, mustard, garlic, the remaining ¼ teaspoon salt, and the remaining ¼ teaspoon of pepper. Still whisking, slowly add the remaining ¼ cup oil in a thin stream until the dressing is emulsified. Stir in the capers, 2 tablespoons of the basil, and the diced peppers. 5. Toast the bread slices and then spoon the pepper mixture over them, drizzling with extra dressing. Garnish with the remaining basil and serve immediately.

Per Serving:

calories: 243 | fat: 6g | protein: 8g | carbs: 39g | fiber: 4g | sodium: 755mg

Cinnamon-Apple Chips

Prep time: 10 minutes | Cook time: 32 minutes |
Serves 4

Oil, for spraying
2 Red Delicious or Honeycrisp apples

¼ teaspoon ground cinnamon, divided

1. Line the air fryer basket with parchment and spray lightly with oil. 2. Trim the uneven ends off the apples. Using a mandoline on the thinnest setting or a sharp knife, cut the apples into very thin slices. Discard the cores. 3. Place half of the apple slices in a single layer in the prepared basket and sprinkle with half of the cinnamon. 4. Place a metal air fryer trivet on top of the apples to keep them from flying around while they are cooking. 5. Air fry at 300°F (149°C) for 16 minutes, flipping every 5 minutes to ensure even cooking. Repeat with the remaining apple slices and cinnamon. 6. Let cool to room temperature before serving. The chips will firm up as they cool.

Per Serving:

calories: 63 | fat: 0g | protein: 0g | carbs: 15g | fiber: 3g | sodium: 1mg

Roasted Pearl Onion Dip

Prep time: 5 minutes | Cook time: 12 minutes |
Serves 4

2 cups peeled pearl onions
3 garlic cloves
3 tablespoons olive oil, divided
½ teaspoon salt
1 cup nonfat plain Greek yogurt
1 tablespoon lemon juice

¼ teaspoon black pepper
⅛ teaspoon red pepper flakes
Pita chips, vegetables, or toasted bread for serving (optional)

1. Preheat the air fryer to 360°F(182°C). 2. In a large bowl, combine the pearl onions and garlic with 2 tablespoons of the olive oil until the onions are well coated. 3. Pour the garlic-and-onion mixture into the air fryer basket and roast for 12 minutes. 4. Transfer the garlic and onions to a food processor. Pulse the vegetables several times, until the onions are minced but still have some chunks. 5. In a large bowl, combine the garlic and onions and the remaining 1 tablespoon of olive oil, along with the salt, yogurt, lemon juice, black pepper, and red pepper flakes. 6. Cover and chill for 1 hour before serving with pita chips, vegetables, or toasted bread.

Per Serving:

calories: 152 | fat: 10g | protein: 4g | carbs: 11g | fiber: 1g | sodium: 341mg

Vegetable Pot Stickers

Prep time: 12 minutes | Cook time: 11 to 18 minutes |
Makes 12 pot stickers

1 cup shredded red cabbage
¼ cup chopped button mushrooms
¼ cup grated carrot
2 tablespoons minced onion

2 garlic cloves, minced
2 teaspoons grated fresh ginger
12 gyoza/pot sticker wrappers
2½ teaspoons olive oil, divided

1. In a baking pan, combine the red cabbage, mushrooms, carrot, onion, garlic, and ginger. Add 1 tablespoon of water. Place in the air fryer and air fry at 370°F (188°C) for 3 to 6 minutes, until the vegetables are crisp-tender. Drain and set aside. 2. Working one at a time, place the pot sticker wrappers on a work surface. Top each wrapper with a scant 1 tablespoon of the filling. Fold half of the wrapper over the other half to form a half circle. Dab one edge with water and press both edges together. 3. To another pan, add 1¼ teaspoons of olive oil. Put half of the pot stickers, seam-side up, in the pan. Air fry for 5 minutes, or until the bottoms are light golden brown. Add 1 tablespoon of water and return the pan to the air fryer. 4. Air fry for 4 to 6 minutes more, or until hot. Repeat with the remaining pot stickers, remaining 1¼ teaspoons of oil, and another tablespoon of water. Serve immediately.

Per Serving:

1 pot stickers: calories: 36 | fat: 1g | protein: 1g | carbs: 6g | fiber: 0g | sodium: 49mg

Sweet Potato Fries

Prep time: 15 minutes | Cook time: 40 minutes |
Serves 4

4 large sweet potatoes, peeled and cut into finger-like strips
2 tablespoons extra-virgin olive oil

½ teaspoon salt
½ teaspoon freshly ground black pepper

1. Preheat the oven to 350°F(180ºC). Line a baking sheet with aluminum foil. Toss the potatoes in a large bowl with the olive oil, salt, and pepper. 2. Arrange the potatoes in a single layer on the baking sheet and bake until brown at the edges, about 40 minutes. Serve piping hot.

Per Serving:
calories: 171 | fat: 7g | protein: 2g | carbs: 26g | fiber: 4g | sodium: 362mg

Red Pepper Tapenade

Prep time: 5 minutes | Cook time: 5 minutes | Serves 4

1 large red bell pepper
2 tablespoons plus 1 teaspoon olive oil, divided
½ cup Kalamata olives, pitted

and roughly chopped
1 garlic clove, minced
½ teaspoon dried oregano
1 tablespoon lemon juice

1. Preheat the air fryer to 380°F(193ºC). 2. Brush the outside of a whole red pepper with 1 teaspoon olive oil and place it inside the air fryer basket. Roast for 5 minutes. 3. Meanwhile, in a medium bowl combine the remaining 2 tablespoons of olive oil with the olives, garlic, oregano, and lemon juice. 4. Remove the red pepper from the air fryer, then gently slice off the stem and remove the seeds. Roughly chop the roasted pepper into small pieces. 5. Add the red pepper to the olive mixture and stir all together until combined. 6. Serve with pita chips, crackers, or crusty bread.

Per Serving:
calories: 94 | fat: 9g | protein: 1g | carbs: 4g | fiber: 2g | sodium: 125mg

Flatbread with Ricotta and Orange-Raisin Relish

Prep time: 5 minutes | Cook time: 8 minutes | Serves 4 to 6

¾ cup golden raisins, roughly chopped
1 shallot, finely diced
1 tablespoon olive oil
1 tablespoon red wine vinegar
1 tablespoon honey
1 tablespoon chopped flat-leaf parsley

1 tablespoon fresh orange zest strips
Pinch of salt
1 oval prebaked whole-wheat flatbread, such as naan or pocketless pita
8 ounces (227 g) whole-milk ricotta cheese

½ cup baby arugula

1. Preheat the oven to 450°F(235ºC). 2. In a small bowl, stir together the raisins, shallot, olive oil, vinegar, honey, parsley, orange zest, and salt. 3. Place the flatbread on a large baking sheet and toast in the preheated oven until the edges are lightly browned, about 8 minutes. 4. Spoon the ricotta cheese onto the flatbread, spreading with the back of the spoon. Scatter the arugula over the cheese. Cut the flatbread into triangles and top each piece with a dollop of the relish. Serve immediately.

Per Serving:
calories: 195 | fat: 9g | protein: 6g | carbs: 25g | fiber: 1g | sodium: 135mg

No-Mayo Tuna Salad Cucumber Bites

Prep time: 5 minutes | Cook time: 0 minutes | Serves 3

1 (5-ounce / 142-g) can water-packed tuna, drained
⅓ cup full-fat Greek yogurt
½ teaspoon extra virgin olive oil
1 tablespoon finely chopped spring onion (white parts only)

1 tablespoon chopped fresh dill
Pinch of coarse sea salt
¼ teaspoon freshly ground black pepper
1 medium cucumber, cut into 15 (¼-inch) thick slices
1 teaspoon red wine vinegar

1. In a medium bowl, combine the tuna, yogurt, olive oil, spring onion, dill, sea salt, and black pepper. Mix well. 2. Arrange the cucumber slices on a plate and sprinkle the vinegar over the slices. 3. Place 1 heaping teaspoon of the tuna salad on top of each cucumber slice 4. Serve promptly. Store the tuna salad mixture covered in the refrigerator for up to 1 day.

Per Serving:
calories: 80 | fat: 3g | protein: 11g | carbs: 4g | fiber: 1g | sodium: 131mg

Mini Lettuce Wraps

Prep time: 10 minutes | Cook time: 0 minutes |
Makes about 1 dozen wraps

1 tomato, diced
1 cucumber, diced
1 red onion, sliced
1 ounce (28 g) low-fat feta cheese, crumbled
Juice of 1 lemon

1 tablespoon olive oil
Sea salt and freshly ground pepper, to taste
12 small, intact iceberg lettuce leaves

1. Combine the tomato, cucumber, onion, and feta in a bowl with the lemon juice and olive oil. 2. Season with sea salt and freshly ground pepper. 3. Without tearing the leaves, gently fill each leaf with a tablespoon of the veggie mixture. 4. Roll them as tightly as you can, and lay them seam-side-down on a serving platter.

Per Serving:
1 wrap: calories: 26 | fat: 2g | protein: 1g | carbs: 2g | fiber: 1g | sodium: 20mg

Garlic-Mint Yogurt Dip

Prep time: 5 minutes | Cook time: 0 minutes | Serves 4 to 6

1 cup plain Greek yogurt
Zest and juice of 1 lemon
1 garlic clove, minced
3 tablespoons chopped fresh mint

¼ teaspoon Aleppo pepper or cayenne pepper
¼ teaspoon salt
Freshly ground black pepper (optional)

1. In a small bowl, stir together all the ingredients until well combined. Season with black pepper, if desired. Refrigerate until ready to serve.

Per Serving:

1 cup: calories: 52 | fat: 2g | protein: 2g | carbs: 7g | fiber: 0g | sodium: 139mg

Roasted Chickpeas

Prep time: 5 minutes | Cook time: 15 minutes | Makes about 1 cup

1 (15-ounce / 425-g) can chickpeas, drained
2 teaspoons curry powder

¼ teaspoon salt
1 tablespoon olive oil

1. Drain chickpeas thoroughly and spread in a single layer on paper towels. Cover with another paper towel and press gently to remove extra moisture. Don't press too hard or you'll crush the chickpeas. 2. Mix curry powder and salt together. 3. Place chickpeas in a medium bowl and sprinkle with seasonings. Stir well to coat. 4. Add olive oil and stir again to distribute oil. 5. Air fry at 390°F (199°C) for 15 minutes, stopping to shake basket about halfway through cooking time. 6. Cool completely and store in airtight container.

Per Serving:

¼ cup: calories: 181 | fat: 6g | protein: 8g | carbs: 24g | fiber: 7g | sodium: 407mg

Mixed-Vegetable Caponata

Prep time: 15 minutes | Cook time: 40 minutes | Serves 8

1 eggplant, chopped
1 zucchini, chopped
1 red bell pepper, seeded and chopped
1 small red onion, chopped
2 tablespoons extra-virgin olive oil, divided
1 cup canned tomato sauce
3 tablespoons red wine vinegar

1 tablespoon honey
¼ teaspoon red-pepper flakes
¼ teaspoon kosher salt
½ cup pitted, chopped green olives
2 tablespoons drained capers
2 tablespoons raisins
2 tablespoons chopped fresh flat-leaf parsley

1. Preheat the oven to 400°F(205°C). 2. On a large rimmed baking sheet, toss the eggplant, zucchini, bell pepper, and onion with 1 tablespoon of the oil. Roast until the vegetables are tender, about 30 minutes. 3. In a medium saucepan over medium heat, warm the remaining 1 tablespoon oil. Add the tomato sauce, vinegar, honey, pepper flakes, and salt and stir to combine. Add the roasted vegetables, olives, capers, raisins, and parsley and cook until bubbly and thickened, 10 minutes. 4. Remove from the heat and cool to room temperature. Serve immediately or store in an airtight container in the refrigerator for up to 1 week.

Per Serving:

calories: 100 | fat: 5g | protein: 2g | carbs: 13g | fiber: 4g | sodium: 464mg

Heart-Healthful Trail Mix

Prep time: 15 minutes | Cook time: 30 minutes | Serves 10

1 cup raw almonds
1 cup walnut halves
1 cup pumpkin seeds
1 cup dried apricots, cut into thin strips
1 cup dried cherries, roughly

chopped
1 cup golden raisins
2 tablespoons extra-virgin olive oil
1 teaspoon salt

1. Preheat the oven to 300°F(150°C). Line a baking sheet with aluminum foil. 2. In a large bowl, combine the almonds, walnuts, pumpkin seeds, apricots, cherries, and raisins. Pour the olive oil over all and toss well with clean hands. Add salt and toss again to distribute. 3. Pour the nut mixture onto the baking sheet in a single layer and bake until the fruits begin to brown, about 30 minutes. Cool on the baking sheet to room temperature. 4. Store in a large airtight container or zipper-top plastic bag.

Per Serving:

calories: 346 | fat: 20g | protein: 8g | carbs: 39g | fiber: 5g | sodium: 240mg

Garlic-Parmesan Croutons

Prep time: 3 minutes | Cook time: 12 minutes | Serves 4

Oil, for spraying
4 cups cubed French bread
1 tablespoon grated Parmesan cheese

3 tablespoons olive oil
1 tablespoon granulated garlic
½ teaspoon unsalted salt

1. Line the air fryer basket with parchment and spray lightly with oil. 2. In a large bowl, mix together the bread, Parmesan cheese, olive oil, garlic, and salt, tossing with your hands to evenly distribute the seasonings. Transfer the coated bread cubes to the prepared basket. 3. Air fry at 350°F (177°C) for 10 to 12 minutes, stirring once after 5 minutes, or until crisp and golden brown.

Per Serving:

calories: 220 | fat: 12g | protein: 5g | carbs: 23g | fiber: 1g | sodium: 285mg

Chapter 8 Vegetables and Sides

Greek Bean Soup

Prep time: 10 minutes | Cook time: 45 minutes |
Serves 4

2 tablespoons olive oil
1 large onion, chopped
1 (15-ounce / 425-g) can diced tomatoes
1 (15-ounce / 425-g) can great northern beans, drained and rinsed
2 celery stalks, chopped

2 carrots, cut into long ribbons
⅓ teaspoon chopped fresh thyme
¼ cup chopped fresh Italian parsley
1 bay leaf
Sea salt
Freshly ground black pepper

1. In a Dutch oven, heat the olive oil over medium-high heat. Add the onion and sauté for 4 minutes, or until softened. Add the tomatoes, beans, celery, carrots, thyme, parsley, and bay leaf, then add water to cover by about 2 inches. 2. Bring the soup to a boil, reduce the heat to low, cover, and simmer for 30 minutes, or until the vegetables are tender. 3. Remove the bay leaf, season with salt and pepper, and serve.

Per Serving:
calories: 185 | fat: 7g | protein: 7g | carbs: 25g | fiber: 8g | sodium: 155mg

Sicilian-Style Roasted Cauliflower with Capers, Currants, and Crispy Breadcrumbs

Prep time: 10 minutes | Cook time: 55 minutes |
Serves 4

1 large head of cauliflower (2 pounds / 907 g), cut into 2-inch florets
6 tablespoons olive oil, divided
1 teaspoon salt
½ teaspoon freshly ground black pepper
3 garlic cloves, thinly sliced
2 tablespoons salt-packed capers, soaked, rinsed, and

patted dry
¾ cup fresh whole-wheat breadcrumbs
½ cup chicken broth
1 teaspoon anchovy paste
⅓ cup golden raisins
1 tablespoon white wine vinegar
2 tablespoons chopped flat-leaf parsley

1. Preheat the oven to 425°F(220°C). 2. In a medium bowl, toss the cauliflower florets with 3 tablespoons olive oil, and the salt and pepper. Spread the cauliflower out in a single layer on a large, rimmed baking sheet and roast in the preheated oven, stirring occasionally, for about 45 minutes, until the cauliflower is golden brown and crispy at the edges. 3. While the cauliflower is roasting, put the remaining 3 tablespoons of olive oil in a small saucepan and heat over medium-low heat. Add the garlic and cook, stirring, for about 5 minutes, until the garlic begins to turn golden. Stir in the capers and cook for 3 minutes more. Add the breadcrumbs, stir to mix well, and cook until the breadcrumbs turn golden brown and are crisp. Use a slotted spoon to transfer the breadcrumbs to a bowl or plate. 4. In the same saucepan, stir together the broth and anchovy paste and bring to a boil over medium-high heat. Stir in the raisins and vinegar and cook, stirring occasionally, for 5 minutes, until the liquid has mostly been absorbed. 5. When the cauliflower is done, transfer it to a large serving bowl. Add the raisin mixture and toss to mix. Top with the breadcrumbs and serve immediately, garnished with parsley.

Per Serving:
calories: 364 | fat: 22g | protein: 8g | carbs: 37g | fiber: 6g | sodium: 657mg

Green Bean Casserole

Prep time: 10 minutes | Cook time: 20 minutes |
Serves 4

1 pound (454 g) fresh green beans, ends trimmed, strings removed, and chopped into 2-inch pieces
1 (8-ounce / 227-g) package sliced brown mushrooms
½ onion, sliced
1 clove garlic, minced

1 tablespoon olive oil
½ teaspoon salt
¼ teaspoon freshly ground black pepper
4 ounces (113 g) cream cheese
½ cup chicken stock
¼ teaspoon ground nutmeg
½ cup grated Cheddar cheese

1. Preheat the air fryer to 400°F (204°C). Coat a casserole dish with olive oil and set aside. 2. In a large bowl, combine the green beans, mushrooms, onion, garlic, olive oil, salt, and pepper. Toss until the vegetables are thoroughly coated with the oil and seasonings. 3. Transfer the mixture to the air fryer basket. Pausing halfway through the cooking time to shake the basket, air fry for 10 minutes until tender. 4. While the vegetables are cooking, in a 2-cup glass measuring cup, warm the cream cheese and chicken stock in the microwave on high for 1 to 2 minutes until the cream cheese is melted. Add the nutmeg and whisk until smooth. 5. Transfer the vegetables to the prepared casserole dish and pour the cream cheese mixture over the top. Top with the Cheddar cheese. Air fry for another 10 minutes until the cheese is melted and beginning to brown.

Per Serving:
calories: 230 | fat: 18g | protein: 8g | carbs: 11g | fiber: 3g | sodium: 502mg

Garlicky Broccoli Rabe with Artichokes

Prep time: 5 minutes | Cook time: 10 minutes | Serves 4

2 pounds (907 g) fresh broccoli rabe	1 (13¾-ounce / 390-g) can artichoke hearts, drained and quartered
½ cup extra-virgin olive oil, divided	1 tablespoon water
3 garlic cloves, finely minced	2 tablespoons red wine vinegar
1 teaspoon salt	Freshly ground black pepper
1 teaspoon red pepper flakes	

1. Trim away any thick lower stems and yellow leaves from the broccoli rabe and discard. Cut into individual florets with a couple inches of thin stem attached. 2. In a large skillet, heat ¼ cup olive oil over medium-high heat. Add the trimmed broccoli, garlic, salt, and red pepper flakes and sauté for 5 minutes, until the broccoli begins to soften. Add the artichoke hearts and sauté for another 2 minutes. 3. Add the water and reduce the heat to low. Cover and simmer until the broccoli stems are tender, 3 to 5 minutes. 4. In a small bowl, whisk together remaining ¼ cup olive oil and the vinegar. Drizzle over the broccoli and artichokes. Season with ground black pepper, if desired.

Per Serving:
calories: 341 | fat: 28g | protein: 11g | carbs: 18g | fiber: 12g | sodium: 750mg

Roasted Vegetables with Lemon Tahini

Prep time: 15 minutes | Cook time: 25 minutes | Serves 4

For the Dressing:

½ cup tahini	lemon juice
½ cup water, as needed	Sea salt
3 tablespoons freshly squeezed	

For the Vegetables:

8 ounces (227 g) baby potatoes, halved	¼ cup olive oil
8 ounces (227 g) baby carrots	1½ teaspoons garlic powder
1 head cauliflower, cored and cut into large chunks	¼ teaspoon dried oregano
2 red bell peppers, quartered	¼ teaspoon dried thyme
1 zucchini, cut into 1-inch pieces	Sea salt
	Freshly ground black pepper
	Red pepper flakes (optional)

Make the Dressing: 1. In a small bowl, stir together the tahini, water, and lemon juice until well blended. 2. Taste, season with salt, and set aside. Make the Vegetables: 3. Preheat the oven to 425°F(220°C). Line a baking sheet with parchment paper. 4. Place the potatoes in a microwave-safe bowl with 3 tablespoons water, cover with a paper plate, and microwave on high for 4 minutes. Drain any excess water. 5. Transfer the potatoes to a large bowl and add the carrots, cauliflower, bell peppers, zucchini, olive oil, garlic powder, oregano, and thyme. Season with salt and black pepper. 6.

Spread the vegetables in a single layer on the prepared baking sheet and roast until fork-tender and a little charred, about 25 minutes. 7. Transfer the vegetables to a large bowl and add the dressing and red pepper flakes, if desired. Toss to coat. 8. Serve the roasted vegetables alongside your favorite chicken or fish dish.

Per Serving:
calories: 412 | fat: 30g | protein: 9g | carbs: 31g | fiber: 9g | sodium: 148mg

Baba Ghanoush

Prep time: 15 minutes | Cook time: 2 to 4 hours | Serves 6

1 large eggplant (2 to 4 pounds / 907 g to 1.8 kg), peeled and diced	oil, plus more as needed
¼ cup freshly squeezed lemon juice	¼ teaspoon sea salt, plus more as needed
2 garlic cloves, minced	⅛ teaspoon freshly ground black pepper, plus more as needed
2 tablespoons tahini	
1 teaspoon extra-virgin olive	2 tablespoons chopped fresh parsley

1. In a slow cooker, combine the eggplant, lemon juice, garlic, tahini, olive oil, salt, and pepper. Stir to mix well. 2. Cover the cooker and cook for 2 to 4 hours on Low heat. 3. Using a spoon or potato masher, mash the mixture. If you prefer a smoother texture, transfer it to a food processor and blend to your desired consistency. Taste and season with olive oil, salt, and pepper as needed. 4. Garnish with fresh parsley for serving.

Per Serving:
calories: 81 | fat: 4g | protein: 3g | carbs: 12g | fiber: 4g | sodium: 108mg

Honey and Spice Glazed Carrots

Prep time: 5 minutes | Cook time: 5 minutes | Serves 4

4 large carrots, peeled and sliced on the diagonal into ½-inch-thick rounds	½ cup honey
	1 tablespoon red wine vinegar
1 teaspoon ground cinnamon	1 tablespoon chopped flat-leaf parsley
1 teaspoon ground ginger	1 tablespoon chopped cilantro
3 tablespoons olive oil	2 tablespoons toasted pine nuts

1. Bring a large saucepan of lightly salted water to a boil and add the carrots. Cover and cook for about 5 minutes, until the carrots are just tender. Drain in a colander, then transfer to a medium bowl. 2. Add the cinnamon, ginger, olive oil, honey, and vinegar and toss to combine well. Add the parsley and cilantro and toss again to incorporate. Garnish with the pine nuts. Serve immediately or let cool to room temperature.

Per Serving:
calories: 281 | fat: 14g | protein: 1g | carbs: 43g | fiber: 2g | sodium: 48mg

Hearty Minestrone Soup

Prep time: 20 minutes | Cook time: 20 minutes | Serves 8

2 cups dried Great Northern beans, soaked overnight and drained
1 cup orzo
2 large carrots, peeled and diced
1 bunch Swiss chard, ribs removed and roughly chopped
1 medium zucchini, trimmed and diced
2 stalks celery, diced
1 medium onion, peeled and

diced
1 teaspoon minced garlic
1 tablespoon Italian seasoning
1 teaspoon salt
½ teaspoon ground black pepper
2 bay leaves
1 (14½-ounce / 411-g) can diced tomatoes, including juice
4 cups vegetable broth
1 cup tomato juice

1. Place all ingredients in the Instant Pot® and stir to combine. Close lid, set steam release to Sealing, press the Soup button, and cook for the default time of 20 minutes. 2. When the timer beeps, let pressure release naturally for 10 minutes. Quick-release any remaining pressure until the float valve drops and open lid. Remove and discard bay leaves. 3. Ladle into bowls and serve warm.

Per Serving:
calories: 207 | fat: 1g | protein: 12g | carbs: 47g | fiber: 10g | sodium: 814mg

Roasted Brussels Sprouts with Delicata Squash and Balsamic Glaze

Prep time: 10 minutes | Cook time: 30 minutes | Serves 2

½ pound (227 g) Brussels sprouts, ends trimmed and outer leaves removed
1 medium delicata squash, halved lengthwise, seeded, and cut into 1-inch pieces
1 cup fresh cranberries
2 teaspoons olive oil

Salt
Freshly ground black pepper
½ cup balsamic vinegar
2 tablespoons roasted pumpkin seeds
2 tablespoons fresh pomegranate arils (seeds)

1. Preheat oven to 400°F (205°C) and set the rack to the middle position. Line a sheet pan with parchment paper. 2. Combine the Brussels sprouts, squash, and cranberries in a large bowl. Drizzle with olive oil, and season liberally with salt and pepper. Toss well to coat and arrange in a single layer on the sheet pan. 3. Roast for 30 minutes, turning vegetables halfway through, or until Brussels sprouts turn brown and crisp in spots and squash has golden-brown spots. 4. While vegetables are roasting, prepare the balsamic glaze by simmering the vinegar for 10 to 12 minutes, or until mixture has reduced to about ¼ cup and turns a syrupy consistency. 5. Remove the vegetables from the oven, drizzle with balsamic syrup, and sprinkle with pumpkin seeds and pomegranate arils before serving.

Per Serving:
calories: 201 | fat: 7g | protein: 6g | carbs: 21g | fiber: 8g | sodium: 34mg

Rosemary-Roasted Red Potatoes

Prep time: 5 minutes | Cook time: 20 minutes | Serves 6

1 pound (454 g) red potatoes, quartered
¼ cup olive oil
½ teaspoon kosher salt

¼ teaspoon black pepper
1 garlic clove, minced
4 rosemary sprigs

1. Preheat the air fryer to 360°F(182°C). 2. In a large bowl, toss the potatoes with the olive oil, salt, pepper, and garlic until well coated. 3. Pour the potatoes into the air fryer basket and top with the sprigs of rosemary. 4. Roast for 10 minutes, then stir or toss the potatoes and roast for 10 minutes more. 5. Remove the rosemary sprigs and serve the potatoes. Season with additional salt and pepper, if needed.

Per Serving:
calories: 134 | fat: 9g | protein: 1g | carbs: 12g | fiber: 1g | sodium: 208mg

Artichokes Provençal

Prep time: 15 minutes | Cook time: 10 minutes | Serves 4

4 large artichokes
1 medium lemon, cut in half
2 tablespoons olive oil
½ medium white onion, peeled and sliced
4 cloves garlic, peeled and chopped
2 tablespoons chopped fresh oregano
2 tablespoons chopped fresh

basil
2 sprigs fresh thyme
2 medium tomatoes, seeded and chopped
¼ cup chopped Kalamata olives
¼ cup red wine
¼ cup water
¼ teaspoon salt
¼ teaspoon ground black pepper

1. Run artichokes under running water, making sure water runs between leaves to flush out any debris. Slice off top ⅓ of artichoke, trim stem, and pull away any tough outer leaves. Rub all cut surfaces with lemon. 2. Press the Sauté button on the Instant Pot® and heat oil. Add onion and cook until just tender, about 2 minutes. Add garlic, oregano, basil, and thyme, and cook until fragrant, about 30 seconds. Add tomatoes and olives and gently mix, then add wine and water and cook for 30 seconds. Press the Cancel button, then add artichokes cut side down to the Instant Pot®. 3. Close lid, set steam release to Sealing, press the Manual button, and set time to 5 minutes. When the timer beeps, quick-release the pressure until the float valve drops. Open lid and transfer artichokes to a serving platter. Pour sauce over top, then season with salt and pepper. Serve warm.

Per Serving:
calories: 449 | fat: 16g | protein: 20g | carbs: 40g | fiber: 12g | sodium: 762mg

Caesar Whole Cauliflower

Prep time: 20 minutes | Cook time: 30 minutes | Serves 2 to 4

3 tablespoons olive oil
2 tablespoons red wine vinegar
2 tablespoons Worcestershire sauce
2 tablespoons grated Parmesan cheese
1 tablespoon Dijon mustard
4 garlic cloves, minced
4 oil-packed anchovy fillets, drained and finely minced

Kosher salt and freshly ground black pepper, to taste
1 small head cauliflower (about 1 pound / 454 g), green leaves trimmed and stem trimmed flush with the bottom of the head
1 tablespoon roughly chopped fresh flat-leaf parsley (optional)

1. In a liquid measuring cup, whisk together the olive oil, vinegar, Worcestershire, Parmesan, mustard, garlic, anchovies, and salt and pepper to taste. Place the cauliflower head upside down on a cutting board and use a paring knife to make an "x" through the full length of the core. Transfer the cauliflower head to a large bowl and pour half the dressing over it. Turn the cauliflower head to coat it in the dressing, then let it rest, stem-side up, in the dressing for at least 10 minutes and up to 30 minutes to allow the dressing to seep into all its nooks and crannies. 2. Transfer the cauliflower head, stem-side down, to the air fryer and air fry at 340ºF (171ºC) for 25 minutes. Drizzle the remaining dressing over the cauliflower and air fry at 400ºF (204ºC) until the top of the cauliflower is golden brown and the core is tender, about 5 minutes more. 3. Remove the basket from the air fryer and transfer the cauliflower to a large plate. Sprinkle with the parsley, if you like, and serve hot.

Per Serving:
calories: 187 | fat: 15g | protein: 5g | carbs: 9g | fiber: 2g | sodium: 453mg

Sesame-Ginger Broccoli

Prep time: 10 minutes | Cook time: 15 minutes | Serves 4

3 tablespoons toasted sesame oil
2 teaspoons sesame seeds
1 tablespoon chili-garlic sauce
2 teaspoons minced fresh ginger

½ teaspoon kosher salt
½ teaspoon black pepper
1 (16-ounce / 454-g) package frozen broccoli florets (do not thaw)

1. In a large bowl, combine the sesame oil, sesame seeds, chili-garlic sauce, ginger, salt, and pepper. Stir until well combined. Add the broccoli and toss until well coated. 2. Arrange the broccoli in the air fryer basket. Set the air fryer to 325ºF (163ºC) for 15 minutes, or until the broccoli is crisp, tender, and the edges are lightly browned, gently tossing halfway through the cooking time.

Per Serving:
calories: 143 | fat: 11g | protein: 4g | carbs: 9g | fiber: 4g | sodium: 385mg

Spinach and Sweet Pepper Poppers

Prep time: 10 minutes | Cook time: 8 minutes | Makes 16 poppers

4 ounces (113 g) cream cheese, softened
1 cup chopped fresh spinach leaves

½ teaspoon garlic powder
8 mini sweet bell peppers, tops removed, seeded, and halved lengthwise

1. In a medium bowl, mix cream cheese, spinach, and garlic powder. Place 1 tablespoon mixture into each sweet pepper half and press down to smooth. 2. Place poppers into ungreased air fryer basket. Adjust the temperature to 400ºF (204ºC) and air fry for 8 minutes. Poppers will be done when cheese is browned on top and peppers are tender-crisp. Serve warm.

Per Serving:
calories: 31 | fat: 2g | protein: 1g | carbs: 3g | fiber: 0g | sodium: 34mg

Zesty Cabbage Soup

Prep time: 25 minutes | Cook time: 30 minutes | Serves 8

2 tablespoons extra-virgin olive oil
3 medium onions, peeled and chopped
1 large carrot, peeled, quartered, and sliced
1 stalk celery, chopped
3 bay leaves
1 teaspoon smoked paprika
3 cups sliced white cabbage
1 teaspoon fresh thyme leaves
3 cloves garlic, peeled and minced
½ cup chopped roasted red

pepper
1 (15-ounce / 425-g) can white navy beans, drained and rinsed
1½ cups low-sodium vegetable cocktail beverage
7 cups low-sodium vegetable stock
1 dried chili pepper
2 medium zucchini, trimmed, halved lengthwise, and thinly sliced
1 teaspoon salt
½ teaspoon ground black pepper

1. Press the Sauté button on the Instant Pot® and heat oil. Add onions, carrot, celery, and bay leaves. Cook for 7–10 minutes or until vegetables are soft. 2. Add paprika, cabbage, thyme, garlic, roasted red pepper, and beans. Stir to combine and cook for 2 minutes. Add vegetable cocktail beverage, stock, and chili pepper. Press the Cancel button. 3. Close lid, set steam release to Sealing, press the Soup button, and cook for default time of 20 minutes. When the timer beeps, quick-release the pressure until the float valve drops and open lid. 4. Remove and discard bay leaves. Add zucchini, close lid, and let stand on the Keep Warm setting for 15 minutes. Season with salt and pepper. Serve hot.

Per Serving:
calories: 157 | fat: 4g | protein: 7g | carbs: 25g | fiber: 8g | sodium: 360mg

Garlicky Sautéed Zucchini with Mint

Prep time: 5 minutes | Cook time: 10 minutes | Serves 4

3 large green zucchini
3 tablespoons extra-virgin olive oil
1 large onion, chopped

3 cloves garlic, minced
1 teaspoon salt
1 teaspoon dried mint

1. Cut the zucchini into ½-inch cubes. 2. In a large skillet over medium heat, cook the olive oil, onions, and garlic for 3 minutes, stirring constantly. 3. Add the zucchini and salt to the skillet and toss to combine with the onions and garlic, cooking for 5 minutes. 4. Add the mint to the skillet, tossing to combine. Cook for another 2 minutes. Serve warm.

Per Serving:

calories: 147 | fat: 11g | protein: 4g | carbs: 12g | fiber: 3g | sodium: 607mg

Garlic Roasted Broccoli

Prep time: 8 minutes | Cook time: 10 to 14 minutes | Serves 6

1 head broccoli, cut into bite-size florets
1 tablespoon avocado oil
2 teaspoons minced garlic
⅛ teaspoon red pepper flakes

Sea salt and freshly ground black pepper, to taste
1 tablespoon freshly squeezed lemon juice
½ teaspoon lemon zest

1. In a large bowl, toss together the broccoli, avocado oil, garlic, red pepper flakes, salt, and pepper. 2. Set the air fryer to 375°F (191°C). Arrange the broccoli in a single layer in the air fryer basket, working in batches if necessary. Roast for 10 to 14 minutes, until the broccoli is lightly charred. 3. Place the florets in a medium bowl and toss with the lemon juice and lemon zest. Serve.

Per Serving:

calories: 58 | fat: 3g | protein: 3g | carbs: 7g | fiber: 3g | sodium: 34mg

Caramelized Eggplant with Harissa Yogurt

Prep time: 10 minutes | Cook time: 15 minutes | Serves 2

1 medium eggplant (about ¾ pound / 340 g), cut crosswise into ½-inch-thick slices and quartered
2 tablespoons vegetable oil
Kosher salt and freshly ground

black pepper, to taste
½ cup plain yogurt (not Greek)
2 tablespoons harissa paste
1 garlic clove, grated
2 teaspoons honey

1. In a bowl, toss together the eggplant and oil, season with salt and pepper, and toss to coat evenly. Transfer to the air fryer and air fry at 400°F (204°C), shaking the basket every 5 minutes, until the eggplant is caramelized and tender, about 15 minutes. 2. Meanwhile, in a small bowl, whisk together the yogurt, harissa, and garlic, then spread onto a serving plate. 3. Pile the warm eggplant over the yogurt and drizzle with the honey just before serving.

Per Serving:

calories: 247 | fat: 16g | protein: 5g | carbs: 25g | fiber: 8g | sodium: 34mg

Toasted Grain and Almond Pilaf

Prep time: 15 minutes | Cook time: 35 minutes | Serves 2

1 tablespoon olive oil
1 garlic clove, minced
3 scallions, minced
2 ounces (57 g) mushrooms, sliced
¼ cup sliced almonds
½ cup uncooked pearled barley

1½ cups low-sodium chicken stock
½ teaspoon dried thyme
1 tablespoon fresh minced parsley
Salt

1. Heat the oil in a saucepan over medium-high heat. Add the garlic, scallions, mushrooms, and almonds, and sauté for 3 minutes. 2. Add the barley and cook, stirring, for 1 minute to toast it. 3. Add the chicken stock and thyme and bring the mixture to a boil. 4. Cover and reduce the heat to low. Simmer the barley for 30 minutes, or until the liquid is absorbed and the barley is tender. 5. Sprinkle with fresh parsley and season with salt before serving.

Per Serving:

calories: 333 | fat: 14g | protein: 10g | carbs: 46g | fiber: 10g | sodium: 141mg

Ratatouille

Prep time: 15 minutes | Cook time: 20 minutes | Serves 2 to 3

2 cups ¾-inch cubed peeled eggplant
1 small red, yellow, or orange bell pepper, stemmed, seeded, and diced
1 cup cherry tomatoes
6 to 8 cloves garlic, peeled and

halved lengthwise
3 tablespoons olive oil
1 teaspoon dried oregano
½ teaspoon dried thyme
1 teaspoon kosher salt
½ teaspoon black pepper

1. In a medium bowl, combine the eggplant, bell pepper, tomatoes, garlic, oil, oregano, thyme, salt, and pepper. Toss to combine. 2. Place the vegetables in the air fryer basket. Set the air fryer to 400°F (204°C) for 20 minutes, or until the vegetables are crisp-tender.

Per Serving:

calories: 161 | fat: 14g | protein: 2g | carbs: 9g | fiber: 3g | sodium: 781mg

Green Beans with Pine Nuts and Garlic

Prep time: 10 minutes | Cook time: 20 minutes |

Serves 4 to 6

1 pound (454 g) green beans, trimmed
1 head garlic (10 to 12 cloves), smashed
2 tablespoons extra-virgin olive oil

½ teaspoon kosher salt
¼ teaspoon red pepper flakes
1 tablespoon white wine vinegar
¼ cup pine nuts, toasted

1. Preheat the oven to 425°F (220°C). Line a baking sheet with parchment paper or foil. 2. In a large bowl, combine the green beans, garlic, olive oil, salt, and red pepper flakes and mix together. Arrange in a single layer on the baking sheet. Roast for 10 minutes, stir, and roast for another 10 minutes, or until golden brown. 3. Mix the cooked green beans with the vinegar and top with the pine nuts.

Per Serving:

calories: 165 | fat: 13g | protein: 4g | carbs: 12g | fiber: 4g | sodium: 150mg

Roasted Radishes with Sea Salt

Prep time: 5 minutes | Cook time: 18 minutes |

Serves 4

1 pound (454 g) radishes, ends trimmed if needed

2 tablespoons olive oil
½ teaspoon sea salt

1. Preheat the air fryer to 360°F(182°C). 2. In a large bowl, combine the radishes with olive oil and sea salt. 3. Pour the radishes into the air fryer and roast for 10 minutes. Stir or turn the radishes over and roast for 8 minutes more, then serve.

Per Serving:

calories: 80 | fat: 7g | protein: 1g | carbs: 5g | fiber: 2g | sodium: 315mg

Puréed Cauliflower Soup

Prep time: 15 minutes | Cook time: 11 minutes |

Serves 6

2 tablespoons olive oil
1 medium onion, peeled and chopped
1 stalk celery, chopped
1 medium carrot, peeled and chopped
3 sprigs fresh thyme

4 cups cauliflower florets
2 cups vegetable stock
½ cup half-and-half
¼ cup low-fat plain Greek yogurt
2 tablespoons chopped fresh chives

1. Press the Sauté button on the Instant Pot® and heat oil. Add onion, celery, and carrot. Cook until just tender, about 6 minutes.

Add thyme, cauliflower, and stock. Stir well, then press the Cancel button. 2. Close lid, set steam release to Sealing, press the Manual button, and set time to 5 minutes. When the timer beeps, let pressure release naturally, about 15 minutes. 3. Open lid, remove and discard thyme stems, and with an immersion blender, purée soup until smooth. Stir in half-and-half and yogurt. Garnish with chives and serve immediately.

Per Serving:

calories: 113 | fat: 7g | protein: 3g | carbs: 9g | fiber: 2g | sodium: 236mg

Asparagus Fries

Prep time: 15 minutes | Cook time: 5 to 7 minutes

per batch | Serves 4

12 ounces (340 g) fresh asparagus spears with tough ends trimmed off
2 egg whites
¼ cup water

¾ cup panko bread crumbs
¼ cup grated Parmesan cheese, plus 2 tablespoons
¼ teaspoon salt
Oil for misting or cooking spray

1. Preheat the air fryer to 390°F (199°C). 2. In a shallow dish, beat egg whites and water until slightly foamy. 3. In another shallow dish, combine panko, Parmesan, and salt. 4. Dip asparagus spears in egg, then roll in crumbs. Spray with oil or cooking spray. 5. Place a layer of asparagus in air fryer basket, leaving just a little space in between each spear. Stack another layer on top, crosswise. Air fry at 390°F (199°C) for 5 to 7 minutes, until crispy and golden brown. 6. Repeat to cook remaining asparagus.

Per Serving:

calories: 132 | fat: 3g | protein: 8g | carbs: 19g | fiber: 3g | sodium: 436mg

Parmesan-Thyme Butternut Squash

Prep time: 15 minutes | Cook time: 20 minutes |

Serves 4

2½ cups butternut squash, cubed into 1-inch pieces (approximately 1 medium)
2 tablespoons olive oil
¼ teaspoon salt

¼ teaspoon garlic powder
¼ teaspoon black pepper
1 tablespoon fresh thyme
¼ cup grated Parmesan

1. Preheat the air fryer to 360°F(182°C). 2. In a large bowl, combine the cubed squash with the olive oil, salt, garlic powder, pepper, and thyme until the squash is well coated. 3. Pour this mixture into the air fryer basket, and roast for 10 minutes. Stir and roast another 8 to 10 minutes more. 4. Remove the squash from the air fryer and toss with freshly grated Parmesan before serving.

Per Serving:

calories: 127 | fat: 9g | protein: 3g | carbs: 12g | fiber: 2g | sodium: 262mg

Roasted Acorn Squash

Prep time: 10 minutes | Cook time: 35 minutes |

Serves 6

2 acorn squash, medium to large
2 tablespoons extra-virgin olive oil
1 teaspoon salt, plus more for seasoning

5 tablespoons unsalted butter
¼ cup chopped sage leaves
2 tablespoons fresh thyme leaves
½ teaspoon freshly ground black pepper

1. Preheat the oven to 400°F(205°C). 2. Cut the acorn squash in half lengthwise. Scrape out the seeds with a spoon and cut it horizontally into ¾-inch-thick slices. 3. In a large bowl, drizzle the squash with the olive oil, sprinkle with salt, and toss together to coat. 4. Lay the acorn squash flat on a baking sheet. 5. Put the baking sheet in the oven and bake the squash for 20 minutes. Flip squash over with a spatula and bake for another 15 minutes. 6. Melt the butter in a medium saucepan over medium heat. 7. Add the sage and thyme to the melted butter and let them cook for 30 seconds. 8. Transfer the cooked squash slices to a plate. Spoon the butter/herb mixture over the squash. Season with salt and black pepper. Serve warm.

Per Serving:

calories: 188 | fat: 15g | protein: 1g | carbs: 16g | fiber: 3g | sodium: 393mg

One-Pan Herb-Roasted Tomatoes, Green Beans, and Baby Potatoes

Prep time: 10 minutes | Cook time: 30 minutes |

Serves 6

¼ cup chopped mixed fresh herbs, such as flat-leaf parsley, oregano, mint, and dill
3 tablespoons olive oil
½ teaspoon kosher salt
½ teaspoon ground black pepper

1 pound (454 g) baby potatoes, halved
1 pound (454 g) green beans, trimmed and halved
2 large shallots, cut into wedges
2 pints cherry tomatoes

1. Preheat the oven to 400°F (205°C). 2. In a small bowl, whisk together the herbs, oil, salt, and pepper. Place the potatoes, string beans, and shallots on a large rimmed baking sheet. Drizzle the herb mixture over the vegetables and toss thoroughly to coat. 3. Roast the vegetables until the potatoes are just tender, about 15 minutes. Remove from the oven and toss in the tomatoes. Roast until the tomatoes blister and the potatoes are completely tender, about 15 minutes.

Per Serving:

calories: 173 | fat: 8g | protein: 5g | carbs: 26g | fiber: 5g | sodium: 185mg

Roasted Brussels Sprouts with Orange and Garlic

Prep time: 5 minutes | Cook time: 10 minutes |

Serves 4

1 pound (454 g) Brussels sprouts, quartered
2 garlic cloves, minced

2 tablespoons olive oil
½ teaspoon salt
1 orange, cut into rings

1. Preheat the air fryer to 360°F(182°C). 2. In a large bowl, toss the quartered Brussels sprouts with the garlic, olive oil, and salt until well coated. 3. Pour the Brussels sprouts into the air fryer, lay the orange slices on top of them, and roast for 10 minutes. 4. Remove from the air fryer and set the orange slices aside. Toss the Brussels sprouts before serving.

Per Serving:

calories: 127 | fat: 7g | protein: 4g | carbs: 15g | fiber: 5g | sodium: 319mg

Roasted Broccoli with Tahini Yogurt Sauce

Prep time: 15 minutes | Cook time: 30 minutes |

Serves 4

For the Broccoli:

1½ to 2 pounds (680 to 907 g) broccoli, stalk trimmed and cut into slices, head cut into florets
1 lemon, sliced into ¼-inch-thick rounds

3 tablespoons extra-virgin olive oil
½ teaspoon kosher salt
¼ teaspoon freshly ground black pepper

For the Tahini Yogurt Sauce:

½ cup plain Greek yogurt
2 tablespoons tahini
1 tablespoon lemon juice

¼ teaspoon kosher salt
1 teaspoon sesame seeds, for garnish (optional)

Make the Broccoli: 1. Preheat the oven to 425°F (220°C). Line a baking sheet with parchment paper or foil. 2. In a large bowl, gently toss the broccoli, lemon slices, olive oil, salt, and black pepper to combine. Arrange the broccoli in a single layer on the prepared baking sheet. Roast 15 minutes, stir, and roast another 15 minutes, until golden brown. Make the Tahini Yogurt Sauce: 3. In a medium bowl, combine the yogurt, tahini, lemon juice, and salt; mix well. 4. Spread the tahini yogurt sauce on a platter or large plate and top with the broccoli and lemon slices. Garnish with the sesame seeds (if desired).

Per Serving:

calories: 245 | fat: 16g | protein: 12g | carbs: 20g | fiber: 7g | sodium: 305mg

Roasted Harissa Carrots

Prep time: 10 minutes | Cook time: 15 minutes |

Serves 4

1 pound (454 g) carrots, peeled and sliced into 1-inch-thick rounds	2 tablespoons harissa
	1 teaspoon honey
	1 teaspoon ground cumin
2 tablespoons extra-virgin olive oil	½ teaspoon kosher salt
	½ cup fresh parsley, chopped

1. Preheat the oven to 450ºF (235ºC). Line a baking sheet with parchment paper or foil. 2. In a large bowl, combine the carrots, olive oil, harissa, honey, cumin, and salt. Arrange in a single layer on the baking sheet. Roast for 15 minutes. Remove from the oven, add the parsley, and toss together.

Per Serving:

calories: 120 | fat: 8g | protein: 1g | carbs: 13g | fiber: 4g | sodium: 255mg

Zesty Fried Asparagus

Prep time: 3 minutes | Cook time: 10 minutes |

Serves 4

Oil, for spraying	1 tablespoon granulated garlic
10 to 12 spears asparagus, trimmed	1 teaspoon chili powder
	½ teaspoon ground cumin
2 tablespoons olive oil	¼ teaspoon salt

1. Line the air fryer basket with parchment and spray lightly with oil. 2. If the asparagus are too long to fit easily in the air fryer, cut them in half. 3. Place the asparagus, olive oil, garlic, chili powder, cumin, and salt in a zip-top plastic bag, seal, and toss until evenly coated. 4. Place the asparagus in the prepared basket. 5. Roast at 390ºF (199ºC) for 5 minutes, flip, and cook for another 5 minutes, or until bright green and firm but tender.

Per Serving:

calories: 74 | fat: 7g | protein: 1g | carbs: 3g | fiber: 1g | sodium: 166mg

Greek Stewed Zucchini

Prep time: 5 minutes | Cook time: 40 minutes |

Serves 4 to 6

¼ cup extra-virgin olive oil	2 cups chopped tomatoes
1 small yellow onion, peeled and slivered	½ cup halved and pitted Kalamata olives
4 medium zucchini squash, cut into ½-inch-thick rounds	¾ cup crumbled feta cheese
4 small garlic cloves, minced	¼ cup chopped fresh flat-leaf Italian parsley, for garnish (optional)
1 to 2 teaspoons dried oregano	

1. In a large skillet, heat the oil over medium-high heat. Add the slivered onion and sauté until just tender, 6 to 8 minutes. Add the zucchini, garlic, and oregano and sauté another 6 to 8 minutes, or until zucchini is just tender. 2. Add the tomatoes and bring to a boil. Reduce the heat to low and add the olives. Cover and simmer on low heat for 20 minutes, or until the flavors have developed and the zucchini is very tender. 3. Serve warm topped with feta and parsley (if using).

Per Serving:

calories: 183 | fat: 15g | protein: 5g | carbs: 10g | fiber: 3g | sodium: 269mg

Indian Eggplant Bharta

Prep time: 15 minutes | Cook time: 20 minutes |

Serves 4

1 medium eggplant	2 tablespoons fresh lemon juice
2 tablespoons vegetable oil	2 tablespoons chopped fresh cilantro
½ cup finely minced onion	
½ cup finely chopped fresh tomato	½ teaspoon kosher salt
	⅛ teaspoon cayenne pepper

1. Rub the eggplant all over with the vegetable oil. Place the eggplant in the air fryer basket. Set the air fryer to 400ºF (204ºC) for 20 minutes, or until the eggplant skin is blistered and charred. 2. Transfer the eggplant to a resealable plastic bag, seal, and set aside for 15 to 20 minutes (the eggplant will finish cooking in the residual heat trapped in the bag). 3. Transfer the eggplant to a large bowl. Peel off and discard the charred skin. Roughly mash the eggplant flesh. Add the onion, tomato, lemon juice, cilantro, salt, and cayenne. Stir to combine.

Per Serving:

calories: 105 | fat: 7g | protein: 2g | carbs: 11g | fiber: 5g | sodium: 295mg

Corn on the Cob

Prep time: 5 minutes | Cook time: 12 to 15 minutes |

Serves 4

2 large ears fresh corn	Salt, to taste (optional)
Olive oil for misting	

1. Shuck corn, remove silks, and wash. 2. Cut or break each ear in half crosswise. 3. Spray corn with olive oil. 4. Air fry at 390ºF (199ºC) for 12 to 15 minutes or until browned as much as you like. 5. Serve plain or with coarsely ground salt.

Per Serving:

calories: 67 | fat: 1g | protein: 2g | carbs: 14g | fiber: 2g | sodium: 156mg

Garlic Zucchini and Red Peppers

Prep time: 5 minutes | Cook time: 15 minutes | Serves 6

2 medium zucchini, cubed
1 red bell pepper, diced
2 garlic cloves, sliced
2 tablespoons olive oil
½ teaspoon salt

1. Preheat the air fryer to 380°F(193ºC). 2. In a large bowl, mix together the zucchini, bell pepper, and garlic with the olive oil and salt. 3. Pour the mixture into the air fryer basket, and roast for 7 minutes. Shake or stir, then roast for 7 to 8 minutes more.

Per Serving:

calories: 59 | fat: 5g | protein: 1g | carbs: 4g | fiber: 1g | sodium: 200mg

Glazed Carrots

Prep time: 10 minutes | Cook time: 8 to 10 minutes | Serves 4

2 teaspoons honey
1 teaspoon orange juice
½ teaspoon grated orange rind
⅛ teaspoon ginger
1 pound (454 g) baby carrots
2 teaspoons olive oil
¼ teaspoon salt

1. Combine honey, orange juice, grated rind, and ginger in a small bowl and set aside. 2. Toss the carrots, oil, and salt together to coat well and pour them into the air fryer basket. 3. Roast at 390°F (199ºC) for 5 minutes. Shake basket to stir a little and cook for 2 to 4 minutes more, until carrots are barely tender. 4. Pour carrots into a baking pan. 5. Stir the honey mixture to combine well, pour glaze over carrots, and stir to coat. 6. Roast at 360ºF (182ºC) for 1 minute or just until heated through.

Per Serving:

calories: 71 | fat: 2g | protein: 1g | carbs: 12g | fiber: 3g | sodium: 234mg

Stuffed Artichokes

Prep time: 20 minutes | Cook time: 5 to 7 hours | Serves 4 to 6

4 to 6 fresh large artichokes
½ cup bread crumbs
½ cup grated Parmesan cheese or Romano cheese
4 garlic cloves, minced
½ teaspoon sea salt
½ teaspoon freshly ground
black pepper
¼ cup water
2 tablespoons extra-virgin olive oil
2 tablespoons chopped fresh parsley for garnish (optional)

1. To trim and prepare the artichokes, cut off the bottom along with 1 inch from the top of each artichoke. Pull off and discard the lowest leaves nearest the stem end. Trim off any pointy tips of artichoke leaves that are poking out. Set aside. 2. In a small bowl, stir together the bread crumbs, Parmesan cheese, garlic, salt, and pepper. 3. Spread apart the artichoke leaves and stuff the bread-crumb mixture into the spaces, down to the base. 4. Pour the water into a slow cooker. 5. Place the artichokes in the slow cooker in a single layer. Drizzle the olive oil over the artichokes. 6. Cover the cooker and cook for 5 to 7 hours on Low heat, or until the artichokes are tender. 7. Garnish with fresh parsley if desired.

Per Serving:

calories: 224 | fat: 12g | protein: 12g | carbs: 23g | fiber: 8g | sodium: 883mg

Parmesan Mushrooms

Prep time: 5 minutes | Cook time: 15 minutes | Serves 4

Oil, for spraying
1 pound (454 g) cremini mushrooms, stems trimmed
2 tablespoons olive oil
2 teaspoons granulated garlic
1 teaspoon dried onion soup
mix
½ teaspoon salt
¼ teaspoon freshly ground black pepper
⅓ cup grated Parmesan cheese, divided

1. Line the air fryer basket with parchment and spray lightly with oil. 2. In a large bowl, toss the mushrooms with the olive oil, garlic, onion soup mix, salt, and black pepper until evenly coated. 3. Place the mushrooms in the prepared basket. 4. Roast at 370ºF (188ºC) for 13 minutes. 5. Sprinkle half of the cheese over the mushrooms and cook for another 2 minutes. 6. Transfer the mushrooms to a serving bowl, add the remaining Parmesan cheese, and toss until evenly coated. Serve immediately.

Per Serving:

calories: 89 | fat: 9g | protein: 5g | carbs: 7g | fiber: 1g | sodium: 451mg

Citrus-Roasted Broccoli Florets

Prep time: 5 minutes | Cook time: 12 minutes | Serves 6

4 cups broccoli florets (approximately 1 large head)
2 tablespoons olive oil
½ teaspoon salt
½ cup orange juice
1 tablespoon raw honey
Orange wedges, for serving (optional)

1. Preheat the air fryer to 360°F(182ºC). 2. In a large bowl, combine the broccoli, olive oil, salt, orange juice, and honey. Toss the broccoli in the liquid until well coated. 3. Pour the broccoli mixture into the air fryer basket and roast for 6 minutes. Stir and roast for 6 minutes more. 4. Serve alone or with orange wedges for additional citrus flavor, if desired.

Per Serving:

calories: 73 | fat: 5g | protein: 2g | carbs: 8g | fiber: 0g | sodium: 207mg

Greek Garlic Dip

Prep time: 10 minutes | Cook time: 30 minutes | Serves 4

2 potatoes (about 1 pound / 454 g), peeled and quartered
½ cup olive oil
¼ cup freshly squeezed lemon juice

4 garlic cloves, minced
Sea salt
Freshly ground black pepper

1. Place the potatoes in a large saucepan and fill the pan three-quarters full with water. Bring the water to a boil over medium-high heat, then reduce the heat to medium and cook the potatoes until fork-tender, 20 to 30 minutes. 2. While the potatoes are boiling, in a medium bowl, stir together the olive oil, lemon juice, and garlic; set aside. 3. Drain the potatoes and return them to the saucepan. Pour in the oil mixture and mash with a potato masher or a fork until well combined and smooth. Taste and season with salt and pepper. Serve.

Per Serving:

calories: 334 | fat: 27g | protein: 3g | carbs: 22g | fiber: 3g | sodium: 47mg

Chapter 9 Vegetarian Mains

Crispy Tofu

Prep time: 30 minutes | Cook time: 15 to 20 minutes | Serves 4

1 (16-ounce / 454-g) block extra-firm tofu
2 tablespoons coconut aminos
1 tablespoon toasted sesame oil
1 tablespoon olive oil

1 tablespoon chili-garlic sauce
1½ teaspoons black sesame seeds
1 scallion, thinly sliced

1. Press the tofu for at least 15 minutes by wrapping it in paper towels and setting a heavy pan on top so that the moisture drains. 2. Slice the tofu into bite-size cubes and transfer to a bowl. Drizzle with the coconut aminos, sesame oil, olive oil, and chili-garlic sauce. Cover and refrigerate for 1 hour or up to overnight. 3. Preheat the air fryer to 400ºF (204ºC). 4. Arrange the tofu in a single layer in the air fryer basket. Pausing to shake the pan halfway through the cooking time, air fry for 15 to 20 minutes until crisp. Serve with any juices that accumulate in the bottom of the air fryer, sprinkled with the sesame seeds and sliced scallion.

Per Serving:
calories: 173 | fat: 14g | protein: 12g | carbs: 3g | fiber: 1g | sodium: 49mg

Turkish Red Lentil and Bulgur Kofte

Prep time: 10 minutes | Cook time: 45 minutes | Serves 4

⅓ cup olive oil, plus 2 tablespoons, divided, plus more for brushing
1 cup red lentils
½ cup bulgur
1 teaspoon salt
1 medium onion, finely diced

2 tablespoons tomato paste
1 teaspoon ground cumin
¼ cup finely chopped flat-leaf parsley
3 scallions, thinly sliced
Juice of ½ lemon

1. Preheat the oven to 400ºF(205ºC). 2. Brush a large, rimmed baking sheet with olive oil. 3. In a medium saucepan, combine the lentils with 2 cups water and bring to a boil. Reduce the heat to low and cook, stirring occasionally, for about 15 minutes, until the lentils are tender and have soaked up most of the liquid. Remove from the heat, stir in the bulgur and salt, cover, and let sit for 15 minutes or so, until the bulgur is tender. 4. Meanwhile, heat ⅓ cup olive oil in a medium skillet over medium-high heat. Add the onion and cook, stirring frequently, until softened, about 5 minutes. Stir

in the tomato paste and cook for 2 minutes more. Remove from the heat and stir in the cumin. 5. Add the cooked onion mixture to the lentil-bulgur mixture and stir to combine. Add the parsley, scallions, and lemon juice and stir to mix well. 6. Shape the mixture into walnut-sized balls and place them on the prepared baking sheet. Brush the balls with the remaining 2 tablespoons of olive oil and bake for 15 to 20 minutes, until golden brown. Serve hot.

Per Serving:
calories: 460 | fat: 25g | protein: 16g | carbs: 48g | fiber: 19g | sodium: 604mg

Baked Tofu with Sun-Dried Tomatoes and Artichokes

Prep time: 15 minutes | Cook time: 30 minutes | Serves 4

1 (16-ounce / 454-g) package extra-firm tofu, drained and patted dry, cut into 1-inch cubes
2 tablespoons extra-virgin olive oil, divided
2 tablespoons lemon juice, divided
1 tablespoon low-sodium soy sauce or gluten-free tamari
1 onion, diced
½ teaspoon kosher salt
2 garlic cloves, minced

1 (14-ounce / 397-g) can artichoke hearts, drained
8 sun-dried tomato halves packed in oil, drained and chopped
¼ teaspoon freshly ground black pepper
1 tablespoon white wine vinegar
Zest of 1 lemon
¼ cup fresh parsley, chopped

1. Preheat the oven to 400ºF (205ºC). Line a baking sheet with foil or parchment paper. 2. In a bowl, combine the tofu, 1 tablespoon of the olive oil, 1 tablespoon of the lemon juice, and the soy sauce. Allow to sit and marinate for 15 to 30 minutes. Arrange the tofu in a single layer on the prepared baking sheet and bake for 20 minutes, turning once, until light golden brown. 3. Heat the remaining 1 tablespoon olive oil in a large skillet or sauté pan over medium heat. Add the onion and salt; sauté until translucent, 5 to 6 minutes. Add the garlic and sauté for 30 seconds. Add the artichoke hearts, sun-dried tomatoes, and black pepper and sauté for 5 minutes. Add the white wine vinegar and the remaining 1 tablespoon lemon juice and deglaze the pan, scraping up any brown bits. Remove the pan from the heat and stir in the lemon zest and parsley. Gently mix in the baked tofu.

Per Serving:
calories: 230 | fat: 14g | protein: 14g | carbs: 13g | fiber: 5g | sodium: 500mg

Sheet Pan Roasted Chickpeas and Vegetables with Harissa Yogurt

Prep time: 10 minutes | Cook time: 30 minutes | Serves 2

4 cups cauliflower florets (about ½ small head)
2 medium carrots, peeled, halved, and then sliced into quarters lengthwise
2 tablespoons olive oil, divided
½ teaspoon garlic powder, divided

½ teaspoon salt, divided
2 teaspoons za'atar spice mix, divided
1 (15-ounce / 425-g) can chickpeas, drained, rinsed, and patted dry
¾ cup plain Greek yogurt
1 teaspoon harissa spice paste

1. Preheat the oven to 400ºF (205ºC) and set the rack to the middle position. Line a sheet pan with foil or parchment paper. 2. Place the cauliflower and carrots in a large bowl. Drizzle with 1 tablespoon olive oil and sprinkle with ¼ teaspoon of garlic powder, ¼ teaspoon of salt, and 1 teaspoon of za'atar. Toss well to combine. 3. Spread the vegetables onto one half of the sheet pan in a single layer. 4. Place the chickpeas in the same bowl and season with the remaining 1 tablespoon of oil, ¼ teaspoon of garlic powder, and ¼ teaspoon of salt, and the remaining za'atar. Toss well to combine. 5. Spread the chickpeas onto the other half of the sheet pan. 6. Roast for 30 minutes, or until the vegetables are tender and the chickpeas start to turn golden. Flip the vegetables halfway through the cooking time, and give the chickpeas a stir so they cook evenly. 7. The chickpeas may need an extra few minutes if you like them crispy. If so, remove the vegetables and leave the chickpeas in until they're cooked to desired crispiness. 8. While the vegetables are roasting, combine the yogurt and harissa in a small bowl. Taste, and add additional harissa as desired.

Per Serving:

calories: 467 | fat: 23g | protein: 18g | carbs: 54g | fiber: 15g | sodium: 632mg

Parmesan Artichokes

Prep time: 10 minutes | Cook time: 10 minutes | Serves 4

2 medium artichokes, trimmed and quartered, center removed
2 tablespoons coconut oil
1 large egg, beaten
½ cup grated vegetarian

Parmesan cheese
¼ cup blanched finely ground almond flour
½ teaspoon crushed red pepper flakes

1. In a large bowl, toss artichokes in coconut oil and then dip each piece into the egg. 2. Mix the Parmesan and almond flour in a large bowl. Add artichoke pieces and toss to cover as completely as possible, sprinkle with pepper flakes. Place into the air fryer basket. 3. Adjust the temperature to 400ºF (204ºC) and air fry for 10 minutes. 4. Toss the basket two times during cooking. Serve warm.

Per Serving:

calories: 207 | fat: 13g | protein: 10g | carbs: 15g | fiber: 5g | sodium: 211mg

Root Vegetable Soup with Garlic Aioli

Prep time: 10 minutes | Cook time 25 minutes | Serves 4

For the Soup:

8 cups vegetable broth
½ teaspoon salt
1 medium leek, cut into thick rounds
1 pound (454 g) carrots, peeled and diced

1 pound (454 g) potatoes, peeled and diced
1 pound (454 g) turnips, peeled and cut into 1-inch cubes
1 red bell pepper, cut into strips
2 tablespoons fresh oregano

For the Aioli:

5 garlic cloves, minced
¼ teaspoon salt

⅔ cup olive oil
1 drop lemon juice

1. Bring the broth and salt to a boil and add the vegetables one at a time, letting the water return to a boil after each addition. Add the carrots first, then the leeks, potatoes, turnips, and finally the red bell peppers. Let the vegetables cook for about 3 minutes after adding the green beans and bringing to a boil. The process will take about 20 minutes in total. 2. Meanwhile, make the aioli. In a mortar and pestle, grind the garlic to a paste with the salt. Using a whisk and whisking constantly, add the olive oil in a thin stream. Continue whisking until the mixture thickens to the consistency of mayonnaise. Add the lemon juice. 3. Serve the vegetables in the broth, dolloped with the aioli and garnished with the fresh oregano.

Per Serving:

calories: 538 | fat: 37g | protein: 5g | carbs: 50g | fiber: 9g | sodium: 773mg

Herbed Ricotta–Stuffed Mushrooms

Prep time: 10 minutes | Cook time: 30 minutes | Serves 4

6 tablespoons extra-virgin olive oil, divided
4 portobello mushroom caps, cleaned and gills removed
1 cup whole-milk ricotta cheese
⅓ cup chopped fresh herbs

(such as basil, parsley, rosemary, oregano, or thyme)
2 garlic cloves, finely minced
½ teaspoon salt
¼ teaspoon freshly ground black pepper

1. Preheat the oven to 400ºF (205ºC). 2. Line a baking sheet with parchment or foil and drizzle with 2 tablespoons olive oil, spreading evenly. Place the mushroom caps on the baking sheet, gill-side up. 3. In a medium bowl, mix together the ricotta, herbs, 2 tablespoons olive oil, garlic, salt, and pepper. Stuff each mushroom cap with one-quarter of the cheese mixture, pressing down if needed. Drizzle with remaining 2 tablespoons olive oil and bake until golden brown and the mushrooms are soft, 30 to 35 minutes, depending on the size of the mushrooms.

Per Serving:

calories: 308 | fat: 29g | protein: 9g | carbs: 6g | fiber: 1g | sodium: 351mg

Cheesy Cauliflower Pizza Crust

Prep time: 15 minutes | Cook time: 11 minutes |
Serves 2

1 (12-ounce / 340-g) steamer
bag cauliflower
½ cup shredded sharp Cheddar
cheese
1 large egg

2 tablespoons blanched finely
ground almond flour
1 teaspoon Italian blend
seasoning

1. Cook cauliflower according to package instructions. Remove from bag and place into cheesecloth or paper towel to remove excess water. Place cauliflower into a large bowl. 2. Add cheese, egg, almond flour, and Italian seasoning to the bowl and mix well. 3. Cut a piece of parchment to fit your air fryer basket. Press cauliflower into 6-inch round circle. Place into the air fryer basket. 4. Adjust the temperature to 360°F (182°C) and air fry for 11 minutes. 5. After 7 minutes, flip the pizza crust. 6. Add preferred toppings to pizza. Place back into air fryer basket and cook an additional 4 minutes or until fully cooked and golden. Serve immediately.

Per Serving:
calories: 251 | fat: 17g | protein: 15g | carbs: 12g | fiber: 5g | sodium: 375mg

Provençal Ratatouille with Herbed Breadcrumbs and Goat Cheese

Prep time: 10 minutes | Cook time: 1 hour 5 minutes | Serves 4

6 tablespoons olive oil, divided
2 medium onions, diced
2 cloves garlic, minced
2 medium eggplants, halved
lengthwise and cut into ¾-inch
thick half rounds
3 medium zucchini, halved
lengthwise and cut into ¾-inch
thick half rounds
2 red bell peppers, seeded and
cut into 1½-inch pieces
1 green bell pepper, seeded and
cut into 1½-inch pieces
1 (14-ounce / 397-g) can diced

tomatoes, drained
1 teaspoon salt
½ teaspoon freshly ground
black pepper
8 ounces (227 g) fresh
breadcrumbs
1 tablespoon chopped fresh
parsley
1 tablespoon chopped fresh
basil
1 tablespoon chopped fresh
chives
6 ounces (170 g) soft, fresh goat
cheese

1. Preheat the oven to 375°F(190°C). 2. Heat 5 tablespoons of the olive oil in a large skillet over medium heat. Add the onions and garlic and cook, stirring frequently, until the onions are soft and beginning to turn golden, about 8 minutes. Add the eggplant, zucchini, and bell peppers and cook, turning the vegetables occasionally, for another 10 minutes. Stir in the tomatoes, salt, and pepper and let simmer for 15 minutes. 3. While the vegetables are simmering, stir together the breadcrumbs, the remaining tablespoon of olive oil, the parsley, basil, and chives. 4. Transfer the vegetable mixture to a large baking dish, spreading it out into an even layer. Crumble the goat cheese over the top, then sprinkle the breadcrumb mixture evenly over the top. Bake in the preheated oven for about 30 minutes, until the topping is golden brown and crisp. Serve hot.

Per Serving:
calories: 644 | fat: 37g | protein: 21g | carbs: 63g | fiber: 16g | sodium: 861mg

Pesto Spinach Flatbread

Prep time: 10 minutes | Cook time: 8 minutes |
Serves 4

1 cup blanched finely ground
almond flour
2 ounces (57 g) cream cheese
2 cups shredded Mozzarella

cheese
1 cup chopped fresh spinach
leaves
2 tablespoons basil pesto

1. Place flour, cream cheese, and Mozzarella in a large microwave-safe bowl and microwave on high 45 seconds, then stir. 2. Fold in spinach and microwave an additional 15 seconds. Stir until a soft dough ball forms. 3. Cut two pieces of parchment paper to fit air fryer basket. Separate dough into two sections and press each out on ungreased parchment to create 6-inch rounds. 4. Spread 1 tablespoon pesto over each flatbread and place rounds on parchment into ungreased air fryer basket. Adjust the temperature to 350°F (177°C) and air fry for 8 minutes, turning crusts halfway through cooking. Flatbread will be golden when done. 5. Let cool 5 minutes before slicing and serving.

Per Serving:
calories: 387 | fat: 28g | protein: 28g | carbs: 10g | fiber: 5g | sodium: 556mg

Tangy Asparagus and Broccoli

Prep time: 25 minutes | Cook time: 22 minutes |
Serves 4

½ pound (227 g) asparagus, cut
into 1½-inch pieces
½ pound (227 g) broccoli, cut
into 1½-inch pieces
2 tablespoons olive oil

Salt and white pepper, to taste
½ cup vegetable broth
2 tablespoons apple cider
vinegar

1. Place the vegetables in a single layer in the lightly greased air fryer basket. Drizzle the olive oil over the vegetables. 2. Sprinkle with salt and white pepper. 3. Cook at 380°F (193°C) for 15 minutes, shaking the basket halfway through the cooking time. 4. Add ½ cup of vegetable broth to a saucepan; bring to a rapid boil and add the vinegar. Cook for 5 to 7 minutes or until the sauce has reduced by half. 5. Spoon the sauce over the warm vegetables and serve immediately. Bon appétit!

Per Serving:
calories: 93 | fat: 7g | protein: 3g | carbs: 6g | fiber: 3g | sodium: 89mg

Stuffed Pepper Stew

Prep time: 20 minutes | Cook time: 50 minutes |
Serves 2

2 tablespoons olive oil
2 sweet peppers, diced (about 2 cups)
½ large onion, minced
1 garlic clove, minced
1 teaspoon oregano
1 tablespoon gluten-free

vegetarian Worcestershire sauce
1 cup low-sodium vegetable stock
1 cup low-sodium tomato juice
¼ cup brown lentils
¼ cup brown rice
Salt

1. Heat olive oil in a Dutch oven over medium-high heat. Add the sweet peppers and onion and sauté for 10 minutes, or until the peppers are wilted and the onion starts to turn golden. 2. Add the garlic, oregano, and Worcestershire sauce, and cook for another 30 seconds. Add the vegetable stock, tomato juice, lentils, and rice. 3. Bring the mixture to a boil. Cover, and reduce the heat to medium-low. Simmer for 45 minutes, or until the rice is cooked and the lentils are softened. Season with salt.

Per Serving:

calories: 379 | fat: 16g | protein: 11g | carbs: 53g | fiber: 7g | sodium: 392mg

Linguine and Brussels Sprouts

Prep time: 10 minutes | Cook time: 25 minutes |
Serves 4

8 ounces (227 g) whole-wheat linguine
⅓ cup, plus 2 tablespoons extra-virgin olive oil, divided
1 medium sweet onion, diced
2 to 3 garlic cloves, smashed
8 ounces (227 g) Brussels

sprouts, chopped
½ cup chicken stock, as needed
⅓ cup dry white wine
½ cup shredded Parmesan cheese
1 lemon, cut in quarters

1. Bring a large pot of water to a boil and cook the pasta according to package directions. Drain, reserving 1 cup of the pasta water. Mix the cooked pasta with 2 tablespoons of olive oil, then set aside. 2. In a large sauté pan or skillet, heat the remaining ⅓ cup of olive oil on medium heat. Add the onion to the pan and cook for about 5 minutes, until softened. Add the smashed garlic cloves and cook for 1 minute, until fragrant. 3. Add the Brussels sprouts and cook covered for 15 minutes. Add chicken stock as needed to prevent burning. Once Brussels sprouts have wilted and are fork-tender, add white wine and cook down for about 7 minutes, until reduced. 4. Add the pasta to the skillet and add the pasta water as needed. 5. Serve with the Parmesan cheese and lemon for squeezing over the dish right before eating.

Per Serving:

calories: 502 | fat: 31g | protein: 15g | carbs: 50g | fiber: 9g | sodium: 246mg

Balsamic Marinated Tofu with Basil and Oregano

Prep time: 10 minutes | Cook time: 30 minutes |
Serves 4

¼ cup extra-virgin olive oil
¼ cup balsamic vinegar
2 tablespoons low-sodium soy sauce or gluten-free tamari
3 garlic cloves, grated
2 teaspoons pure maple syrup
Zest of 1 lemon
1 teaspoon dried basil
1 teaspoon dried oregano
½ teaspoon dried thyme

½ teaspoon dried sage
¼ teaspoon kosher salt
¼ teaspoon freshly ground black pepper
¼ teaspoon red pepper flakes (optional)
1 (16-ounce / 454-g) block extra firm tofu, drained and patted dry, cut into ½-inch or 1-inch cubes

1. In a bowl or gallon zip-top bag, mix together the olive oil, vinegar, soy sauce, garlic, maple syrup, lemon zest, basil, oregano, thyme, sage, salt, black pepper, and red pepper flakes, if desired. Add the tofu and mix gently. Put in the refrigerator and marinate for 30 minutes, or up to overnight if you desire. 2. Preheat the oven to 425ºF (220ºC). Line a baking sheet with parchment paper or foil. Arrange the marinated tofu in a single layer on the prepared baking sheet. Bake for 20 to 30 minutes, turning over halfway through, until slightly crispy on the outside and tender on the inside.

Per Serving:

calories: 225 | fat: 16g | protein: 13g | carbs: 9g | fiber: 2g | sodium: 265mg

Freekeh, Chickpea, and Herb Salad

Prep time: 15 minutes | Cook time: 10 minutes |
Serves 4 to 6

1 (15-ounce / 425-g) can chickpeas, rinsed and drained
1 cup cooked freekeh
1 cup thinly sliced celery
1 bunch scallions, both white and green parts, finely chopped
½ cup chopped fresh flat-leaf parsley
¼ cup chopped fresh mint

3 tablespoons chopped celery leaves
½ teaspoon kosher salt
⅓ cup extra-virgin olive oil
¼ cup freshly squeezed lemon juice
¼ teaspoon cumin seeds
1 teaspoon garlic powder

1. In a large bowl, combine the chickpeas, freekeh, celery, scallions, parsley, mint, celery leaves, and salt and toss lightly. 2. In a small bowl, whisk together the olive oil, lemon juice, cumin seeds, and garlic powder. Once combined, add to freekeh salad.

Per Serving:

calories: 350 | fat: 19g | protein: 9g | carbs: 38g | fiber: 9g | sodium: 329mg

Crispy Eggplant Rounds

Prep time: 15 minutes | Cook time: 10 minutes |
Serves 4

1 large eggplant, ends trimmed, cut into ½-inch slices	cheese crisps, finely ground
½ teaspoon salt	½ teaspoon paprika
2 ounces (57 g) Parmesan 100%	¼ teaspoon garlic powder
	1 large egg

1. Sprinkle eggplant rounds with salt. Place rounds on a kitchen towel for 30 minutes to draw out excess water. Pat rounds dry. 2. In a medium bowl, mix cheese crisps, paprika, and garlic powder. In a separate medium bowl, whisk egg. Dip each eggplant round in egg, then gently press into cheese crisps to coat both sides. 3. Place eggplant rounds into ungreased air fryer basket. Adjust the temperature to 400ºF (204ºC) and air fry for 10 minutes, turning rounds halfway through cooking. Eggplant will be golden and crispy when done. Serve warm.

Per Serving:
calories: 113 | fat: 5g | protein: 7g | carbs: 10g | fiber: 4g | sodium: 567mg

Baked Mediterranean Tempeh with Tomatoes and Garlic

Prep time: 25 minutes | Cook time: 35 minutes |
Serves 4

For the Tempeh:

12 ounces (340 g) tempeh	Zest of 1 lemon
¼ cup white wine	¼ teaspoon kosher salt
2 tablespoons extra-virgin olive oil	¼ teaspoon freshly ground black pepper
2 tablespoons lemon juice	

For the Tomatoes and Garlic Sauce:

1 tablespoon extra-virgin olive oil	1 dried bay leaf
1 onion, diced	1 teaspoon white wine vinegar
3 garlic cloves, minced	1 teaspoon lemon juice
1 (14½-ounce / 411-g) can no-salt-added crushed tomatoes	1 teaspoon dried oregano
1 beefsteak tomato, diced	1 teaspoon dried thyme
	¾ teaspoon kosher salt
	¼ cup basil, cut into ribbons

Make the Tempeh: 1. Place the tempeh in a medium saucepan. Add enough water to cover it by 1 to 2 inches. Bring to a boil over medium-high heat, cover, and lower heat to a simmer. Cook for 10 to 15 minutes. Remove the tempeh, pat dry, cool, and cut into 1-inch cubes. 2. In a large bowl, combine the white wine, olive oil, lemon juice, lemon zest, salt, and black pepper. Add the tempeh, cover the bowl, and put in the refrigerator for 4 hours, or up to overnight. 3. Preheat the oven to 375ºF (190ºC). Place the marinated tempeh and the marinade in a baking dish and cook for 15 minutes. Make the Tomatoes and Garlic Sauce: 4. Heat the olive oil in a large skillet over medium heat. Add the onion and sauté until transparent, 3 to 5 minutes. Add the garlic and sauté for 30 seconds. Add the crushed tomatoes, beefsteak tomato, bay leaf, vinegar, lemon juice, oregano, thyme, and salt. Mix well. Simmer for 15 minutes. 5. Add the baked tempeh to the tomato mixture and gently mix together. Garnish with the basil.

Per Serving:
calories: 330 | fat: 20g | protein: 18g | carbs: 22g | fiber: 4g | sodium: 305mg

Broccoli Crust Pizza

Prep time: 15 minutes | Cook time: 12 minutes |
Serves 4

3 cups riced broccoli, steamed and drained well	3 tablespoons low-carb Alfredo sauce
1 large egg	½ cup shredded Mozzarella cheese
½ cup grated vegetarian Parmesan cheese	

1. In a large bowl, mix broccoli, egg, and Parmesan. 2. Cut a piece of parchment to fit your air fryer basket. Press out the pizza mixture to fit on the parchment, working in two batches if necessary. Place into the air fryer basket. 3. Adjust the temperature to 370ºF (188ºC) and air fry for 5 minutes. 4. The crust should be firm enough to flip. If not, add 2 additional minutes. Flip crust. 5. Top with Alfredo sauce and Mozzarella. Return to the air fryer basket and cook an additional 7 minutes or until cheese is golden and bubbling. Serve warm.

Per Serving:
calories: 87 | fat: 2g | protein: 11g | carbs: 5g | fiber: 1g | sodium: 253mg

Pesto Vegetable Skewers

Prep time: 30 minutes | Cook time: 8 minutes |
Makes 8 skewers

1 medium zucchini, trimmed and cut into ½-inch slices	squares
½ medium yellow onion, peeled and cut into 1-inch squares	16 whole cremini mushrooms
1 medium red bell pepper, seeded and cut into 1-inch	⅓ cup basil pesto
	½ teaspoon salt
	¼ teaspoon ground black pepper

1. Divide zucchini slices, onion, and bell pepper into eight even portions. Place on 6-inch skewers for a total of eight kebabs. Add 2 mushrooms to each skewer and brush kebabs generously with pesto. 2. Sprinkle each kebab with salt and black pepper on all sides, then place into ungreased air fryer basket. Adjust the temperature to 375ºF (191ºC) and air fry for 8 minutes, turning kebabs halfway through cooking. Vegetables will be browned at the edges and tender-crisp when done. Serve warm.

Per Serving:
calories: 75 | fat: 6g | protein: 3g | carbs: 4g | fiber: 1g | sodium: 243mg

Cauliflower Rice-Stuffed Peppers

Prep time: 10 minutes | Cook time: 15 minutes |

Serves 4

2 cups uncooked cauliflower rice	cheese
¾ cup drained canned petite diced tomatoes	¼ teaspoon salt
2 tablespoons olive oil	¼ teaspoon ground black pepper
1 cup shredded Mozzarella	4 medium green bell peppers, tops removed, seeded

1. In a large bowl, mix all ingredients except bell peppers. Scoop mixture evenly into peppers. 2. Place peppers into ungreased air fryer basket. Adjust the temperature to 350ºF (177ºC) and air fry for 15 minutes. Peppers will be tender and cheese will be melted when done. Serve warm.

Per Serving:

calories: 144 | fat: 7g | protein: 11g | carbs: 11g | fiber: 5g | sodium: 380mg

Stuffed Portobellos

Prep time: 10 minutes | Cook time: 8 minutes |

Serves 4

3 ounces (85 g) cream cheese, softened	leaves
½ medium zucchini, trimmed and chopped	4 large portobello mushrooms, stems removed
¼ cup seeded and chopped red bell pepper	2 tablespoons coconut oil, melted
1½ cups chopped fresh spinach	½ teaspoon salt

1. In a medium bowl, mix cream cheese, zucchini, pepper, and spinach. 2. Drizzle mushrooms with coconut oil and sprinkle with salt. Scoop ¼ zucchini mixture into each mushroom. 3. Place mushrooms into ungreased air fryer basket. Adjust the temperature to 400ºF (204ºC) and air fry for 8 minutes. Portobellos will be tender and tops will be browned when done. Serve warm.

Per Serving:

calories: 151 | fat: 13g | protein: 4g | carbs: 6g | fiber: 2g | sodium: 427mg

Roasted Ratatouille Pasta

Prep time: 10 minutes | Cook time: 20 minutes |

Serves 2

1 small eggplant (about 8 ounces / 227 g)	seeded
1 small zucchini	½ teaspoon salt, plus additional for the pasta water
1 portobello mushroom	1 teaspoon Italian herb seasoning
1 Roma tomato, halved	
½ medium sweet red pepper,	1 tablespoon olive oil

2 cups farfalle pasta (about 8 ounces / 227 g)	tomatoes in olive oil with herbs
2 tablespoons minced sun-dried	2 tablespoons prepared pesto

1. Slice the ends off the eggplant and zucchini. Cut them lengthwise into ½-inch slices. 2. Place the eggplant, zucchini, mushroom, tomato, and red pepper in a large bowl and sprinkle with ½ teaspoon of salt. Using your hands, toss the vegetables well so that they're covered evenly with the salt. Let them rest for about 10 minutes. 3. While the vegetables are resting, preheat the oven to 400°F (205ºC) and set the rack to the bottom position. Line a baking sheet with parchment paper. 4. When the oven is hot, drain off any liquid from the vegetables and pat them dry with a paper towel. Add the Italian herb seasoning and olive oil to the vegetables and toss well to coat both sides. 5. Lay the vegetables out in a single layer on the baking sheet. Roast them for 15 to 20 minutes, flipping them over after about 10 minutes or once they start to brown on the underside. When the vegetables are charred in spots, remove them from the oven. 6. While the vegetables are roasting, fill a large saucepan with water. Add salt and cook the pasta according to package directions. Drain the pasta, reserving ½ cup of the pasta water. 7. When cool enough to handle, cut the vegetables into large chunks (about 2 inches) and add them to the hot pasta. 8. Stir in the sun-dried tomatoes and pesto and toss everything well.

Per Serving:

calories: 612 | fat: 16g | protein: 23g | carbs: 110g | fiber: 23g | sodium: 776mg

Fava Bean Purée with Chicory

Prep time: 5 minutes | Cook time: 2 hours 10

minutes | Serves 4

½ pound (227 g) dried fava beans, soaked in water overnight and drained	¼ cup olive oil
	1 small onion, chopped
1 pound (454 g) chicory leaves	1 clove garlic, minced
	Salt

1. In a saucepan, cover the fava beans by at least an inch of water and bring to a boil over medium-high heat. Reduce the heat to low, cover, and simmer until very tender, about 2 hours. Check the pot from time to time to make sure there is enough water and add more as needed. 2. Drain off any excess water and then mash the beans with a potato masher. 3. While the beans are cooking, bring a large pot of salted water to a boil. Add the chicory and cook for about 3 minutes, until tender. Drain. 4. In a medium skillet, heat the olive oil over medium-high heat. Add the onion and a pinch of salt and cook, stirring frequently, until softened and beginning to brown, about 5 minutes. Add the garlic and cook, stirring, for another minute. Transfer half of the onion mixture, along with the oil, to the bowl with the mashed beans and stir to mix. Taste and add salt as needed. 5. Serve the purée topped with some of the remaining onions and oil, with the chicory leaves on the side.

Per Serving:

calories: 336 | fat: 14g | protein: 17g | carbs: 40g | fiber: 19g | sodium: 59mg

One-Pan Mushroom Pasta with Mascarpone

Prep time: 10 minutes | Cook time: 20 minutes | Serves 2

2 tablespoons olive oil	stock
1 large shallot, minced	6 ounces (170 g) dry
8 ounces (227 g) baby bella	pappardelle pasta
(cremini) mushrooms, sliced	2 tablespoons mascarpone
¼ cup dry sherry	cheese
1 teaspoon dried thyme	Salt
2 cups low-sodium vegetable	Freshly ground black pepper

1. Heat olive oil in a large sauté pan over medium-high heat. Add the shallot and mushrooms and sauté for 10 minutes, or until the mushrooms have given up much of their liquid. 2. Add the sherry, thyme, and vegetable stock. Bring the mixture to a boil. 3. Add the pasta, breaking it up as needed so it fits into the pan and is covered by the liquid. Return the mixture to a boil. Cover, and reduce the heat to medium-low. Let the pasta cook for 10 minutes, or until al dente. Stir it occasionally so it doesn't stick. If the sauce gets too dry, add some water or additional chicken stock. 4. When the pasta is tender, stir in the mascarpone cheese and season with salt and pepper. 5. The sauce will thicken up a bit when it's off the heat.

Per Serving:

calories: 517 | fat: 18g | protein: 16g | carbs: 69g | fiber: 3g | sodium: 141mg

Mushroom Ragù with Parmesan Polenta

Prep time: 20 minutes | Cook time: 30 minutes | Serves 2

½ ounce (14 g) dried porcini mushrooms (optional but recommended)	1 cup mushroom stock (or reserved liquid from soaking the porcini mushrooms, if using)
2 tablespoons olive oil	½ teaspoon dried thyme
1 pound (454 g) baby bella (cremini) mushrooms, quartered	1 fresh rosemary sprig
1 large shallot, minced (about ⅓ cup)	1½ cups water
1 garlic clove, minced	½ teaspoon salt
1 tablespoon flour	⅓ cup instant polenta
2 teaspoons tomato paste	2 tablespoons grated Parmesan cheese
½ cup red wine	

1. If using the dried porcini mushrooms, soak them in 1 cup of hot water for about 15 minutes to soften them. When they're softened, scoop them out of the water, reserving the soaking liquid. (I strain it through a coffee filter to remove any possible grit.) Mince the porcini mushrooms. 2. Heat the olive oil in a large sauté pan over medium-high heat. Add the mushrooms, shallot, and garlic, and sauté for 10 minutes, or until the vegetables are wilted and starting to caramelize. 3. Add the flour and tomato paste, and cook for

another 30 seconds. Add the red wine, mushroom stock or porcini soaking liquid, thyme, and rosemary. Bring the mixture to a boil, stirring constantly until it thickens. Reduce the heat and let it simmer for 10 minutes. 4. While the mushrooms are simmering, bring the water to a boil in a saucepan and add salt. 5. Add the instant polenta and stir quickly while it thickens. Stir in the Parmesan cheese. Taste and add additional salt if needed.

Per Serving:

calories: 451 | fat: 16g | protein: 14g | carbs: 58g | fiber: 5g | sodium: 165mg

Pistachio Mint Pesto Pasta

Prep time: 10 minutes | Cook time: 10 minutes | Serves 4

8 ounces (227 g) whole-wheat pasta	shelled
	1 garlic clove, peeled
1 cup fresh mint	½ teaspoon kosher salt
½ cup fresh basil	Juice of ½ lime
⅓ cup unsalted pistachios,	⅓ cup extra-virgin olive oil

1. Cook the pasta according to the package directions. Drain, reserving ½ cup of the pasta water, and set aside. 2. In a food processor, add the mint, basil, pistachios, garlic, salt, and lime juice. Process until the pistachios are coarsely ground. Add the olive oil in a slow, steady stream and process until incorporated. 3. In a large bowl, mix the pasta with the pistachio pesto; toss well to incorporate. If a thinner, more saucy consistency is desired, add some of the reserved pasta water and toss well.

Per Serving:

calories: 420 | fat: 3g | protein: 11g | carbs: 48g | fiber: 2g | sodium: 150mg

Mediterranean Pan Pizza

Prep time: 5 minutes | Cook time: 8 minutes | Serves 2

1 cup shredded Mozzarella cheese	leaves
	2 tablespoons chopped black
¼ medium red bell pepper, seeded and chopped	olives
	2 tablespoons crumbled feta
½ cup chopped fresh spinach	cheese

1. Sprinkle Mozzarella into an ungreased round nonstick baking dish in an even layer. Add remaining ingredients on top. 2. Place dish into air fryer basket. Adjust the temperature to 350ºF (177ºC) and bake for 8 minutes, checking halfway through to avoid burning. Top of pizza will be golden brown and the cheese melted when done. 3. Remove dish from fryer and let cool 5 minutes before slicing and serving.

Per Serving:

calories: 108 | fat: 1g | protein: 20g | carbs: 5g | fiber: 3g | sodium: 521mg

Rustic Vegetable and Brown Rice Bowl

Prep time: 15 minutes | Cook time: 20 minutes |

Serves 4

Nonstick cooking spray	2 to 3 tablespoons sesame
2 cups broccoli florets	seeds, for garnish
2 cups cauliflower florets	2 cups cooked brown rice
1 (15-ounce / 425-g) can	For the Dressing:
chickpeas, drained and rinsed	3 to 4 tablespoons tahini
1 cup carrots sliced 1 inch thick	2 tablespoons honey
2 to 3 tablespoons extra-virgin	1 lemon, juiced
olive oil, divided	1 garlic clove, minced
Salt	Salt
Freshly ground black pepper	Freshly ground black pepper

1. Preheat the oven to 400ºF (205ºC). Spray two baking sheets with cooking spray. 2. Cover the first baking sheet with the broccoli and cauliflower and the second with the chickpeas and carrots. Toss each sheet with half of the oil and season with salt and pepper before placing in oven. 3. Cook the carrots and chickpeas for 10 minutes, leaving the carrots still just crisp, and the broccoli and cauliflower for 20 minutes, until tender. Stir each halfway through cooking. 4. To make the dressing, in a small bowl, mix the tahini, honey, lemon juice, and garlic. Season with salt and pepper and set aside. 5. Divide the rice into individual bowls, then layer with vegetables and drizzle dressing over the dish.

Per Serving:

calories: 454 | fat: 18g | protein: 12g | carbs: 62g | fiber: 11g | sodium: 61mg

Beet and Carrot Fritters with Yogurt Sauce

Prep time: 15 minutes | Cook time: 15 minutes |

Serves 2

For the Yogurt Sauce:

⅓ cup plain Greek yogurt	Zest of ½ lemon
1 tablespoon freshly squeezed	¼ teaspoon garlic powder
lemon juice	¼ teaspoon salt

For the Fritters:

1 large carrot, peeled	unseasoned bread crumbs
1 small potato, peeled	¼ teaspoon garlic powder
1 medium golden or red beet,	¼ teaspoon salt
peeled	1 large egg, beaten
1 scallion, minced	¼ cup feta cheese, crumbled
2 tablespoons fresh minced	2 tablespoons olive oil (more if
parsley	needed)
¼ cup brown rice flour or	

Make the Yogurt Sauce: In a small bowl, mix together the yogurt,

lemon juice and zest, garlic powder, and salt. Set aside. Make the Fritters: 1. Shred the carrot, potato, and beet in a food processor with the shredding blade. You can also use a mandoline with a julienne shredding blade or a vegetable peeler. Squeeze out any moisture from the vegetables and place them in a large bowl. 2. Add the scallion, parsley, rice flour, garlic powder, salt, and egg. Stir the mixture well to combine. Add the feta cheese and stir briefly, leaving chunks of feta cheese throughout. 3. Heat a large nonstick sauté pan over medium-high heat and add 1 tablespoon of the olive oil. 4. Make the fritters by scooping about 3 tablespoons of the vegetable mixture into your hands and flattening it into a firm disc about 3 inches in diameter. 5. Place 2 fritters at a time in the pan and let them cook for about two minutes. Check to see if the underside is golden, and then flip and repeat on the other side. Remove from the heat, add the rest of the olive oil to the pan, and repeat with the remaining vegetable mixture. 6. To serve, spoon about 1 tablespoon of the yogurt sauce on top of each fritter.

Per Serving:

calories: 295 | fat: 14g | protein: 6g | carbs: 44g | fiber: 5g | sodium: 482mg

Crustless Spanakopita

Prep time: 15 minutes | Cook time: 45 minutes |

Serves 6

12 tablespoons extra-virgin	½ teaspoon salt
olive oil, divided	½ teaspoon freshly ground
1 small yellow onion, diced	black pepper
1 (32-ounce / 907-g) bag frozen	1 cup whole-milk ricotta cheese
chopped spinach, thawed, fully	4 large eggs
drained, and patted dry (about 4	¾ cup crumbled traditional feta
cups)	cheese
4 garlic cloves, minced	¼ cup pine nuts

1. Preheat the oven to 375ºF (190ºC). 2. In a large skillet, heat 4 tablespoons olive oil over medium-high heat. Add the onion and sauté until softened, 6 to 8 minutes. 3. Add the spinach, garlic, salt, and pepper and sauté another 5 minutes. Remove from the heat and allow to cool slightly. 4. In a medium bowl, whisk together the ricotta and eggs. Add to the cooled spinach and stir to combine. 5. Pour 4 tablespoons olive oil in the bottom of a 9-by-13-inch glass baking dish and swirl to coat the bottom and sides. Add the spinach-ricotta mixture and spread into an even layer. 6. Bake for 20 minutes or until the mixture begins to set. Remove from the oven and crumble the feta evenly across the top of the spinach. Add the pine nuts and drizzle with the remaining 4 tablespoons olive oil. Return to the oven and bake for an additional 15 to 20 minutes, or until the spinach is fully set and the top is starting to turn golden brown. Allow to cool slightly before cutting to serve.

Per Serving:

calories: 497 | fat: 44g | protein: 18g | carbs: 11g | fiber: 5g | sodium: 561mg

Chapter 10 Desserts

Blueberry Panna Cotta

Prep time: 5 minutes | Cook time: 0 minutes | Serves 6

1 tablespoon gelatin powder
2 tablespoons water
2 cups goat's cream, coconut cream, or heavy whipping cream
2 cups wild blueberries, fresh or frozen, divided
½ teaspoon vanilla powder or 1½ teaspoons unsweetened vanilla extract
Optional: low-carb sweetener, to taste

1. In a bowl, sprinkle the gelatin powder over the cold water. Set aside to let it bloom. 2. Place the goat's cream, half of the blueberries, and the vanilla in a blender and process until smooth and creamy. Alternatively, use an immersion blender. 3. Pour the blueberry cream into a saucepan. Gently heat; do not boil. Scrape the gelatin into the hot cream mixture together with the sweetener, if using. Mix well until all the gelatin has dissolved. 4. Divide among 6 (4-ounce / 113-g) jars or serving glasses and fill them about two-thirds full, leaving enough space for the remaining blueberries. Place in the fridge for 3 to 4 hours, or until set. 5. When the panna cotta has set, evenly distribute the remaining blueberries among the jars. Serve immediately or store in the fridge for up to 4 days.

Per Serving:
calories: 172 | fat: 15g | protein: 2g | carbs: 8g | fiber: 2g | sodium: 19mg

Creamy Spiced Almond Milk

Prep time: 5 minutes | Cook time: 1 minute | Serves 6

1 cup raw almonds
5 cups filtered water, divided
1 teaspoon vanilla bean paste
½ teaspoon pumpkin pie spice

1. Add almonds and 1 cup water to the Instant Pot®. Close lid, set steam release to Sealing, press the Manual button, and set time to 1 minute. 2. When the timer beeps, quick-release the pressure until the float valve drops. Press the Cancel button and open lid. Strain almonds and rinse under cool water. Transfer to a high-powered blender with remaining 3.cups water. Purée for 2 minutes on high speed. 4. Pour mixture into a nut milk bag set over a large bowl. Squeeze bag to extract all liquid. Stir in vanilla and pumpkin pie spice. Transfer to a Mason jar or sealed jug and refrigerate for 8 hours. Stir or shake gently before serving.

Per Serving:
calories: 86 | fat: 8g | protein: 3g | carbs: 3g | fiber: 2g | sodium: 0mg

Date and Honey Almond Milk Ice Cream

Prep time: 10 minutes | Cook time: 5 minutes | Serves 4

¾ cup (about 4 ounces/ 113 g) pitted dates
¼ cup honey
½ cup water
2 cups cold unsweetened almond milk
2 teaspoons vanilla extract

1. Combine the dates and water in a small saucepan and bring to a boil over high heat. Remove the pan from the heat, cover, and let stand for 15 minutes. 2. In a blender, combine the almond milk, dates, the date soaking water, honey, and the vanilla and process until very smooth. 3. Cover the blender jar and refrigerate the mixture until cold, at least 1 hour. 4. Transfer the mixture to an electric ice cream maker and freeze according to the manufacturer's instructions. 5. Serve immediately or transfer to a freezer-safe storage container and freeze for 4 hours (or longer). Serve frozen.

Per Serving:
calories: 106 | fat: 2g | protein: 1g | carbs: 23g | fiber: 3g | sodium: 92mg

Ricotta with Balsamic Cherries and Black Pepper

Prep time: 10 minutes | Cook time: 0 minutes | Serves 4

1 cup (8 ounces/ 227 g) ricotta
2 tablespoons honey
1 teaspoon vanilla extract
3 cups pitted sweet cherries (thawed if frozen), halved
1½ teaspoons aged balsamic vinegar
Pinch of freshly ground black pepper

1. In a food processor, combine the ricotta, honey, and vanilla and process until smooth. Transfer the mixture to a medium bowl, cover, and refrigerate for 1 hour. 2. In a small bowl, combine the cherries, vinegar, and pepper and stir to mix well. Chill along with the ricotta mixture. 3. To serve, spoon the ricotta mixture into 4 serving bowls or glasses. Top with the cherries, dividing them equally and spooning a bit of the accumulated juice over the top of each bowl. Serve chilled.

Per Serving:
calories: 236 | fat: 5g | protein: 7g | carbs: 42g | fiber: 1g | sodium: 93mg

Strawberry-Pomegranate Molasses Sauce

Prep time: 10 minutes | Cook time: 5 minutes | Serves 6

3 tablespoons olive oil
¼ cup honey
2 pints strawberries, hulled and halved
1 to 2 tablespoons pomegranate molasses
2 tablespoons chopped fresh mint
Greek yogurt, for serving

1. In a medium saucepan, heat the olive oil over medium heat. Add the strawberries; cook until their juices are released. Stir in the honey and cook for 1 to 2 minutes. Stir in the molasses and mint. Serve warm over Greek yogurt.

Per Serving:
calories: 189 | fat: 7g | protein: 4g | carbs: 24g | fiber: 3g | sodium: 12mg

Flourless Chocolate Brownies with Raspberry Balsamic Sauce

Prep time: 10 minutes | Cook time: 20 minutes | Serves 2

For the raspberry sauce

¼ cup good-quality balsamic vinegar
1 cup frozen raspberries

For the brownie

½ cup black beans with no added salt, rinsed
1 large egg
1 tablespoon olive oil
½ teaspoon vanilla extract
4 tablespoons unsweetened cocoa powder
¼ cup sugar
¼ teaspoon baking powder
Pinch salt
¼ cup dark chocolate chips

Make the raspberry sauce Combine the balsamic vinegar and raspberries in a saucepan and bring the mixture to a boil. Reduce the heat to medium and let the sauce simmer for 15 minutes, or until reduced to ½ cup. If desired, strain the seeds and set the sauce aside until the brownie is ready. Make the brownie 1. Preheat the oven to 350°F (180°C) and set the rack to the middle position. Grease two 8-ounce ramekins and place them on a baking sheet. 2. In a food processor, combine the black beans, egg, olive oil, and vanilla. Purée the mixture for 1 to 2 minutes, or until it's smooth and the beans are completely broken down. Scrape down the sides of the bowl a few times to make sure everything is well-incorporated. 3. Add the cocoa powder, sugar, baking powder, and salt and purée again to combine the dry ingredients, scraping down the sides of the bowl as needed. 4. Stir the chocolate chips into the batter by hand. Reserve a few if you like, to sprinkle over the top of the brownies when they come out of the oven. 5. Pour the brownies into the prepared ramekins and bake for 15 minutes, or until firm. The center will look slightly undercooked. If you prefer a firmer brownie, leave it in the oven for another 5 minutes, or until a toothpick inserted in the middle comes out clean. 6. Remove the brownies from the oven. If desired, sprinkle any remaining chocolate chips over the top and let them melt into the warm brownies. 7. Let the brownies cool for a few minutes and top with warm raspberry sauce to serve.

Per Serving:
calories: 510 | fat: 16g | protein: 10g | carbs: 88g | fiber: 14g | sodium: 124mg

Nut Butter Cup Fat Bomb

Prep time: 5 minutes | Cook time: 0 minutes | Serves 8

½ cup crunchy almond butter (no sugar added)
½ cup light fruity extra-virgin olive oil
¼ cup ground flaxseed
2 tablespoons unsweetened cocoa powder
1 teaspoon vanilla extract
1 teaspoon ground cinnamon (optional)
1 to 2 teaspoons sugar-free sweetener of choice (optional)

1. In a mixing bowl, combine the almond butter, olive oil, flaxseed, cocoa powder, vanilla, cinnamon (if using), and sweetener (if using) and stir well with a spatula to combine. Mixture will be a thick liquid. 2. Pour into 8 mini muffin liners and freeze until solid, at least 12 hours. Store in the freezer to maintain their shape.

Per Serving:
calories: 239 | fat: 24g | protein: 4g | carbs: 5g | fiber: 3g | sodium: 3mg

Red Wine–Poached Figs with Ricotta and Almond

Prep time: 5 minutes | Cook time: 1 minute | Serves 4

2 cups water
2 cups red wine
¼ cup honey
1 cinnamon stick
1 star anise
1 teaspoon vanilla bean paste
12 dried mission figs
1 cup ricotta cheese
1 tablespoon confectioners' sugar
¼ teaspoon almond extract
1 cup toasted sliced almonds

1. Add water, wine, honey, cinnamon, star anise, and vanilla to the Instant Pot® and whisk well. Add figs, close lid, set steam release to Sealing, press the Manual button, and set time to 1 minute. 2. When the timer beeps, quick-release the pressure until the float valve drops. Press the Cancel button and open lid. With a slotted spoon, transfer figs to a plate and set aside to cool for 5 minutes. 3. In a small bowl, mix together ricotta, sugar, and almond extract. Serve figs with a dollop of sweetened ricotta and a sprinkling of almonds.

Per Serving:
calories: 597 | fat: 21g | protein: 13g | carbs: 56g | fiber: 9g | sodium: 255mg

Slow-Cooked Fruit Medley

Prep time: 10 minutes | Cook time: 3 to 5 hours |
Serves 4 to 6

Nonstick cooking spray
1 pound (454 g) fresh or frozen fruit of your choice, stemmed and chopped as needed
⅓ cup almond milk or low-sugar fruit juice of your choice
½ cup honey

1. Generously coat a slow cooker with cooking spray, or line the bottom and sides with parchment paper or aluminum foil. 2. In a slow cooker, combine the fruit and milk. Gently stir to mix. 3. Drizzle the fruit with the honey. 4. Cover the cooker and cook for 3 to 5 hours on Low heat.

Per Serving:
calories: 192 | fat: 0g | protein: 1g | carbs: 50g | fiber: 3g | sodium: 27mg

Apple and Brown Rice Pudding

Prep time: 10 minutes | Cook time: 20 minutes |
Serves 6

2 cups almond milk
1 cup long-grain brown rice
½ cup golden raisins
1 Granny Smith apple, peeled,
cored, and chopped
¼ cup honey
1 teaspoon vanilla extract
½ teaspoon ground cinnamon

1. Place all ingredients in the Instant Pot®. Stir to combine. Close lid, set steam release to Sealing, press the Manual button, and set time to 20 minutes. 2. When the timer beeps, let pressure release naturally for 15 minutes, then quick-release the remaining pressure. Press the Cancel button and open lid. Serve warm or at room temperature.

Per Serving:
calories: 218 | fat: 2g | protein: 3g | carbs: 51g | fiber: 4g | sodium: 54mg

Individual Apple Pockets

Prep time: 5 minutes | Cook time: 15 minutes |
Serves 6

1 organic puff pastry, rolled out, at room temperature
1 Gala apple, peeled and sliced
¼ cup brown sugar
⅛ teaspoon ground cinnamon
⅛ teaspoon ground cardamom
Nonstick cooking spray
Honey, for topping

1. Preheat the oven to 350°F(180°C). 2. Cut the pastry dough into 4 even discs. Peel and slice the apple. In a small bowl, toss the slices with brown sugar, cinnamon, and cardamom. 3. Spray a muffin tin very well with nonstick cooking spray. Be sure to spray only the muffin holders you plan to use. 4. Once sprayed, line the bottom of the muffin tin with the dough and place 1 or 2 broken apple slices on top. Fold the remaining dough over the apple and drizzle with honey. 5. Bake for 15 minutes or until brown and bubbly.

Per Serving:
calories: 250 | fat: 15g | protein: 3g | carbs: 30g | fiber: 1g | sodium: 98mg

Almond Cookies

Prep time: 5 minutes | Cook time: 10 minutes |
Serves 4 to 6

½ cup sugar
8 tablespoons (1 stick) room temperature salted butter
1 large egg
1½ cups all-purpose flour
1 cup ground almonds or almond flour

1. Preheat the oven to 375°F(190°C). 2. Using a mixer, cream together the sugar and butter. 3. Add the egg and mix until combined. 4. Alternately add the flour and ground almonds, ½ cup at a time, while the mixer is on slow. 5. Once everything is combined, line a baking sheet with parchment paper. Drop a tablespoon of dough on the baking sheet, keeping the cookies at least 2 inches apart. 6. Put the baking sheet in the oven and bake just until the cookies start to turn brown around the edges, about 5 to 7 minutes.

Per Serving:
calories: 604 | fat: 36g | protein: 11g | carbs: 63g | fiber: 4g | sodium: 181mg

Halva Protein Slices

Prep time: 5 minutes | Cook time: 0 minutes | Serves
16

¾ cup tahini
⅓ cup coconut butter
¼ cup virgin coconut oil
1 cup collagen powder
½ teaspoon vanilla powder or 1½ teaspoons unsweetened
vanilla extract
½ teaspoon cinnamon
⅛ teaspoon salt
Optional: low-carb sweetener, to taste

1. To soften the tahini and the coconut butter, place them in a small saucepan over low heat with the coconut oil. Remove from the heat and set aside to cool for a few minutes. 2. Add the remaining ingredients and optional sweetener. Stir to combine, then pour the mixture into an 8 × 8-inch (20 × 20 cm) parchment-lined pan or a silicone pan, or any pan or container lined with parchment paper. Place in the fridge for at least 1 hour or until fully set. 3. Cut into 16 pieces and serve. To store, keep refrigerated for up to 2 weeks or freeze to up to 3 months.

Per Serving:
calories: 131 | fat: 13g | protein: 2g | carbs: 3g | fiber: 1g | sodium: 33mg

Golden Coconut Cream Pops

Prep time: 5 minutes | Cook time: 0 minutes | Makes

8 cream pops

1½ cups coconut cream	tablespoon unsweetened vanilla
½ cup coconut milk	extract
4 egg yolks	¼ teaspoon ground black
2 teaspoons ground turmeric	pepper
1 teaspoon ground ginger	Optional: low-carb sweetener,
1 teaspoon cinnamon	to taste
1 teaspoon vanilla powder or 1	

1. Place all of the ingredients in a blender (including the optional sweetener) and process until well combined. Pour into eight ⅓-cup (80 ml) ice pop molds. Freeze until solid for 3 hours, or until set. 2. To easily remove the ice pops from the molds, fill a pot as tall as the ice pops with warm (not hot) water and dip the ice pop molds in for 15 to 20 seconds. Remove the ice pops from the molds and then freeze again. Store in the freezer in a resealable bag for up to 3 months.

Per Serving:

calories: 219 | fat: 21g | protein: 3g | carbs: 5g | fiber: 2g | sodium: 9mg

Greek Yogurt Ricotta Mousse

Prep time: 1 hour 5 minutes | Cook time: 0 minutes |

Serves 4

9 ounces (255 g) full-fat ricotta cheese	3 teaspoons fresh lemon juice
	½ teaspoon pure vanilla extract
4½ ounces (128 g) 2% Greek yogurt	2 tablespoons granulated sugar

1. Combine all of the ingredients in a food processor. Blend until smooth, about 1 minute. 2. Divide the mousse between 4 serving glasses. Cover and transfer to the refrigerator to chill for 1 hour before serving. Store covered in the refrigerator for up to 4 days.

Per Serving:

calories: 156 | fat: 8g | protein: 10g | carbs: 10g | fiber: 0g | sodium: 65mg

Strawberry Ricotta Parfaits

Prep time: 10 minutes | Cook time: 0 minutes |

Serves 4

2 cups ricotta cheese	Toppings such as sliced
¼ cup honey	almonds, fresh mint, and lemon
2 cups sliced strawberries	zest (optional)
1 teaspoon sugar	

1. In a medium bowl, whisk together the ricotta and honey until well blended. Place the bowl in the refrigerator for a few minutes to firm up the mixture. 2. In a medium bowl, toss together the strawberries and sugar. 3. In each of four small glasses, layer 1 tablespoon of the ricotta mixture, then top with a layer of the strawberries and finally another layer of the ricotta. 4. Finish with your preferred toppings, if desired, then serve.

Per Serving:

calories: 311 | fat: 16g | protein: 14g | carbs: 29g | fiber: 2g | sodium: 106mg

Grilled Peaches with Greek Yogurt

Prep time: 5 minutes | Cook time: 30 minutes |

Serves 4

4 ripe peaches, halved and pitted	plus extra for topping
	2 cups plain full-fat Greek
2 tablespoons olive oil	yogurt
1 teaspoon ground cinnamon,	¼ cup honey, for drizzling

1. Preheat the oven to 350°F (180ºC). 2. Place the peaches in a baking dish, cut-side up. 3. In a small bowl, stir together the olive oil and cinnamon, then brush the mixture over the peach halves. 4. Bake the peaches for about 30 minutes, until they are soft. 5. Top the peaches with the yogurt and drizzle them with the honey, then serve.

Per Serving:

calories: 259 | fat: 11g | protein: 6g | carbs: 38g | fiber: 3g | sodium: 57mg

Blueberry Pomegranate Granita

Prep time: 5 minutes | Cook time: 10 minutes |

Serves 2

1 cup frozen wild blueberries	¼ cup sugar
1 cup pomegranate or pomegranate blueberry juice	¼ cup water

1. Combine the frozen blueberries and pomegranate juice in a saucepan and bring to a boil. Reduce the heat and simmer for 5 minutes, or until the blueberries start to break down. 2. While the juice and berries are cooking, combine the sugar and water in a small microwave-safe bowl. Microwave for 60 seconds, or until it comes to a rolling boil. Stir to make sure all of the sugar is dissolved and set the syrup aside. 3. Combine the blueberry mixture and the sugar syrup in a blender and blend for 1 minute, or until the fruit is completely puréed. 4. Pour the mixture into an 8-by-8-inch baking pan or a similar-sized bowl. The liquid should come about ½ inch up the sides. Let the mixture cool for 30 minutes, and then put it into the freezer. 5. Every 30 minutes for the next 2 hours, scrape the granita with a fork to keep it from freezing solid. 6. Serve it after 2 hours, or store it in a covered container in the freezer.

Per Serving:

calories: 214 | fat: 0g | protein: 1g | carbs: 54g | fiber: 2g | sodium: 15mg

Banana Cream Pie Parfaits

Prep time: 10 minutes | Cook time: 0 minutes | Serves 2

1 cup nonfat vanilla pudding
2 low-sugar graham crackers, crushed
1 banana, peeled and sliced
¼ cup walnuts, chopped
Honey for drizzling

1. In small parfait dishes or glasses, layer the ingredients, starting with the pudding and ending with chopped walnuts. 2. You can repeat the layers, depending on the size of the glass and your preferences. 3. Drizzle with the honey. Serve chilled.

Per Serving:

calories: 312 | fat: 11g | protein: 7g | carbs: 50g | fiber: 3g | sodium: 273mg

Honey Ricotta with Espresso and Chocolate Chips

Prep time: 5 minutes | Cook time: 0 minutes | Serves 2

8 ounces (227 g) ricotta cheese
2 tablespoons honey
2 tablespoons espresso, chilled
or room temperature
1 teaspoon dark chocolate chips or chocolate shavings

1. In a medium bowl, whip together the ricotta cheese and honey until light and smooth, 4 to 5 minutes. 2. Spoon the ricotta cheese-honey mixture evenly into 2 dessert bowls. Drizzle 1 tablespoon espresso into each dish and sprinkle with chocolate chips or shavings.

Per Serving:

calories: 235 | fat: 10g | protein: 13g | carbs: 25g | fiber: 0g | sodium: 115mg

Vanilla-Poached Apricots

Prep time: 10 minutes | Cook time: 1 minute | Serves 6

1¼ cups water
¼ cup marsala wine
¼ cup sugar
1 teaspoon vanilla bean paste
8 medium apricots, sliced in half and pitted

1. Place all ingredients in the Instant Pot®. Stir to combine. Close lid, set steam release to Sealing, press the Manual button, and set time to 1 minute. 2. When the timer beeps, quick-release the pressure until the float valve drops. Press the Cancel button and open lid. Let stand for 10 minutes. Carefully remove apricots from poaching liquid with a slotted spoon. Serve warm or at room temperature.

Per Serving:

calories: 62 | fat: 0g | protein: 2g | carbs: 14g | fiber: 1g | sodium: 10mg

Dried Fruit Compote

Prep time: 15 minutes | Cook time: 8 minutes | Serves 6

8 ounces (227 g) dried apricots, quartered
8 ounces (227 g) dried peaches, quartered
1 cup golden raisins
1½ cups orange juice
1 cinnamon stick
4 whole cloves

1. Place all ingredients in the Instant Pot®. Stir to combine. Close lid, set steam release to Sealing, press the Manual button, and set time to 3 minutes. When the timer beeps, let pressure release naturally, about 20 minutes. Press the Cancel button and open lid. 2. Remove and discard cinnamon stick and cloves. Press the Sauté button and simmer for 5–6 minutes. Serve warm or allow to cool, and then cover and refrigerate for up to a week.

Per Serving:

calories: 258 | fat: 0g | protein: 4g | carbs: 63g | fiber: 5g | sodium: 7mg

Chocolate Turtle Hummus

Prep time: 15 minutes | Cook time: 0 minutes | Serves 2

For the Caramel:

2 tablespoons coconut oil
1 tablespoon maple syrup
1 tablespoon almond butter
Pinch salt

For the Hummus:

½ cup chickpeas, drained and rinsed
2 tablespoons unsweetened cocoa powder
1 tablespoon maple syrup, plus
more to taste
2 tablespoons almond milk, or more as needed, to thin
Pinch salt
2 tablespoons pecans

Make the caramel 1. put the coconut oil in a small microwave-safe bowl. If it's solid, microwave it for about 15 seconds to melt it. 2. Stir in the maple syrup, almond butter, and salt. 3. Place the caramel in the refrigerator for 5 to 10 minutes to thicken. Make the hummus 1. In a food processor, combine the chickpeas, cocoa powder, maple syrup, almond milk, and pinch of salt, and process until smooth. Scrape down the sides to make sure everything is incorporated. 2. If the hummus seems too thick, add another tablespoon of almond milk. 3. Add the pecans and pulse 6 times to roughly chop them. 4. Transfer the hummus to a serving bowl and when the caramel is thickened, swirl it into the hummus. Gently fold it in, but don't mix it in completely. 5. Serve with fresh fruit or pretzels.

Per Serving:

calories: 321 | fat: 22g | protein: 7g | carbs: 30g | fiber: 6g | sodium: 100mg

Chocolate-Dipped Fruit Bites

Prep time: 10 minutes | Cook time: 0 minutes |

Serves 4 to 6

½ cup semisweet chocolate chips
¼ cup low-fat milk
½ teaspoon pure vanilla extract
½ teaspoon ground nutmeg
¼ teaspoon salt

2 kiwis, peeled and sliced
1 cup honeydew melon chunks (about 2-inch chunks)
1 pound (454 g) whole strawberries

1. Place the chocolate chips in a small bowl. 2. In another small bowl, microwave the milk until hot, about 30 seconds. Pour the milk over the chocolate chips and let sit for 1 minute, then whisk until the chocolate is melted and smooth. Stir in the vanilla, nutmeg, and salt and allow to cool for 5 minutes. 3. Line a baking sheet with wax paper. Dip each piece of fruit halfway into the chocolate, tap gently to remove excess chocolate, and place the fruit on the baking sheet. 4. Once all the fruit has been dipped, allow it to sit until dry, about 30 minutes. Arrange on a platter and serve.

Per Serving:

calories: 125 | fat: 5g | protein: 2g | carbs: 21g | fiber: 3g | sodium: 110mg

Figs with Mascarpone and Honey

Prep time: 5 minutes | Cook time: 5 minutes | Serves 4

⅓ cup walnuts, chopped
8 fresh figs, halved
¼ cup mascarpone cheese

1 tablespoon honey
¼ teaspoon flaked sea salt

1. In a skillet over medium heat, toast the walnuts, stirring often, 3 to 5 minutes. 2. Arrange the figs cut-side up on a plate or platter. Using your finger, make a small depression in the cut side of each fig and fill with mascarpone cheese. Sprinkle with a bit of the walnuts, drizzle with the honey, and add a tiny pinch of sea salt.

Per Serving:

calories: 200 | fat: 13g | protein: 3g | carbs: 24g | fiber: 3g | sodium: 105mg

Poached Apricots and Pistachios with Greek Yogurt

Prep time: 2 minutes | Cook time: 18 minutes |

Serves 4

½ cup orange juice
2 tablespoons brandy
2 tablespoons honey
¾ cup water
1 cinnamon stick

12 dried apricots
⅓ cup 2% Greek yogurt
2 tablespoons mascarpone cheese
2 tablespoons shelled pistachios

1. Place a saucepan over medium heat and add the orange juice, brandy, honey, and water. Stir to combine, then add the cinnamon stick. 2. Once the honey has dissolved, add the apricots. Bring the mixture to a boil, then cover, reduce the heat to low, and simmer for 15 minutes. 3. While the apricots are simmering, combine the Greek yogurt and mascarpone cheese in a small serving bowl. Stir until smooth, then set aside. 4. When the cooking time for the apricots is complete, uncover, add the pistachios, and continue simmering for 3 more minutes. Remove the pan from the heat. 5. To serve, divide the Greek yogurt–mascarpone cheese mixture into 4 serving bowls and top each serving with 3 apricots, a few pistachios, and 1 teaspoon of the syrup. The apricots and syrup can be stored in a jar at room temperature for up to 1 month.

Per Serving:

calories: 146 | fat: 3g | protein: 4g | carbs: 28g | fiber: 4g | sodium: 62mg

Fresh Figs with Chocolate Sauce

Prep time: 5 minutes | Cook time: 0 minutes | Serves 4

¼ cup honey
2 tablespoons cocoa powder

8 fresh figs

1. Combine the honey and cocoa powder in a small bowl, and mix well to form a syrup. 2. Cut the figs in half and place cut side up. Drizzle with the syrup and serve.

Per Serving:

calories: 112 | fat: 1g | protein: 1g | carbs: 30g | fiber: 3g | sodium: 3mg

Mediterranean Orange Yogurt Cake

Prep time: 10 minutes | Cook time: 3 to 5 hours |

Serves 4 to 6

Nonstick cooking spray
¾ cup all-purpose flour
¾ cup whole-wheat flour
2 teaspoons baking powder
¼ teaspoon salt
1 cup coconut palm sugar
½ cup plain Greek yogurt

½ cup mild-flavored, extra-virgin olive oil
3 large eggs
2 teaspoons vanilla extract
Grated zest of 1 orange
Juice of 1 orange

1. Generously coat a slow cooker with cooking spray, or line the bottom and sides with parchment paper or aluminum foil. 2. In a large bowl, whisk together the all-purpose and whole-wheat flours, baking powder, and salt. 3. In another large bowl, whisk together the sugar, yogurt, olive oil, eggs, vanilla, orange zest, and orange juice until smooth. 4. Add the dry ingredients to the wet ingredients and mix together until well-blended. Pour the batter into the prepared slow cooker. 5. Cover the cooker and cook for 3 to 5 hours on Low heat, or until the middle has set and a knife inserted into it comes out clean.

Per Serving:

calories: 544 | fat: 33g | protein: 11g | carbs: 53g | fiber: 4g | sodium: 482mg

Cinnamon-Stewed Dried Plums with Greek Yogurt

Prep time: 5 minutes | Cook time: 3 minutes | Serves 6

3 cups dried plums
2 cups water
2 tablespoons sugar

2 cinnamon sticks
3 cups low-fat plain Greek yogurt

1. Add dried plums, water, sugar, and cinnamon to the Instant Pot®. Close lid, set steam release to Sealing, press the Manual button, and set time to 3 minutes. 2. When the timer beeps, quick-release the pressure until the float valve drops. Press the Cancel button and open lid. Remove and discard cinnamon sticks. Serve warm over Greek yogurt.

Per Serving:

calories: 301 | fat: 2g | protein: 14g | carbs: 61g | fiber: 4g | sodium: 50mg

Tortilla Fried Pies

Prep time: 10 minutes | Cook time: 5 minutes per batch | Makes 12 pies

12 small flour tortillas (4-inch diameter)
½ cup fig preserves
¼ cup sliced almonds

2 tablespoons shredded, unsweetened coconut
Oil for misting or cooking spray

1. Wrap refrigerated tortillas in damp paper towels and heat in microwave 30 seconds to warm. 2. Working with one tortilla at a time, place 2 teaspoons fig preserves, 1 teaspoon sliced almonds, and ½ teaspoon coconut in the center of each. 3. Moisten outer edges of tortilla all around. 4. Fold one side of tortilla over filling to make a half-moon shape and press down lightly on center. Using the tines of a fork, press down firmly on edges of tortilla to seal in filling. 5. Mist both sides with oil or cooking spray. 6. Place hand pies in air fryer basket close but not overlapping. It's fine to lean some against the sides and corners of the basket. You may need to cook in 2 batches. 7. Air fry at 390ºF (199ºC) for 5 minutes or until lightly browned. Serve hot. 8. Refrigerate any leftover pies in a closed container. To serve later, toss them back in the air fryer basket and cook for 2 or 3 minutes to reheat.

Per Serving:

1 pie: calories: 137 | fat: 4g | protein: 4g | carbs: 22g | fiber: 2g | sodium: 279mg

Chapter 11 Salads

Tabbouleh

Prep time: 15 minutes | Cook time: 12 minutes |
Serves 4 to 6

1 cup water
½ cup dried bulgur
½ English cucumber, quartered lengthwise and sliced
2 tomatoes on the vine, diced
2 scallions, chopped
Juice of 1 lemon
2 cups coarsely chopped fresh

Italian parsley
⅓ cup coarsely chopped fresh mint leaves
1 garlic clove
¼ cup extra-virgin olive oil
Sea salt
Freshly ground black pepper

1. In a medium saucepan, combine the water and bulgur and bring to a boil over medium heat. Reduce the heat to low, cover, and cook until the bulgur is tender, about 12 minutes. Drain off any excess liquid, fluff the bulgur with a fork, and set aside to cool. 2. In a large bowl, toss together the bulgur, cucumber, tomatoes, scallions, and lemon juice. 3. In a food processor, combine the parsley, mint, and garlic and process until finely chopped. 4. Add the chopped herb mixture to the bulgur mixture and stir to combine. Add the olive oil and stir to incorporate. 5. Season with salt and pepper and serve.

Per Serving:

calories: 215 | fat: 14g | protein: 4g | carbs: 21g | fiber: 5g | sodium: 66mg

Citrus Fennel Salad

Prep time: 15 minutes | Cook time: 0 minutes |
Serves 2

For the Dressing:

2 tablespoons fresh orange juice
3 tablespoons olive oil
1 tablespoon blood orange vinegar, other orange vinegar,

or cider vinegar
1 tablespoon honey
Salt
Freshly ground black pepper

For the Salad:

2 cups packed baby kale
1 medium navel or blood orange, segmented
½ small fennel bulb, stems and leaves removed, sliced into

matchsticks
3 tablespoons toasted pecans, chopped
2 ounces (57 g) goat cheese, crumbled

Make the Dressing: Combine the orange juice, olive oil, vinegar, and honey in a small bowl and whisk to combine. Season with salt and pepper. Set the dressing aside. Make the Salad: 1. Divide the baby kale, orange segments, fennel, pecans, and goat cheese evenly between two plates. 2. Drizzle half of the dressing over each salad.

Per Serving:

calories: 502 | fat: 39g | protein: 13g | carbs: 31g | fiber: 6g | sodium: 158mg

Superfood Salmon Salad Bowl

Prep time: 5 minutes | Cook time: 10 minutes |
Serves 2

Salmon:

2 fillets wild salmon
Salt and black pepper, to taste
2 teaspoons extra-virgin avocado oil
Dressing:
1 tablespoon capers
1 teaspoon Dijon or whole-

grain mustard
1 tablespoon apple cider vinegar or fresh lemon juice
3 tablespoons extra-virgin olive oil
1 teaspoon coconut aminos
Salt and black pepper, to taste

Salad:

½ medium cucumber, diced
1 cup sugar snap peas, sliced into matchsticks
½ small red bell pepper, sliced
⅓ cup pitted Kalamata olives, halved
2 sun-dried tomatoes, chopped

1 medium avocado, diced
3 tablespoons chopped fresh herbs, such as dill, chives, parsley, and/or basil
1 tablespoon pumpkin seeds
1 tablespoon sunflower seeds

1. Make the salmon: Season the salmon with salt and pepper. Heat a pan greased with the avocado oil over medium heat. Add the salmon, skin-side down, and cook for 4 to 5 minutes. Flip and cook for 1 to 2 minutes or until cooked through. Remove from the heat and transfer to a plate to cool. Remove the skin from the salmon and flake into chunks. 2. Make the dressing: Mix all the dressing ingredients together in a small bowl. Set aside. 3. Make the salad: Place the cucumber, sugar snap peas, bell pepper, olives, sun-dried tomatoes, avocado, and herbs in a mixing bowl, and combine well. Add the flaked salmon. Dry-fry the seeds in a pan placed over medium-low heat until lightly golden. Allow to cool, then add to the bowl. Drizzle with the prepared dressing and serve. This salad can be stored in the fridge for up to 1 day.

Per Serving:

calories: 660 | fat: 54g | protein: 31g | carbs: 18g | fiber: 9g | sodium: 509mg

Spanish Potato Salad

Prep time: 10 minutes | Cook time: 10 minutes |

Serves 6 to 8

4 russet potatoes, peeled and chopped
3 large hard-boiled eggs, chopped
1 cup frozen mixed vegetables, thawed
½ cup plain, unsweetened, full-fat Greek yogurt
5 tablespoons pitted Spanish

olives
½ teaspoon freshly ground black pepper
½ teaspoon dried mustard seed
½ tablespoon freshly squeezed lemon juice
½ teaspoon dried dill
Salt
Freshly ground black pepper

1. Boil potatoes for 5 to 7 minutes, until just fork-tender, checking periodically for doneness. You don't want to overcook them. 2. While the potatoes are cooking, in a large bowl, mix the eggs, vegetables, yogurt, olives, pepper, mustard, lemon juice, and dill. Season with salt and pepper. Once the potatoes are cooled somewhat, add them to the large bowl, then mix well and serve.

Per Serving:

calories: 192 | fat: 5g | protein: 9g | carbs: 30g | fiber: 2g | sodium: 59mg

Panzanella (Tuscan Bread and Tomatoes Salad)

Prep time: 10 minutes | Cook time: 20 minutes |

Serves 6

4 ounces (113 g) sourdough bread, cut into 1' slices
3 tablespoons extra-virgin olive oil, divided
2 tablespoons red wine vinegar
2 cloves garlic, mashed to a paste
1 teaspoon finely chopped fresh oregano or ½ teaspoon dried
1 teaspoon fresh thyme leaves
½ teaspoon Dijon mustard
Pinch of kosher salt

Few grinds of ground black pepper
2 pounds (907 g) ripe tomatoes (mixed colors)
6 ounces (170 g) fresh mozzarella pearls
1 cucumber, cut into ½'-thick half-moons
1 small red onion, thinly sliced
1 cup baby arugula
½ cup torn fresh basil

1. Coat a grill rack or grill pan with olive oil and prepare to medium-high heat. 2. Brush 1 tablespoon of the oil all over the bread slices. Grill the bread on both sides until grill marks appear, about 2 minutes per side. Cut the bread into 1' cubes. 3. In a large bowl, whisk together the vinegar, garlic, oregano, thyme, mustard, salt, pepper, and the remaining 2 tablespoons oil until emulsified. 4. Add the bread, tomatoes, mozzarella, cucumber, onion, arugula, and basil. Toss to combine and let sit for 10 minutes to soak up the flavors.

Per Serving:

calories: 219 | fat: 12g | protein: 10g | carbs: 19g | fiber: 3g | sodium: 222mg

Greek Potato Salad

Prep time: 15 minutes | Cook time: 15 to 18 minutes | Serves 6

1½ pounds (680 g) small red or new potatoes
½ cup olive oil
⅓ cup red wine vinegar
1 teaspoon fresh Greek oregano
4 ounces (113 g) feta cheese, crumbled, if desired, or 4 ounces (113 g) grated Swiss

cheese (for a less salty option)
1 green bell pepper, seeded and chopped (1¼ cups)
1 small red onion, halved and thinly sliced (generous 1 cup)
½ cup Kalamata olives, pitted and halved

1. Put the potatoes in a large saucepan and add water to cover. Bring the water to a boil and cook until tender, 15 to 18 minutes. Drain and set aside until cool enough to handle. 2. Meanwhile, in a large bowl, whisk together the olive oil, vinegar, and oregano. 3. When the potatoes are just cool enough to handle, cut them into 1-inch pieces and add them to the bowl with the dressing. Toss to combine. Add the cheese, bell pepper, onion, and olives and toss gently. Let stand for 30 minutes before serving.

Per Serving:

calories: 315 | fat: 23g | protein: 5g | carbs: 21g | fiber: 3g | sodium: 360mg

Toasted Pita Bread Salad

Prep time: 10 minutes | Cook time: 0 minutes |

Serves 4

For the Dressing:

½ cup lemon juice
½ cup olive oil
1 small clove garlic, minced
1 teaspoon salt

½ teaspoon ground sumac
¼ teaspoon freshly ground black pepper

For the Salad:

2 cups shredded romaine lettuce
1 large or 2 small cucumbers, seeded and diced
2 medium tomatoes, diced
½ cup chopped fresh flat-leaf parsley leaves
¼ cup chopped fresh mint

leaves
1 small green bell pepper, diced
1 bunch scallions, thinly sliced
2 whole-wheat pita bread rounds, toasted and broken into quarter-sized pieces
Ground sumac for garnish

1. To make the dressing, whisk together the lemon juice, olive oil, garlic, salt, sumac, and pepper in a small bowl. 2. To make the salad, in a large bowl, combine the lettuce, cucumber, tomatoes, parsley, mint, bell pepper, scallions, and pita bread. Toss to combine. Add the dressing and toss again to coat well. 3. Serve immediately sprinkled with sumac.

Per Serving:

calories: 359 | fat: 27g | protein: 6g | carbs: 29g | fiber: 6g | sodium: 777mg

Greek Village Salad

Prep time: 10 minutes | Cook time: 0 minutes | Serves 4

5 large tomatoes, cut into medium chunks
2 red onions, cut into medium chunks or sliced
1 English cucumber, peeled and cut into medium chunks
2 green bell peppers, cut into medium chunks
¼ cup extra-virgin olive oil,

plus extra for drizzling
1 cup kalamata olives, for topping
¼ teaspoon dried oregano, plus extra for garnish
¼ lemon
4 ounces (113 g) Greek feta cheese, sliced

1. In a large bowl, mix the tomatoes, onions, cucumber, bell peppers, olive oil, olives, and oregano. 2. Divide the vegetable mixture evenly among four bowls and top each with a squirt of lemon juice and 1 slice of feta. Drizzle with olive oil, garnish with oregano, and serve.

Per Serving:
calories: 315 | fat: 24g | protein: 8g | carbs: 21g | fiber: 6g | sodium: 524mg

Four-Bean Salad

Prep time: 20 minutes | Cook time: 0 minutes | Serves 4

½ cup white beans, cooked
½ cup black-eyed peas, cooked
½ cup fava beans, cooked
½ cup lima beans, cooked
1 red bell pepper, diced
1 small bunch flat-leaf parsley,

chopped
2 tablespoons olive oil
1 teaspoon ground cumin
Juice of 1 lemon
Sea salt and freshly ground pepper, to taste

1. You can cook the beans a day or two in advance to speed up the preparation of this dish. 2. Combine all ingredients in a large bowl and mix well. Season to taste. 3. Allow to sit for 30 minutes, so the flavors can come together before serving.

Per Serving:
calories: 189 | fat: 7g | protein: 8g | carbs: 24g | fiber: 7g | sodium: 14mg

Wilted Kale Salad

Prep time: 10 minutes | Cook time: 5 minutes | Serves 4

2 heads kale
1 tablespoon olive oil, plus 1 teaspoon
2 cloves garlic, minced

1 cup cherry tomatoes, sliced
Sea salt and freshly ground pepper, to taste
Juice of 1 lemon

1. Rinse and dry kale. 2. Tear the kale into bite-sized pieces. 3. Heat 1 tablespoon of the olive oil in a large skillet, and add the garlic. Cook for 1 minute and then add the kale. 4. Cook just until wilted, then add the tomatoes. 5. Cook until tomatoes are softened, then remove from heat. 6. Place tomatoes and kale in a bowl, and season with sea salt and freshly ground pepper. 7. Drizzle with remaining olive oil and lemon juice, serve, and enjoy.

Per Serving:
calories: 153 | fat: 6g | protein: 10g | carbs: 23g | fiber: 9g | sodium: 88mg

Arugula and Fennel Salad with Fresh Basil

Prep time: 5 minutes | Cook time: 0 minutes | Serves 4

3 tablespoons olive oil
3 tablespoons lemon juice
1 teaspoon honey
½ teaspoon salt
1 medium bulb fennel, very thinly sliced
1 small cucumber, very thinly

sliced
2 cups arugula
¼ cup toasted pine nuts
½ cup crumbled feta cheese
¼ cup julienned fresh basil leaves

1. In a medium bowl, whisk together the olive oil, lemon juice, honey, and salt. Add the fennel and cucumber and toss to coat and let sit for 10 minutes or so. 2. Put the arugula in a large salad bowl. Add the marinated cucumber and fennel, along with the dressing, to the bowl and toss well. Serve immediately, sprinkled with pine nuts, feta cheese, and basil.

Per Serving:
calories: 237 | fat: 21g | protein: 6g | carbs: 11g | fiber: 3g | sodium: 537mg

No-Mayo Florence Tuna Salad

Prep time: 10 minutes | Cook time: 0 minutes | Serves 4

4 cups spring mix greens
1 (15-ounce / 425-g) can cannellini beans, drained
2 (5-ounce / 142-g) cans water-packed, white albacore tuna, drained (I prefer Wild Planet brand)
⅔ cup crumbled feta cheese
½ cup thinly sliced sun-dried tomatoes
¼ cup sliced pitted kalamata

olives
¼ cup thinly sliced scallions, both green and white parts
3 tablespoons extra-virgin olive oil
½ teaspoon dried cilantro
2 or 3 leaves thinly chopped fresh sweet basil
1 lime, zested and juiced
Kosher salt
Freshly ground black pepper

1. In a large bowl, combine greens, beans, tuna, feta, tomatoes, olives, scallions, olive oil, cilantro, basil, and lime juice and zest. Season with salt and pepper, mix, and enjoy!

Per Serving:
1 cup: calories: 355 | fat: 19g | protein: 22g | carbs: 25g | fiber: 8g | sodium: 744mg

Italian Coleslaw

Prep time: 10 minutes | Cook time: 0 minutes |

Serves 6

1 cup shredded green cabbage
½ cup shredded red cabbage
½ cup shredded carrot
1 small yellow bell pepper, seeded and cut into thin strips

¼ cup sliced red onion or shallot
2 tablespoons olive oil
3 tablespoons red wine vinegar
¼ teaspoon celery seeds

1. In a large bowl, mix all the ingredients. Refrigerate until chilled before serving.

Per Serving:

calories: 62 | fat: 4g | protein: 1g | carbs: 5g | fiber: 1g | sodium: 14mg

Fruited Chicken Salad

Prep time: 10 minutes | Cook time: 0 minutes |

Serves 2

2 cups chopped cooked chicken breast
2 Granny Smith apples, peeled, cored, and diced
½ cup dried cranberries
¼ cup diced red onion
¼ cup diced celery

2 tablespoons honey Dijon mustard
1 tablespoon olive oil mayonnaise
½ teaspoon salt
¼ teaspoon freshly ground black pepper

1. In a medium bowl, combine the chicken, apples, cranberries, onion, and celery and mix well. 2. In a small bowl, combine the mustard, mayonnaise, salt, and pepper and whisk together until well blended. 3. Stir the dressing into the chicken mixture until thoroughly combined.

Per Serving:

calories: 384 | fat: 9g | protein: 45g | carbs: 28g | fiber: 7g | sodium: 638mg

Valencia-Inspired Salad

Prep time: 5 minutes | Cook time: 0 minutes | Serves 4

2 small oranges, peeled, thinly sliced, and pitted
1 small blood orange, peeled, thinly sliced, and pitted
1 (7-ounce / 198-g) bag butter lettuce
½ English cucumber, thinly sliced into rounds
1 (6-ounce / 170-g) can pitted black olives, halved

1 small shallot, thinly sliced (optional)
¼ cup raw hulled pumpkin seeds
8 slices Manchego cheese, roughly broken
2 to 3 tablespoons extra-virgin olive oil
Juice of 1 orange

1. In a large bowl, toss together the oranges, lettuce, cucumber,

olives, shallot (if desired), pumpkin seeds, and cheese until well mixed. Evenly divide the mixture among four plates. 2. Drizzle the salads with the olive oil and orange juice. Serve.

Per Serving:

calories: 419 | fat: 31g | protein: 17g | carbs: 22g | fiber: 5g | sodium: 513mg

Greek Black-Eyed Pea Salad

Prep time: 10 minutes | Cook time: 0 minutes |

Serves 4

2 tablespoons olive oil
Juice of 1 lemon (about 2 tablespoons)
1 garlic clove, minced
1 teaspoon ground cumin
1 (15½-ounce / 439-g) can no-salt-added black-eyed peas, drained and rinsed
1 red bell pepper, seeded and chopped

1 shallot, finely chopped
2 scallions (green onions), chopped
2 tablespoons chopped fresh dill
¼ cup chopped fresh parsley
½ cup pitted Kalamata olives, sliced
½ cup crumbled feta cheese (optional)

1. In a large bowl, whisk together the olive oil, lemon juice, garlic, and cumin. 2. Add the black-eyed peas, bell pepper, shallot, scallions, dill, parsley, olives, and feta (if using) and toss to combine. Serve.

Per Serving:

calories: 213 | fat: 14g | protein: 7g | carbs: 16g | fiber: 5g | sodium: 426mg

Marinated Greek Salad with Oregano and Goat Cheese

Prep time: 10 minutes | Cook time: 0 minutes |

Serves 4

½ cup white wine vinegar
1 small garlic clove, minced
1 teaspoon crumbled dried Greek oregano
½ teaspoon salt
¼ teaspoon freshly ground black pepper
2 Persian cucumbers, sliced
2 ounces (57 g) crumbled goat cheese or feta

thinly
4 to 6 long, skinny red or yellow banana peppers or other mild peppers
1 medium red onion, cut into rings
1 pint mixed small heirloom tomatoes, halved

1. In a large, nonreactive (glass, ceramic, or plastic) bowl, whisk together the vinegar, garlic, oregano, salt, and pepper. Add the cucumbers, peppers, and onion and toss to mix. Cover and refrigerate for at least 1 hour. 2. Add the tomatoes to the bowl and toss to coat. Serve topped with the cheese.

Per Serving:

calories: 98 | fat: 4g | protein: 4g | carbs: 13g | fiber: 3g | sodium: 460mg

Simple Insalata Mista (Mixed Salad) with Honey Balsamic Dressing

Serves 2

For the Dressing:

¼ cup balsamic vinegar
¼ cup olive oil
1 tablespoon honey
1 teaspoon Dijon mustard
¼ teaspoon salt, plus more to

taste
¼ teaspoon garlic powder
Pinch freshly ground black pepper

For the Salad:

4 cups chopped red leaf lettuce
½ cup cherry or grape tomatoes, halved
½ English cucumber, sliced in quarters lengthwise and then cut into bite-size pieces

Any combination fresh, torn herbs (parsley, oregano, basil, chives, etc.)
1 tablespoon roasted sunflower seeds

Make the Dressing: Combine the vinegar, olive oil, honey, mustard, salt, garlic powder, and pepper in a jar with a lid. Shake well. Make the Salad: 1. In a large bowl, combine the lettuce, tomatoes, cucumber, and herbs. 2. Toss well to combine. 3. Pour all or as much dressing as desired over the tossed salad and toss again to coat the salad with dressing. 4. Top with the sunflower seeds.

Per Serving:

calories: 339 | fat: 26g | protein: 4g | carbs: 24g | fiber: 3g | sodium: 171mg

Italian White Bean Salad with Bell Peppers

Prep time: 15 minutes | Cook time: 0 minutes |

Serves 4

2 tablespoons extra-virgin olive oil
2 tablespoons white wine vinegar
½ shallot, minced
½ teaspoon kosher salt
¼ teaspoon freshly ground black pepper
3 cups cooked cannellini beans,

or 2 (15-ounce / 425-g) cans no-salt-added or low-sodium cannellini beans, drained and rinsed
2 celery stalks, diced
½ red bell pepper, diced
¼ cup fresh parsley, chopped
¼ cup fresh mint, chopped

1. In a large bowl, whisk together the olive oil, vinegar, shallot, salt, and black pepper. 2. Add the beans, celery, red bell pepper, parsley, and mint; mix well.

Per Serving:

calories: 300 | fat: 8g | protein: 15g | carbs: 46g | fiber: 11g | sodium: 175mg

Pistachio-Parmesan Kale-Arugula Salad

Prep time: 20 minutes |Cook time: 0 minutes|

Serves: 6

6 cups raw kale, center ribs removed and discarded, leaves coarsely chopped
¼ cup extra-virgin olive oil
2 tablespoons freshly squeezed lemon juice (from about 1 small lemon)

½ teaspoon smoked paprika
2 cups arugula
⅓ cup unsalted shelled pistachios
6 tablespoons grated Parmesan or Pecorino Romano cheese

1. In a large salad bowl, combine the kale, oil, lemon juice, and smoked paprika. With your hands, gently massage the leaves for about 15 seconds or so, until all are thoroughly coated. Let the kale sit for 10 minutes. 2. When you're ready to serve, gently mix in the arugula and pistachios. Divide the salad among six serving bowls, sprinkle 1 tablespoon of grated cheese over each, and serve.

Per Serving:

calories: 150 | fat: 14g | protein: 4g | carbs: 5g | fiber: 1g | sodium: 99mg

Moroccan Tomato and Roasted Chile Salad

Prep time: 15 minutes | Cook time: 0 minutes |

Serves 6

2 large green bell peppers
1 hot red chili Fresno or jalapeño pepper
4 large tomatoes, peeled, seeded, and diced
1 large cucumber, peeled and diced

1 small bunch flat-leaf parsley, chopped
4 tablespoons olive oil
1 teaspoon ground cumin
Juice of 1 lemon
Sea salt and freshly ground pepper, to taste

1. Preheat broiler on high. Broil all of the peppers and chilies until the skin blackens and blisters. 2. Place the peppers and chilies in a paper bag. Seal and set aside to cool. Combine the rest of the ingredients in a medium bowl and mix well. 3. Take peppers and chilies out from the bag and remove the skins. Seed and chop the peppers and add them to the salad. 4. Season with sea salt and freshly ground pepper. 5. Toss to combine and let sit for 15–20 minutes before serving.

Per Serving:

calories: 128 | fat: 10g | protein: 2g | carbs: 10g | fiber: 3g | sodium: 16mg

Traditional Greek Salad

Prep time: 10 minutes | Cook time: 0 minutes |

Serves 4

2 large English cucumbers
4 Roma tomatoes, quartered
1 green bell pepper, cut into 1-
to 1½-inch chunks
¼ small red onion, thinly sliced
4 ounces (113 g) pitted
Kalamata olives
¼ cup extra-virgin olive oil
2 tablespoons freshly squeezed

lemon juice
1 tablespoon red wine vinegar
1 tablespoon chopped fresh
oregano or 1 teaspoon dried
oregano
¼ teaspoon freshly ground
black pepper
4 ounces (113 g) crumbled
traditional feta cheese

1. Cut the cucumbers in half lengthwise and then into ½-inch-thick half-moons. Place in a large bowl. 2. Add the quartered tomatoes, bell pepper, red onion, and olives. 3. In a small bowl, whisk together the olive oil, lemon juice, vinegar, oregano, and pepper. Drizzle over the vegetables and toss to coat. 4. Divide between salad plates and top each with 1 ounce (28 g) of feta.

Per Serving:

calories: 256 | fat: 22g | protein: 6g | carbs: 11g | fiber: 3g | sodium: 476mg

Red Pepper, Pomegranate, and Walnut Salad

Prep time: 5 minutes | Cook time: 40 minutes |

Serves 4

2 red bell peppers, halved and
seeded
1 teaspoon plus 2 tablespoons
olive oil
4 teaspoons pomegranate
molasses, divided
2 teaspoons fresh lemon juice
¼ teaspoon kosher salt

⅛ teaspoon ground black
pepper
4 plum tomatoes, halved,
seeded, and chopped
¼ cup walnut halves, chopped
¼ cup chopped fresh flat-leaf
parsley

1. Preheat the oven to 450°F(235°C). 2. Brush the bell peppers all over with 1 teaspoon of the oil and place cut side up on a large rimmed baking sheet. Drizzle 2 teaspoons of the pomegranate molasses in the cavities of the bell peppers. Roast the bell peppers until they have softened and the skins have charred, turning once during cooking, 30 to 40 minutes. Remove from the oven and cool to room temperature. Remove the skins and chop the peppers coarsely. 3. In a large bowl, whisk together the lemon juice, salt, black pepper, the remaining 2 tablespoons oil, and the remaining 2 teaspoons pomegranate molasses. Add the bell peppers, tomatoes, walnuts, and parsley and toss gently to combine. Serve at room temperature.

Per Serving:

calories: 166 | fat: 13g | protein: 2g | carbs: 11g | fiber: 3g | sodium: 153mg

Turkish Shepherd'S Salad

Prep time: 15 minutes | Cook time: 0 minutes |

Serves 6

¼ cup extra-virgin olive oil
2 tablespoons apple cider
vinegar
2 tablespoons lemon juice
½ teaspoon kosher salt
¼ teaspoon ground black
pepper
3 plum tomatoes, seeded and
chopped
2 cucumbers, seeded and
chopped
1 red bell pepper, seeded and

chopped
1 green bell pepper, seeded and
chopped
1 small red onion, chopped
⅓ cup pitted black olives (such
as kalamata), halved
½ cup chopped fresh flat-leaf
parsley
¼ cup chopped fresh mint
¼ cup chopped fresh dill
6 ounces (170 g) feta cheese,
cubed

1. In a small bowl, whisk together the oil, vinegar, lemon juice, salt, and black pepper. 2. In a large serving bowl, combine the tomatoes, cucumber, bell peppers, onion, olives, parsley, mint, and dill. Pour the dressing over the salad, toss gently, and sprinkle with the cheese.

Per Serving:

calories: 238 | fat: 20g | protein: 6g | carbs: 10g | fiber: 2g | sodium: 806mg

Beets with Goat Cheese and Chermoula

Prep time: 10 minutes | Cook time: 40 minutes |

Serves 4

6 beets, trimmed
Chermoula:
1 cup fresh cilantro leaves
1 cup fresh flat-leaf parsley
leaves
¼ cup fresh lemon juice
3 cloves garlic, minced
2 teaspoons ground cumin

1 teaspoon smoked paprika
½ teaspoon kosher salt
¼ teaspoon chili powder
(optional)
¼ cup extra-virgin olive oil
2 ounces (57 g) goat cheese,
crumbled

1. Preheat the oven to 400°F(205°C). 2. Wrap the beets in a piece of foil and place on a baking sheet. Roast until the beets are tender enough to be pierced with a fork, 30 to 40 minutes. When cool enough to handle, remove the skins and slice the beets into ¼' rounds. Arrange the beet slices on a large serving platter. 3. To make the chermoula: In a food processor, pulse the cilantro, parsley, lemon juice, garlic, cumin, paprika, salt, and chili powder (if using) until the herbs are just coarsely chopped and the ingredients are combined. Stir in the oil. 4. To serve, dollop the chermoula over the beets and scatter the cheese on top.

Per Serving:

calories: 249 | fat: 19g | protein: 6g | carbs: 15g | fiber: 5g | sodium: 472mg

Chapter 12 Pizzas, Wraps, and Sandwiches

Grilled Chicken Salad Pita

Prep time: 15 minutes | Cook time: 16 minutes | Serves 1

1 boneless, skinless chicken breast	½ small red onion, thinly sliced
Sea salt and freshly ground pepper, to taste	½ small cucumber, chopped
	1 tablespoon olive oil
1 cup baby spinach	Juice of 1 lemon
1 roasted red pepper, sliced	1 whole-wheat pita pocket
1 tomato, chopped	2 tablespoons crumbled feta cheese

1. Preheat a gas or charcoal grill to medium-high heat. 2. Season the chicken breast with sea salt and freshly ground pepper, and grill until cooked through, about 7–8 minutes per side. 3. Allow chicken to rest for 5 minutes before slicing into strips. 4. While the chicken is cooking, put all the chopped vegetables into a medium-mixing bowl and season with sea salt and freshly ground pepper. 5. Chop the chicken into cubes and add to salad. Add the olive oil and lemon juice and toss well. 6. Stuff the mixture onto a pita pocket and top with the feta cheese. Serve immediately.

Per Serving:
calories: 653 | fat: 26g | protein: 71g | carbs: 34g | fiber: 6g | sodium: 464mg

Turkish Pizza

Prep time: 20 minutes | Cook time: 10 minutes | Serves 4

4 ounces (113 g) ground lamb or 85% lean ground beef	2 teaspoons tomato paste
¼ cup finely chopped green bell pepper	¼ teaspoon sweet paprika
	¼ teaspoon ground cumin
¼ cup chopped fresh parsley	⅛ to ¼ teaspoon red pepper flakes
1 small plum tomato, seeded and finely chopped	⅛ teaspoon ground allspice
2 tablespoons finely chopped yellow onion	⅛ teaspoon kosher salt
	⅛ teaspoon black pepper
1 garlic clove, minced	4 (6-inch) flour tortillas

For Serving:

Chopped fresh mint	Lemon wedges
Extra-virgin olive oil	

1. In a medium bowl, gently mix the ground lamb, bell pepper, parsley, chopped tomato, onion, garlic, tomato paste, paprika, cumin, red pepper flakes, allspice, salt, and black pepper until well combined. 2. Divide the meat mixture evenly among the tortillas, spreading it all the way to the edge of each tortilla. 3. Place 1 tortilla in the air fryer basket. Set the air fryer to 400°F (204°C) for 10 minutes, or until the meat topping has browned and the edge of the tortilla is golden. Transfer to a plate and repeat to cook the remaining tortillas. 4. Serve the pizzas warm, topped with chopped fresh mint and a drizzle of extra-virgin olive oil and with lemon wedges alongside.

Per Serving:
calories: 172 | fat: 8g | protein: 8g | carbs: 18g | fiber: 2g | sodium: 318mg

Croatian Double-Crust Pizza with Greens and Garlic

Prep time: 15 minutes | Cook time: 20 minutes | Serves 4

4½ cups all-purpose flour	leaves julienned
1¼ teaspoons salt, divided	¼ small head of green cabbage, thinly sliced
1½ cups olive oil, plus 3 tablespoons, divided	¼ teaspoon freshly ground black pepper
1 cup warm water	
1 pound (454 g) Swiss chard or kale, tough center ribs removed,	4 cloves garlic, minced

1. In a medium bowl, combine the flour and 1 teaspoon salt. Add 1½ cups olive oil and the warm water and stir with a fork until the mixture comes together and forms a ball. Wrap the ball in plastic wrap and refrigerate for at least 30 minutes. 2. While the dough is chilling, in a large bowl, toss together the greens, cabbage, 2 tablespoons olive oil, the remaining ¼ teaspoon salt, and the pepper. 3. Preheat the oven to 400°F(205°C). 4. Halve the dough and place the halves on two sheets of lightly floured parchment paper. Roll or pat the dough out into two ¼-inch-thick, 11-inch-diameter rounds. 5. Spread the greens mixture over one of the dough rounds, leaving about an inch clear around the edge. Place the second dough round over the greens and fold the edges together to seal the two rounds together. Bake in the preheated oven until the crust is golden brown, about 20 minutes. 6. While the pizza is in the oven, combine 1 tablespoon of olive oil with the garlic. When the pizza is done, remove it from the oven and immediately brush the garlic-oil mixture over the crust. Cut into wedges and serve hot.

Per Serving:
calories: 670 | fat: 45g | protein: 10g | carbs: 62g | fiber: 5g | sodium: 504mg

Greek Salad Wraps

Prep time: 15 minutes |Cook time: 0 minutes|

Serves: 4

1½ cups seedless cucumber, peeled and chopped (about 1 large cucumber)
1 cup chopped tomato (about 1 large tomato)
½ cup finely chopped fresh mint
1 (2¼-ounce / 64-g) can sliced black olives (about ½ cup), drained
¼ cup diced red onion (about ¼ onion)
2 tablespoons extra-virgin olive oil
1 tablespoon red wine vinegar
¼ teaspoon freshly ground black pepper
¼ teaspoon kosher or sea salt
½ cup crumbled goat cheese (about 2 ounces / 57 g)
4 whole-wheat flatbread wraps or soft whole-wheat tortillas

1. In a large bowl, mix together the cucumber, tomato, mint, olives, and onion until well combined. 2. In a small bowl, whisk together the oil, vinegar, pepper, and salt. Drizzle the dressing over the salad, and mix gently. 3. With a knife, spread the goat cheese evenly over the four wraps. Spoon a quarter of the salad filling down the middle of each wrap. 4. Fold up each wrap: Start by folding up the bottom, then fold one side over and fold the other side over the top. Repeat with the remaining wraps and serve.

Per Serving:

calories: 217 | fat: 14g | protein: 7g | carbs: 17g | fiber: 3g | sodium: 329mg

Herbed Focaccia Panini with Anchovies and Burrata

Prep time: 5 minutes | Cook time: 8 minutes | Serves 4

8 ounces (227 g) burrata cheese, chilled and sliced
1 pound (454 g) whole-wheat herbed focaccia, cut crosswise into 4 rectangles and split horizontally
1 can anchovy fillets packed in oil, drained
8 slices tomato, sliced
2 cups arugula
1 tablespoon olive oil

1. Divide the cheese evenly among the bottom halves of the focaccia rectangles. Top each with 3 or 4 anchovy fillets, 2 slices of tomato, and ½ cup arugula. Place the top halves of the focaccia on top of the sandwiches. 2. To make the panini, heat a skillet or grill pan over high heat and brush with the olive oil. 3. Place the sandwiches in the hot pan and place another heavy pan, such as a cast-iron skillet, on top to weigh them down. Cook for about 3 to 4 minutes, until crisp and golden on the bottom, and then flip over and repeat on the second side, cooking for an additional 3 to 4 minutes until golden and crisp. Slice each sandwich in half and serve hot.

Per Serving:

calories: 596 | fat: 30g | protein: 27g | carbs: 58g | fiber: 5g | sodium: 626mg

Classic Margherita Pizza

Prep time: 10 minutes | Cook time: 10 minutes |

Serves 4

All-purpose flour, for dusting
1 pound (454 g) premade pizza dough
1 (15-ounce / 425-g) can crushed San Marzano tomatoes, with their juices
2 garlic cloves
1 teaspoon Italian seasoning
Pinch sea salt, plus more as needed
1½ teaspoons olive oil, for drizzling
10 slices mozzarella cheese
12 to 15 fresh basil leaves

1. Preheat the oven to 475ºF (245ºC). 2. On a floured surface, roll out the dough to a 12-inch round and place it on a lightly floured pizza pan or baking sheet. 3. In a food processor, combine the tomatoes with their juices, garlic, Italian seasoning, and salt and process until smooth. Taste and adjust the seasoning. 4. Drizzle the olive oil over the pizza dough, then spoon the pizza sauce over the dough and spread it out evenly with the back of the spoon, leaving a 1-inch border. Evenly distribute the mozzarella over the pizza. 5. Bake until the crust is cooked through and golden, 8 to 10 minutes. Remove from the oven and let sit for 1 to 2 minutes. Top with the basil right before serving.

Per Serving:

calories: 570 | fat: 21g | protein: 28g | carbs: 66g | fiber: 4g | sodium: 570mg

Margherita Open-Face Sandwiches

Prep time: 10 minutes |Cook time: 5 minutes|

Serves: 4

2 (6- to 7-inch) whole-wheat submarine or hoagie rolls, sliced open horizontally
1 tablespoon extra-virgin olive oil
1 garlic clove, halved
1 large ripe tomato, cut into 8 slices
¼ teaspoon dried oregano
1 cup fresh mozzarella (about 4 ounces / 113 g), patted dry and sliced
¼ cup lightly packed fresh basil leaves, torn into small pieces
¼ teaspoon freshly ground black pepper

1. Preheat the broiler to high with the rack 4 inches under the heating element. 2. Place the sliced bread on a large, rimmed baking sheet. Place under the broiler for 1 minute, until the bread is just lightly toasted. Remove from the oven. 3. Brush each piece of the toasted bread with the oil, and rub a garlic half over each piece. 4. Place the toasted bread back on the baking sheet. Evenly distribute the tomato slices on each piece, sprinkle with the oregano, and layer the cheese on top. 5. Place the baking sheet under the broiler. Set the timer for 1½ minutes, but check after 1 minute. When the cheese is melted and the edges are just starting to get dark brown, remove the sandwiches from the oven (this can take anywhere from 1½ to 2 minutes). 6. Top each sandwich with the fresh basil and pepper.

Per Serving:

calories: 176 | fat: 9g | protein: 10g | carbs: 14g | fiber: 2g | sodium: 119mg

Greek Salad Pita

Prep time: 15 minutes | Cook time: 0 minutes |

Serves 4

1 cup chopped romaine lettuce	1 tablespoon crumbled feta cheese
1 tomato, chopped and seeded	½ tablespoon red wine vinegar
½ cup baby spinach leaves	1 teaspoon Dijon mustard
½ small red onion, thinly sliced	Sea salt and freshly ground
½ small cucumber, chopped and deseeded	pepper, to taste
2 tablespoons olive oil	1 whole-wheat pita

1. Combine everything except the sea salt, freshly ground pepper, and pita bread in a medium bowl. 2. Toss until the salad is well combined. 3. Season with sea salt and freshly ground pepper to taste. Fill the pita with the salad mixture, serve, and enjoy!

Per Serving:

calories: 123 | fat: 8g | protein: 3g | carbs: 12g | fiber: 2g | sodium: 125mg

Turkey and Provolone Panini with Roasted Peppers and Onions

Prep time: 15 minutes | Cook time: 1 hour 5 minutes | Serves 4

For the peppers and onions

2 red bell pepper, seeded and quartered	2 tablespoons olive oil
2 red onions, peeled and quartered	½ teaspoon salt
	½ teaspoon freshly ground black pepper

For the panini

2 tablespoons olive oil	provolone cheese
8 slices whole-wheat bread	8 ounces (227 g) sliced roasted turkey or chicken breast
8 ounces (227 g) thinly sliced	

1. Preheat the oven to 375°F(190ºC). 2. To roast the peppers and onions, toss them together with the olive oil, salt, and pepper on a large, rimmed baking sheet. Spread them out in a single layer and then bake in the preheated oven for 45 to 60 minutes, turning occasionally, until they are tender and beginning to brown. Remove the peppers and onions from the oven and let them cool for a few minutes until they are cool enough to handle. Skin the peppers and thinly slice them. Thinly slice the onions. 3. Preheat a skillet or grill pan over medium-high heat. 4. To make the panini, brush one side of each of the 8 slices of bread with olive oil. Place 4 of the bread slices, oiled side down, on your work surface. Top each with ¼ of the cheese and ¼ of the turkey, and top with some of the roasted peppers and onions. Place the remaining 4 bread slices on top of the sandwiches, oiled side up. 5. Place the sandwiches in the skillet or grill pan (you may have to cook them in two batches), cover the pan, and cook until the bottoms have golden brown grill marks and the cheese is beginning to melt, about 2 minutes. Turn the sandwiches over and cook, covered, until the second side is golden brown and the cheese is melted, another 2 minutes or so. Cut each

sandwich in half and serve immediately.

Per Serving:

calories: 603 | fat: 32g | protein: 41g | carbs: 37g | fiber: 6g | sodium: 792mg

Sautéed Mushroom, Onion, and Pecorino Romano Panini

Prep time: 10 minutes | Cook time: 20 minutes | Serves 4

3 tablespoons olive oil, divided	¼ teaspoon freshly ground black pepper
1 small onion, diced	4 crusty Italian sandwich rolls
10 ounces (283 g) button or cremini mushrooms, sliced	4 ounces (113 g) freshly grated Pecorino Romano
½ teaspoon salt	

1. Heat 1 tablespoon of the olive oil in a skillet over medium-high heat. Add the onion and cook, stirring, until it begins to soften, about 3 minutes. Add the mushrooms, season with salt and pepper, and cook, stirring, until they soften and the liquid they release evaporates, about 7 minutes. 2. To make the panini, heat a skillet or grill pan over high heat and brush with 1 tablespoon olive oil. Brush the inside of the rolls with the remaining 1 tablespoon olive oil. Divide the mushroom mixture evenly among the rolls and top each with ¼ of the grated cheese. 3. Place the sandwiches in the hot pan and place another heavy pan, such as a cast-iron skillet, on top to weigh them down. Cook for about 3 to 4 minutes, until crisp and golden on the bottom, and then flip over and repeat on the second side, cooking for an additional 3 to 4 minutes until golden and crisp. Slice each sandwich in half and serve hot.

Per Serving:

calories: 348 | fat: 20g | protein: 14g | carbs: 30g | fiber: 2g | sodium: 506mg

Mediterranean-Pita Wraps

Prep time: 5 minutes | Cook time: 14 minutes | Serves 4

1 pound (454 g) mackerel fish fillets	Sea salt and freshly ground black pepper, to taste
2 tablespoons olive oil	2 ounces (57 g) feta cheese, crumbled
1 tablespoon Mediterranean seasoning mix	4 tortillas
½ teaspoon chili powder	

1. Toss the fish fillets with the olive oil; place them in the lightly oiled air fryer basket. 2. Air fry the fish fillets at 400ºF (204ºC) for about 14 minutes, turning them over halfway through the cooking time. 3. Assemble your pitas with the chopped fish and remaining ingredients and serve warm.

Per Serving:

calories: 275 | fat: 13g | protein: 27g | carbs: 13g | fiber: 2g | sodium: 322mg

Chicken and Goat Cheese Pizza

Prep time: 10 minutes | Cook time: 10 minutes |
Serves 4

All-purpose flour, for dusting
1 pound (454 g) premade pizza dough
2 tablespoons olive oil
1 cup shredded cooked chicken
3 ounces (85 g) goat cheese, crumbled
Sea salt
Freshly ground black pepper

1. Preheat the oven to 475°F (245°C) . 2. On a floured surface, roll out the dough to a 12-inch round and place it on a lightly floured pizza pan or baking sheet. Drizzle the dough with the olive oil and spread it out evenly. Top the dough with the chicken and goat cheese. 3. Bake the pizza for 8 to 10 minutes, until the crust is cooked through and golden. 4. Season with salt and pepper and serve.

Per Serving:
calories: 555 | fat: 23g | protein: 24g | carbs: 60g | fiber: 2g | sodium: 660mg

Mediterranean Tuna Salad Sandwiches

Prep time: 10 minutes | Cook time: 5 minutes |
Serves 2

1 can white tuna, packed in water or olive oil, drained
1 roasted red pepper, diced
½ small red onion, diced
10 low-salt olives, pitted and finely chopped
¼ cup plain Greek yogurt
1 tablespoon flat-leaf parsley, chopped
Juice of 1 lemon
Sea salt and freshly ground pepper, to taste
4 whole-grain pieces of bread

1. In a small bowl, combine all of the ingredients except the bread, and mix well. 2. Season with sea salt and freshly ground pepper to taste. Toast the bread or warm in a pan. 3. Make the sandwich and serve immediately.

Per Serving:
calories: 307 | fat: 7g | protein: 30g | carbs: 31g | fiber: 5g | sodium: 564mg

Jerk Chicken Wraps

Prep time: 30 minutes | Cook time: 15 minutes |
Serves 4

1 pound (454 g) boneless, skinless chicken tenderloins
1 cup jerk marinade
Olive oil
4 large low-carb tortillas
1 cup julienned carrots
1 cup peeled cucumber ribbons
1 cup shredded lettuce
1 cup mango or pineapple chunks

1. In a medium bowl, coat the chicken with the jerk marinade, cover, and refrigerate for 1 hour. 2. Spray the air fryer basket lightly with olive oil. 3. Place the chicken in the air fryer basket in a single layer and spray lightly with olive oil. You may need to cook the chicken in batches. Reserve any leftover marinade. 4. Air fry at 375°F (191°C) for 8 minutes. Turn the chicken over and brush with some of the remaining marinade. Cook until the chicken reaches an internal temperature of at least 165°F (74°C), an additional 5 to 7 minutes. 5. To assemble the wraps, fill each tortilla with ¼ cup carrots, ¼ cup cucumber, ¼ cup lettuce, and ¼ cup mango. Place one quarter of the chicken tenderloins on top and roll up the tortilla. These are great served warm or cold.

Per Serving:
calories: 241 | fat: 4g | protein: 28g | carbs: 23g | fiber: 4g | sodium: 85mg

Avocado and Asparagus Wraps

Prep time: 10 minutes | Cook time: 10 minutes |
Serves 6

12 spears asparagus
1 ripe avocado, mashed slightly
Juice of 1 lime
2 cloves garlic, minced
2 cups brown rice, cooked and chilled
3 tablespoons Greek yogurt
Sea salt and freshly ground pepper, to taste
3 (8-inch) whole-grain tortillas
½ cup cilantro, diced
2 tablespoons red onion, diced

1. Steam asparagus in microwave or stove top steamer until tender. Mash the avocado, lime juice, and garlic in a medium mixing bowl. In a separate bowl, mix the rice and yogurt. 2. Season both mixtures with sea salt and freshly ground pepper to taste. Heat the tortillas in a dry nonstick skillet. 3. Spread each tortilla with the avocado mixture, and top with the rice, cilantro, and onion, followed by the asparagus. 4. Fold up both sides of the tortilla, and roll tightly to close. Cut in half diagonally before serving.

Per Serving:
calories: 361 | fat: 9g | protein: 9g | carbs: 63g | fiber: 7g | sodium: 117mg

Pesto Chicken Mini Pizzas

Prep time: 5 minutes | Cook time: 10 minutes |
Serves 4

2 cups shredded cooked chicken
¾ cup pesto
4 English muffins, split
2 cups shredded Mozzarella cheese

1. In a medium bowl, toss the chicken with the pesto. Place one-eighth of the chicken on each English muffin half. Top each English muffin with ¼ cup of the Mozzarella cheese. 2. Put four pizzas at a time in the air fryer and air fry at 350°F (177°C) for 5 minutes. Repeat this process with the other four pizzas.

Per Serving:
calories: 617 | fat: 36g | protein: 45g | carbs: 29g | fiber: 3g | sodium: 544mg

Vegetable Pita Sandwiches

Prep time: 15 minutes | Cook time: 9 to 12 minutes | Serves 4

1 baby eggplant, peeled and chopped
1 red bell pepper, sliced
½ cup diced red onion
½ cup shredded carrot

1 teaspoon olive oil
⅓ cup low-fat Greek yogurt
½ teaspoon dried tarragon
2 low-sodium whole-wheat pita breads, halved crosswise

1. In a baking pan, stir together the eggplant, red bell pepper, red onion, carrot, and olive oil. Put the vegetable mixture into the air fryer basket and roast at 390ºF (199ºC) for 7 to 9 minutes, stirring once, until the vegetables are tender. Drain if necessary. 2. In a small bowl, thoroughly mix the yogurt and tarragon until well combined. 3. Stir the yogurt mixture into the vegetables. Stuff one-fourth of this mixture into each pita pocket. 4. Place the sandwiches in the air fryer and cook for 2 to 3 minutes, or until the bread is toasted. Serve immediately.

Per Serving:

calories: 115 | fat: 2g | protein: 4g | carbs: 22g | fiber: 6g | sodium: 90mg

Open-Faced Eggplant Parmesan Sandwich

Prep time: 10 minutes | Cook time: 10 minutes | Serves 2

1 small eggplant, sliced into ¼-inch rounds
Pinch sea salt
2 tablespoons olive oil
Sea salt and freshly ground pepper, to taste

2 slices whole-grain bread, thickly cut and toasted
1 cup marinara sauce (no added sugar)
¼ cup freshly grated, low-fat Parmesan cheese

1. Preheat broiler to high heat. 2. Salt both sides of the sliced eggplant, and let sit for 20 minutes to draw out the bitter juices. 3. Rinse the eggplant and pat dry with a paper towel. 4. Brush the eggplant with the olive oil, and season with sea salt and freshly ground pepper. 5. Lay the eggplant on a sheet pan, and broil until crisp, about 4 minutes. Flip over and crisp the other side. 6. Lay the toasted bread on a sheet pan. Spoon some marinara sauce on each slice of bread, and layer the eggplant on top. 7. Sprinkle half of the cheese on top of the eggplant and top with more marinara sauce. 8. Sprinkle with remaining cheese. 9. Put the sandwiches under the broiler until the cheese has melted, about 2 minutes. 10. Using a spatula, transfer the sandwiches to plates and serve.

Per Serving:

calories: 355 | fat: 19g | protein: 10g | carbs: 38g | fiber: 13g | sodium: 334mg

Beans and Greens Pizza

Prep time: 11 minutes | Cook time: 14 to 19 minutes | Serves 4

¾ cup whole-wheat pastry flour
½ teaspoon low-sodium baking powder
1 tablespoon olive oil, divided
1 cup chopped kale
2 cups chopped fresh baby spinach

1 cup canned no-salt-added cannellini beans, rinsed and drained
½ teaspoon dried thyme
1 piece low-sodium string cheese, torn into pieces

1. In a small bowl, mix the pastry flour and baking powder until well combined. 2. Add ¼ cup of water and 2 teaspoons of olive oil. Mix until a dough forms. 3. On a floured surface, press or roll the dough into a 7-inch round. Set aside while you cook the greens. 4. In a baking pan, mix the kale, spinach, and remaining teaspoon of the olive oil. Air fry at 350ºF (177ºC) for 3 to 5 minutes, until the greens are wilted. Drain well. 5. Put the pizza dough into the air fryer basket. Top with the greens, cannellini beans, thyme, and string cheese. Air fry for 11 to 14 minutes, or until the crust is golden brown and the cheese is melted. Cut into quarters to serve.

Per Serving:

calories: 181 | fat: 6g | protein: 8g | carbs: 27g | fiber: 6g | sodium: 103mg

Grilled Eggplant and Feta Sandwiches

Prep time: 10 minutes | Cook time: 8 minutes | Serves 2

1 medium eggplant, sliced into ½-inch-thick slices
2 tablespoons olive oil
Sea salt and freshly ground pepper, to taste
5 to 6 tablespoons hummus

4 slices whole-wheat bread, toasted
1 cup baby spinach leaves
2 ounces (57 g) feta cheese, softened

1. Preheat a gas or charcoal grill to medium-high heat. 2. Salt both sides of the sliced eggplant, and let sit for 20 minutes to draw out the bitter juices. 3. Rinse the eggplant and pat dry with a paper towel. 4. Brush the eggplant slices with olive oil and season with sea salt and freshly ground pepper. 5. Grill the eggplant until lightly charred on both sides but still slightly firm in the middle, about 3–4 minutes a side. 6. Spread the hummus on the bread and top with the spinach leaves, feta, and eggplant. Top with the other slice of bread and serve warm.

Per Serving:

calories: 516 | fat: 27g | protein: 14g | carbs: 59g | fiber: 14g | sodium: 597mg

Chapter 13 Pasta

Toasted Orzo with Shrimp and Feta

Prep time: 10 minutes | Cook time: 15 minutes |
Serves 4 to 6

1 pound (454 g) large shrimp (26 to 30 per pound), peeled and deveined	2 cups orzo
1 tablespoon grated lemon zest plus 1 tablespoon juice	2 cups chicken broth, plus extra as needed
¼ teaspoon table salt	1¼ cups water
¼ teaspoon pepper	½ cup pitted kalamata olives, chopped coarse
2 tablespoons extra-virgin olive oil, plus extra for serving	1 ounce (28 g) feta cheese, crumbled (¼ cup), plus extra for serving
1 onion, chopped fine	1 tablespoon chopped fresh dill
2 garlic cloves, minced	

1. Toss shrimp with lemon zest, salt, and pepper in bowl; refrigerate until ready to use. 2. Using highest sauté function, heat oil in Instant Pot until shimmering. Add onion and cook until softened, about 5 minutes. Stir in garlic and cook until fragrant, about 30 seconds. Add orzo and cook, stirring frequently, until orzo is coated with oil and lightly browned, about 5 minutes. Stir in broth and water, scraping up any browned bits. 3. Lock lid in place and close pressure release valve. Select high pressure cook function and cook for 2 minutes. Turn off Instant Pot and quick-release pressure. Carefully remove lid, allowing steam to escape away from you. 4. Stir shrimp, olives, and feta into orzo. Cover and let sit until shrimp are opaque throughout, 5 to 7 minutes. Adjust consistency with extra hot broth as needed. Stir in dill and lemon juice, and season with salt and pepper to taste. Sprinkle individual portions with extra feta and drizzle with extra oil before serving.

Per Serving:

calories: 320 | fat: 8g | protein: 18g | carbs: 46g | fiber: 2g | sodium: 670mg

Creamy Spring Vegetable Linguine

Prep time: 10 minutes | Cook time: 10 minutes |
Serves 4 to 6

1 pound (454 g) linguine	quartered
5 cups water, plus extra as needed	1 cup frozen peas, thawed
1 tablespoon extra-virgin olive oil	4 ounces (113 g) finely grated Pecorino Romano (2 cups), plus extra for serving
1 teaspoon table salt	½ teaspoon pepper
1 cup jarred whole baby artichokes packed in water,	2 teaspoons grated lemon zest
	2 tablespoons chopped fresh

tarragon

1. Loosely wrap half of pasta in dish towel, then press bundle against corner of counter to break noodles into 6-inch lengths; repeat with remaining pasta. 2. Add pasta, water, oil, and salt to Instant Pot, making sure pasta is completely submerged. Lock lid in place and close pressure release valve. Select high pressure cook function and cook for 4 minutes. Turn off Instant Pot and quick-release pressure. Carefully remove lid, allowing steam to escape away from you. 3. Stir artichokes and peas into pasta, cover, and let sit until heated through, about 3 minutes. Gently stir in Pecorino and pepper until cheese is melted and fully combined, 1 to 2 minutes. Adjust consistency with extra hot water as needed. Stir in lemon zest and tarragon, and season with salt and pepper to taste. Serve, passing extra Pecorino separately.

Per Serving:

calories: 390 | fat: 8g | protein: 17g | carbs: 59g | fiber: 4g | sodium: 680mg

Penne with Roasted Vegetables

Prep time: 20 minutes | Cook time: 25 to 30 minutes
| Serves 6

1 large butternut squash, peeled and diced	1 teaspoon paprika
1 large zucchini, diced	½ teaspoon garlic powder
1 large yellow onion, chopped	1 pound (454 g) whole-grain penne
2 tablespoons extra-virgin olive oil	½ cup dry white wine or chicken stock
½ teaspoon salt	2 tablespoons grated Parmesan cheese
½ teaspoon freshly ground black pepper	

1. Preheat the oven to 400°F(205°C). Line a baking sheet with aluminum foil. 2. In a large bowl, toss the vegetables with the olive oil, then spread them out on the baking sheet. Sprinkle the vegetables with the salt, pepper, paprika, and garlic powder and bake just until fork-tender, 25 to 30 minutes. 3. Meanwhile, bring a large stockpot of water to a boil over high heat and cook the penne according to the package instructions until al dente (still slightly firm). Drain but do not rinse. 4. Place ½ cup of the roasted vegetables and the wine or stock in a blender or food processor and blend until smooth. 5. Place the purée in a large skillet and heat over medium-high heat. Add the pasta and cook, stirring, just until heated through. 6. Serve the pasta and sauce topped with the roasted vegetables. Sprinkle with Parmesan cheese.

Per Serving:

calories: 456 | fat: 7g | protein: 9g | carbs: 92g | fiber: 14g | sodium: 241mg

Neapolitan Pasta and Zucchini

Prep time: 5 minutes | Cook time: 28 minutes |

Serves 3

⅓ cup extra virgin olive oil
1 large onion (any variety), diced
1 teaspoon fine sea salt, divided
2 large zucchini, quartered lengthwise and cut into ½-inch pieces
10 ounces (283 g) uncooked spaghetti, broken into 1-inch

pieces
2 tablespoons grated Parmesan cheese
2 ounces (57 g) grated or shaved Parmesan cheese for serving
½ teaspoon freshly ground black pepper

1. Add the olive oil to a medium pot over medium heat. When the oil begins to shimmer, add the onions and ¼ teaspoon of the sea salt. Sauté for 3 minutes, add the zucchini, and continue sautéing for 3 more minutes. 2. Add 2 cups of hot water to the pot or enough to just cover the zucchini (the amount of water may vary depending on the size of the pot). Cover, reduce the heat to low, and simmer for 10 minutes. 3. Add the pasta to the pot, stir, then add 2 more cups of hot water. Continue simmering, stirring occasionally, until the pasta is cooked and the mixture has thickened, about 12 minutes. (If the pasta appears to be dry or undercooked, add small amounts of hot water to the pot to ensure the pasta is covered in the water.). When the pasta is cooked, remove the pot from the heat. Add 2 tablespoons of the grated Parmesan and stir. 4. Divide the pasta into three servings and then top each with 1 ounce (28 g) of the grated or shaved Parmesan. Sprinkle the remaining sea salt and black pepper over the top of each serving. Store covered in the refrigerator for up to 3 days.

Per Serving:

calories: 718 | fat: 33g | protein: 24g | carbs: 83g | fiber: 6g | sodium: 815mg

Avgolemono

Prep time: 10 minutes | Cook time: 3 minutes |

Serves 6

6 cups chicken stock
½ cup orzo
1 tablespoon olive oil
12 ounces (340 g) cooked chicken breast, shredded
½ teaspoon salt
½ teaspoon ground black

pepper
¼ cup lemon juice
2 large eggs
2 tablespoons chopped fresh dill
1 tablespoon chopped fresh flat-leaf parsley

1. Add stock, orzo, and olive oil to the Instant Pot®. Close lid, set steam release to Sealing, press the Manual button, and set time to 3 minutes. When the timer beeps, quick-release the pressure until the float valve drops. Open lid and stir in chicken, salt, and pepper. 2. In a medium bowl, combine lemon juice and eggs, then slowly whisk in hot cooking liquid from the pot, ¼ cup at a time, until 1 cup of liquid has been added. Immediately add egg mixture to soup and stir well. Let stand on the Keep Warm setting, stirring occasionally, for 10 minutes. Add dill and parsley. Serve immediately.

Per Serving:

calories: 193 | fat: 5g | protein: 21g | carbs: 15g | fiber: 1g | sodium: 552mg

Whole-Wheat Spaghetti à la Puttanesca

Prep time: 5 minutes | Cook time: 20 minutes |

Serves 6

1 pound (454 g) dried whole-wheat spaghetti
⅓ cup olive oil
5 garlic cloves, minced or pressed
4 anchovy fillets, chopped
½ teaspoon red pepper flakes
1 teaspoon salt
½ teaspoon freshly ground

black pepper
1 (28-ounce / 794-g) can tomato purée
1 pint cherry tomatoes, halved
½ cup pitted green olives, halved
2 tablespoons drained capers
¾ cup coarsely chopped basil

1. Cook the pasta according to the package instructions. 2. Meanwhile, heat the oil in a large skillet over medium-high heat. Add the garlic, anchovies, red pepper flakes, salt, and pepper. Cook, stirring frequently, until the garlic just begins to turn golden brown, 2 to 3 minutes. Add the tomato purée, olives, cherry tomatoes, and capers and let the mixture simmer, reducing the heat if necessary, and stirring occasionally, until the pasta is done, about 10 minutes. 3. Drain the pasta in a colander and then add it to the sauce, tossing with tongs until the pasta is well coated. Serve hot, garnished with the basil.

Per Serving:

calories: 464 | fat: 17g | protein: 12g | carbs: 70g | fiber: 12g | sodium: 707mg

Penne with Tuna and Green Olives

Prep time: 5 minutes | Cook time: 5 minutes | Serves 4

2 tablespoons olive oil
3 garlic cloves, minced
½ cup green olives
½ teaspoon salt
¼ teaspoon freshly ground black pepper
2 (6-ounce / 170-g) cans tuna in

olive oil (don't drain off the oil)
½ teaspoon wine vinegar
12 ounces (340 g) penne pasta, cooked according to package directions
2 tablespoons chopped flat-leaf parsley

1. Heat the olive oil in a medium skillet over medium heat. Add the garlic and cook, stirring, 2 to 3 minutes, just until the garlic begins to brown. Add the olives, salt, pepper, and the tuna along with its oil. Cook, stirring, for a minute or two to heat the ingredients through. Remove from the heat and stir in the vinegar. 2. Add the cooked pasta to the skillet and toss to combine the pasta with the sauce. Serve immediately, garnished with the parsley.

Per Serving:

calories: 511 | fat: 22g | protein: 31g | carbs: 52g | fiber: 1g | sodium: 826mg

Greek Spaghetti with Meat Sauce

Prep time: 10 minutes | Cook time: 17 minutes |

Serves 6

1 pound (454 g) spaghetti
4 cups water
3 tablespoons olive oil, divided
1 medium white onion, peeled and diced
½ pound (227 g) lean ground veal
½ teaspoon salt
¼ teaspoon ground black

pepper
¼ cup white wine
½ cup tomato sauce
1 cinnamon stick
2 bay leaves
1 clove garlic, peeled
¼ cup grated aged myzithra or Parmesan cheese

1. Add pasta, water, and 1 tablespoon oil to the Instant Pot®. Close lid, set steam release to Sealing, press the Manual button, and set time to 4 minutes. When the timer beeps, quick-release the pressure until the float valve drops, open lid, and drain. Press the Cancel button. Set aside. 2. Press the Sauté button and heat remaining 2 tablespoons oil. Add onion and cook until soft, about 3 minutes. Add veal and crumble well. Keep stirring until meat is browned, about 5 minutes. Add salt, pepper, wine, and tomato sauce, and mix well. 3. Stir in cinnamon stick, bay leaves, and garlic. Press the Cancel button. Close lid, set steam release to Sealing, press the Manual button, and set time to 5 minutes. When the timer beeps, quick-release the pressure until the float valve drops and open lid. Remove and discard cinnamon stick and bay leaves. 4. Place pasta in a large bowl. Sprinkle with cheese and spoon meat sauce over top. Serve immediately.

Per Serving:

calories: 447 | fat: 15g | protein: 18g | carbs: 60g | fiber: 4g | sodium: 394mg

Shrimp with Angel Hair Pasta

Prep time: 10 minutes | Cook time: 5 minutes |

Serves 4

1 pound (454 g) dried angel hair pasta
2 tablespoons olive oil
3 garlic cloves, minced
1 pound (454 g) large shrimp, peeled and deveined

Zest of ½ lemon
¼ cup chopped fresh Italian parsley
¼ teaspoon red pepper flakes (optional)

1. Fill a large stockpot three-quarters full with water and bring to a boil over high heat. Add the pasta and cook according to the package instructions until al dente, about 5 minutes. Drain the pasta and set aside. 2. In the same pot, heat the olive oil over medium heat. Add the garlic and sauté until fragrant, about 3 minutes. Add the shrimp and cook for about 2 minutes on each side, until pink and fully cooked. 3. Turn off the heat and return the pasta to the pot. Add the lemon zest and mix well. 4. Serve garnished with the parsley and red pepper flakes, if desired.

Per Serving:

calories: 567 | fat: 10g | protein: 31g | carbs: 87g | fiber: 4g | sodium: 651mg

Spaghetti with Fresh Mint Pesto and Ricotta Salata

Prep time: 5 minutes | Cook time: 15 minutes |

Serves 4

1 pound (454 g) spaghetti
¼ cup slivered almonds
2 cups packed fresh mint leaves, plus more for garnish
3 medium garlic cloves
1 tablespoon lemon juice and ½ teaspoon lemon zest from 1

lemon
⅓ cup olive oil
¼ teaspoon freshly ground black pepper
½ cup freshly grated ricotta salata, plus more for garnish

1. Set a large pot of salted water over high heat to boil for the pasta. 2. In a food processor, combine the almonds, mint leaves, garlic, lemon juice and zest, olive oil, and pepper and pulse to a smooth paste. Add the cheese and pulse to combine. 3. When the water is boiling, add the pasta and cook according to the package instructions. Drain the pasta and return it to the pot. Add the pesto to the pasta and toss until the pasta is well coated. Serve hot, garnished with additional mint leaves and cheese, if desired.

Per Serving:

calories: 619 | fat: 31g | protein: 21g | carbs: 70g | fiber: 4g | sodium: 113mg

Yogurt and Dill Pasta Salad

Prep time: 10 minutes | Cook time: 4 minutes |

Serves 8

½ cup low-fat plain Greek yogurt
1 tablespoon apple cider vinegar
2 tablespoons chopped fresh dill
1 teaspoon honey
1 pound (454 g) whole-wheat elbow macaroni
4 cups water

1 tablespoon extra-virgin olive oil
1 medium red bell pepper, seeded and chopped
1 medium sweet onion, peeled and diced
1 stalk celery, diced
½ teaspoon ground black pepper

1. In a small bowl, combine yogurt and vinegar. Add dill and honey, and mix well. Refrigerate until ready to use. 2. Place pasta, water, and olive oil to the Instant Pot®. Close lid, set steam release to Sealing, press the Manual button, and set time to 4 minutes. 3. When the timer beeps, quick-release the pressure until the float valve drops and open lid. Drain off any excess liquid. Cool pasta to room temperature, about 30 minutes. Add prepared dressing and toss until pasta is well coated. Add bell pepper, onion, celery, and black pepper, and toss to coat. Refrigerate for 2 hours. Stir well before serving.

Per Serving:

calories: 295 | fat: 5g | protein: 19g | carbs: 47g | fiber: 8g | sodium: 51mg

Mixed Vegetable Couscous

Prep time: 20 minutes | Cook time: 10 minutes |
Serves 8

1 tablespoon light olive oil
1 medium zucchini, trimmed and chopped
1 medium yellow squash, chopped
1 large red bell pepper, seeded and chopped
1 large orange bell pepper, seeded and chopped
2 tablespoons chopped fresh

oregano
2 cups Israeli couscous
3 cups vegetable broth
½ cup crumbled feta cheese
¼ cup red wine vinegar
¼ cup extra-virgin olive oil
½ teaspoon ground black pepper
¼ cup chopped fresh basil

1. Press the Sauté button on the Instant Pot® and heat light olive oil. Add zucchini, squash, bell peppers, and oregano, and sauté 8 minutes. Press the Cancel button. Transfer to a serving bowl and set aside to cool. 2. Add couscous and broth to the Instant Pot® and stir well. Close lid, set steam release to Sealing, press the Manual button, and set time to 2 minutes. When the timer beeps, let pressure release naturally for 5 minutes, then quick-release the remaining pressure and open lid. 3. Fluff with a fork and stir in cooked vegetables, cheese, vinegar, extra-virgin olive oil, black pepper, and basil. Serve warm.

Per Serving:

calories: 355 | fat: 9g | protein: 14g | carbs: 61g | fiber: 7g | sodium: 588mg

Rotini with Red Wine Marinara

Prep time: 10 minutes | Cook time: 25 minutes |
Serves 6

1 pound (454 g) rotini
4 cups water
1 tablespoon olive oil
½ medium yellow onion, peeled and diced
3 cloves garlic, peeled and minced
1 (15-ounce / 425-g) can

crushed tomatoes
½ cup red wine
1 teaspoon sugar
2 tablespoons chopped fresh basil
½ teaspoon salt
¼ teaspoon ground black pepper

1. Add pasta and water to the Instant Pot®. Close lid, set steam release to Sealing, press the Manual button, and set time to 4 minutes. When the timer beeps, quick-release the pressure until the float valve drops and open the lid. Press the Cancel button. Drain pasta and set aside. 2. Clean pot and return to machine. Press the Sauté button and heat oil. Add onion and cook until it begins to caramelize, about 10 minutes. Add garlic and cook 30 seconds. Add tomatoes, red wine, and sugar, and simmer for 10 minutes. Add basil, salt, pepper, and pasta. Serve immediately.

Per Serving:

calories: 320 | fat: 4g | protein: 10g | carbs: 59g | fiber: 4g | sodium: 215mg

Greek Chicken Pasta Casserole

Prep time: 15 minutes | Cook time: 4 to 6 hours |
Serves 4

2 pounds (907 g) boneless, skinless chicken thighs or breasts, cut into 1-inch pieces
8 ounces (227 g) dried rotini pasta
7 cups low-sodium chicken broth
½ red onion, diced
3 garlic cloves, minced
¼ cup whole Kalamata olives,

pitted
3 Roma tomatoes, diced
2 tablespoons red wine vinegar
1 teaspoon extra-virgin olive oil
2 teaspoons dried oregano
1 teaspoon sea salt
½ teaspoon freshly ground black pepper
¼ cup crumbled feta cheese

1. In a slow cooker, combine the chicken, pasta, chicken broth, onion, garlic, olives, tomatoes, vinegar, olive oil, oregano, salt, and pepper. Stir to mix well. 2. Cover the cooker and cook for 4 to 6 hours on Low heat. 3. Garnish with the feta cheese for serving.

Per Serving:

calories: 608 | fat: 17g | protein: 59g | carbs: 55g | fiber: 8g | sodium: 775mg

Rotini with Spinach, Cherry Tomatoes, and Feta

Prep time: 5 minutes | Cook time: 30 minutes |
Serves 2

6 ounces (170 g) uncooked rotini pasta (penne pasta will also work)
1 garlic clove, minced
3 tablespoons extra virgin olive oil, divided
1½ cups cherry tomatoes, halved and divided

9 ounces (255 g) baby leaf spinach, washed and chopped
1½ ounces (43 g) crumbled feta, divided
Kosher salt, to taste
Freshly ground black pepper, to taste

1. Cook the pasta according to the package instructions, reserving ½ cup of the cooking water. Drain and set aside. 2. While the pasta is cooking, combine the garlic with 2 tablespoons of the olive oil in a small bowl. Set aside. 3. Add the remaining tablespoon of olive oil to a medium pan placed over medium heat and then add 1 cup of the tomatoes. Cook for 2–3 minutes, then use a fork to mash lightly. 4. Add the spinach to the pan and continue cooking, stirring occasionally, until the spinach is wilted and the liquid is absorbed, about 4–5 minutes. 5. Transfer the cooked pasta to the pan with the spinach and tomatoes. Add 3 tablespoons of the pasta water, the garlic and olive oil mixture, and 1 ounce (28 g) of the crumbled feta. Increase the heat to high and cook for 1 minute. 6. Top with the remaining cherry tomatoes and feta, and season to taste with kosher salt and black pepper. Store covered in the refrigerator for up to 2 days.

Per Serving:

calories: 602 | fat: 27g | protein: 19g | carbs: 74g | fiber: 7g | sodium: 307mg

Whole-Wheat Capellini with Sardines, Olives, and Manchego

Prep time: 5 minutes | Cook time: 15 minutes | Serves 4

1 (7-ounce / 198-g) jar Spanish sardines in olive oil, chopped (reserve the oil)
1 medium onion, diced
4 cloves garlic, minced
2 medium tomatoes, sliced
1 pound (454 g) whole-wheat capellini pasta, cooked according to package instructions
1 cup pitted, chopped cured black olives, such as Kalamata
3 ounces (85 g) freshly grated manchego cheese

1. Heat the olive oil from the sardines in a large skillet over medium-high heat. Add the onion and garlic and cook, stirring frequently, until softened, about 5 minutes. Add the tomatoes and sardines and cook, stirring, 2 minutes more. 2. Add the cooked and drained pasta to the skillet with the sauce and toss to combine. 3. Stir in the olives and serve immediately, topped with the grated cheese.

Per Serving:

calories: 307 | fat: 11g | protein: 8g | carbs: 38g | fiber: 6g | sodium: 433mg

Fresh Tomato Pasta Bowl

Prep time: 10 minutes | Cook time: 15 minutes | Serves 4

8 ounces (227 g) whole-grain linguine
1 tablespoon extra-virgin olive oil
2 garlic cloves, minced
¼ cup chopped yellow onion
1 teaspoon chopped fresh oregano
½ teaspoon salt
¼ teaspoon freshly ground black pepper
1 teaspoon tomato paste
8 ounces (227 g) cherry tomatoes, halved
½ cup grated Parmesan cheese
1 tablespoon chopped fresh parsley

1. Bring a large saucepan of water to a boil over high heat and cook the linguine according to the package instructions until al dente (still slightly firm). Drain, reserving ½ cup of the pasta water. Do not rinse the pasta. 2. In a large, heavy skillet, heat the olive oil over medium-high heat. Sauté the garlic, onion, and oregano until the onion is just translucent, about 5 minutes. 3. Add the salt, pepper, tomato paste, and ¼ cup of the reserved pasta water. Stir well and allow it to cook for 1 minute. 4. Stir in the tomatoes and cooked pasta, tossing everything well to coat. Add more pasta water if needed. 5. To serve, mound the pasta in shallow bowls and top with Parmesan cheese and parsley.

Per Serving:

calories: 310 | fat: 9g | protein: 10g | carbs: 49g | fiber: 7g | sodium: 305mg

Orzo with Feta and Marinated Peppers

Prep time:1 hour 25 minutes | Cook time: 37 minutes | Serves 2

2 medium red bell peppers
¼ cup extra virgin olive oil
1 tablespoon balsamic vinegar plus 1 teaspoon for serving
¼ teaspoon ground cumin
Pinch of ground cinnamon
Pinch of ground cloves
¼ teaspoon fine sea salt plus a pinch for the orzo
1 cup uncooked orzo
3 ounces (85 g) crumbled feta
1 tablespoon chopped fresh basil
¼ teaspoon freshly ground black pepper

1. Preheat the oven at 350°F (180°C). Place the peppers on a baking pan and roast in the oven for 25 minutes or until they're soft and can be pierced with a fork. Set aside to cool for 10 minutes. 2. While the peppers are roasting, combine the olive oil, 1 tablespoon of the balsamic vinegar, cumin, cinnamon, cloves, and ¼ teaspoon of the sea salt. Stir to combine, then set aside. 3. Peel the cooled peppers, remove the seeds, and then chop into large pieces. Place the peppers in the olive oil and vinegar mixture and then toss to coat, ensuring the peppers are covered in the marinade. Cover and place in the refrigerator to marinate for 20 minutes. 4. While the peppers are marinating, prepare the orzo by bringing 3 cups of water and a pinch of salt to a boil in a large pot over high heat. When the water is boiling, add the orzo, reduce the heat to medium, and cook, stirring occasionally, for 10–12 minutes or until soft, then drain and transfer to a serving bowl. 5. Add the peppers and marinade to the orzo, mixing well, then place in the refrigerator and to cool for at least 1 hour. 6. To serve, top with the feta, basil, black pepper, and 1 teaspoon of the balsamic vinegar. Mix well, and serve promptly. Store covered in the refrigerator for up to 3 days.

Per Serving:

calories: 600 | fat: 37g | protein: 15g | carbs: 51g | fiber: 4g | sodium: 690mg

Meaty Baked Penne

Prep time: 10 minutes | Cook time: 40 minutes | Serves 8

1 pound (454 g) penne pasta
1 pound (454 g) ground beef
1 teaspoon salt

1 (25-ounce / 709-g) jar marinara sauce
1 (1-pound / 454-g) bag baby spinach, washed
3 cups shredded mozzarella cheese, divided

1. Bring a large pot of salted water to a boil, add the penne, and cook for 7 minutes. Reserve 2 cups of the pasta water and drain the pasta. 2. Preheat the oven to 350°F(180°C). 3. In a large saucepan over medium heat, cook the ground beef and salt. Brown the ground beef for about 5 minutes. 4. Stir in marinara sauce, and 2 cups of pasta water. Let simmer for 5 minutes. 5. Add a handful of spinach at a time into the sauce, and cook for another 3 minutes. 6. To assemble, in a 9-by-13-inch baking dish, add the pasta and pour the pasta sauce over it. Stir in 1½ cups of the mozzarella cheese. Cover the dish with foil and bake for 20 minutes. 7. After 20 minutes, remove the foil, top with the rest of the mozzarella, and bake for another 10 minutes. Serve warm.

Per Serving:

calories: 454 | fat: 13g | protein: 31g | carbs: 55g | fiber: 9g | sodium: 408mg

Roasted Asparagus Caprese Pasta

Prep time: 10 minutes |Cook time: 15 minutes| Serves: 6

8 ounces (227 g) uncooked small pasta, like orecchiette (little ears) or farfalle (bow ties)
1½ pounds (680 g) fresh asparagus, ends trimmed and stalks chopped into 1-inch pieces (about 3 cups)
1 pint grape tomatoes, halved (about 1½ cups)
2 tablespoons extra-virgin olive oil

¼ teaspoon freshly ground black pepper
¼ teaspoon kosher or sea salt
2 cups fresh mozzarella, drained and cut into bite-size pieces (about 8 ounces / 227 g)
⅓ cup torn fresh basil leaves
2 tablespoons balsamic vinegar

1. Preheat the oven to 400°F(205°C). 2. In a large stockpot, cook the pasta according to the package directions. Drain, reserving about ¼ cup of the pasta water. 3. While the pasta is cooking, in a large bowl, toss the asparagus, tomatoes, oil, pepper, and salt together. Spread the mixture onto a large, rimmed baking sheet and bake for 15 minutes, stirring twice as it cooks. 4. Remove the vegetables from the oven, and add the cooked pasta to the baking sheet. Mix with a few tablespoons of pasta water to help the sauce become smoother and the saucy vegetables stick to the pasta. 5. Gently mix in the mozzarella and basil. Drizzle with the balsamic vinegar. Serve from the baking sheet or pour the pasta into a large bowl. 6. If you want to make this dish ahead of time or to serve it cold, follow the recipe up to step 4, then refrigerate the pasta and vegetables. When you are ready to serve, follow step 5 either with the cold pasta or with warm pasta that's been gently reheated in a pot on the stove.

Per Serving:

calories: 317 | fat: 12g | protein: 16g | carbs: 38g | fiber: 7g | sodium: 110mg

Chapter 14 Staples, Sauces, Dips, and Dressings

Sweet Red Wine Vinaigrette

Prep time: 5 minutes | Cook time: 0 minutes | Serves 2

¼ cup plus 2 tablespoons extra-virgin olive oil
2 tablespoons red wine vinegar
1 tablespoon apple cider vinegar
2 teaspoons honey

2 teaspoons Dijon mustard
½ teaspoon minced garlic
⅛ teaspoon kosher salt
⅛ teaspoon freshly ground black pepper

1. In a jar, combine the olive oil, vinegars, honey, mustard, garlic, salt, and pepper and shake well.

Per Serving:

calories: 386 | fat: 41g | protein: 0g | carbs: 6g | fiber: 0g | sodium: 198mg

Kidney Bean Dip with Cilantro, Cumin, and Lime

Prep time: 10 minutes | Cook time: 30 minutes |

Serves 16

1 cup dried kidney beans, soaked overnight and drained
4 cups water
3 cloves garlic, peeled and crushed
¼ cup roughly chopped

cilantro, divided
¼ cup extra-virgin olive oil
1 tablespoon lime juice
2 teaspoons grated lime zest
1 teaspoon ground cumin
½ teaspoon salt

1. Place beans, water, garlic, and 2 tablespoons cilantro in the Instant Pot®. Close the lid, set steam release to Sealing, press the Bean button, and cook for the default time of 30 minutes. 2. When the timer beeps, let pressure release naturally, about 20 minutes. Press the Cancel button, open lid, and check that beans are tender. Drain off excess water and transfer beans to a medium bowl. Gently mash beans with potato masher or fork until beans are mashed but chunky. Add oil, lime juice, lime zest, cumin, salt, and remaining 2 tablespoons cilantro and stir to combine. Serve warm or at room temperature.

Per Serving:

calories: 65 | fat: 3g | protein: 2g | carbs: 7g | fiber: 2g | sodium: 75mg

Berry and Honey Compote

Prep time: 5 minutes | Cook time: 15 minutes |

Serves 2 to 3

½ cup honey
¼ cup fresh berries

2 tablespoons grated orange zest

1. In a small saucepan, heat the honey, berries, and orange zest over medium-low heat for 2 to 5 minutes, until the sauce thickens, or heat for 15 seconds in the microwave. Serve the compote drizzled over pancakes, muffins, or French toast.

Per Serving:

calories: 272 | fat: 0g | protein: 1g | carbs: 74g | fiber: 1g | sodium: 4mg

Roasted Harissa

Prep time: 5 minutes | Cook time: 15 minutes |

Makes ¾ cup

1 red bell pepper
2 small fresh red chiles, or more to taste
4 garlic cloves, unpeeled
½ teaspoon ground coriander

½ teaspoon ground cumin
½ teaspoon ground caraway
1 tablespoon fresh lemon juice
½ teaspoon salt

1. Preheat the broiler to high. 2. Put the bell pepper, chiles, and garlic on a baking sheet and broil for 6 to 8 minutes. Turn the vegetables over and broil for 5 to 6 minutes more, until the pepper and chiles are softened and blackened. Remove from the broiler and set aside until cool enough to handle. Remove and discard the stems, skin, and seeds from the pepper and chiles. Remove and discard the papery skin from the garlic. 3. Put the flesh of the pepper and chiles with the garlic cloves in a blender or food processor. Add the coriander, cumin, caraway, lemon juice, and salt and blend until smooth. 4. This may be stored refrigerated for up to 3 days. Store in an airtight container, and cover the sauce with a ¼-inch layer of oil.

Per Serving:

calories: 28 | fat: 0g | protein: 1g | carbs: 6g | fiber: 1g | sodium: 393mg

Cucumber Yogurt Dip

Prep time: 5 minutes | Cook time: 0 minutes | Serves 2 to 3

1 cup plain, unsweetened, full-fat Greek yogurt
½ cup cucumber, peeled, seeded, and diced
1 tablespoon freshly squeezed lemon juice

1 tablespoon chopped fresh mint
1 small garlic clove, minced
Salt and freshly ground black pepper, to taste

1. In a food processor, combine the yogurt, cucumber, lemon juice, mint, and garlic. Pulse several times to combine, leaving noticeable cucumber chunks. 2. Taste and season with salt and pepper.

Per Serving:

calories: 55 | fat: 3g | protein: 3g | carbs: 5g | fiber: 0g | sodium: 38mg

Harissa Spice Mix

Prep time: 5 minutes | Cook time: 0 minutes | Makes about 7 tablespoons

2 tablespoons ground cumin
4 teaspoons paprika
4 teaspoons ground turmeric
2 teaspoons ground coriander
2 teaspoons chili powder

1 teaspoon garlic powder
1 teaspoon ground caraway seeds
½ teaspoon cayenne powder

1. Place all of the ingredients in a jar. Seal and shake well to combine. Store in a sealed jar at room temperature for up to 6 months.

Per Serving:

1 tablespoon: calories: 21 | fat: 1g | protein: 1g | carbs: 4g | fiber: 2g | sodium: 27mg

Red Pepper Chimichurri

Prep time: 10 minutes | Cook time: 0 minutes | Serves 4

1 garlic clove, minced
3 tablespoons olive oil
1 tablespoon red wine vinegar or sherry vinegar
¼ teaspoon freshly ground black pepper
1 shallot, finely chopped

1 large red bell pepper, roasted, peeled, seeded, and finely chopped (about 1 cup)
3 tablespoons capers, rinsed
3 tablespoons chopped fresh parsley
½ teaspoon red pepper flakes

1. In a small bowl, stir together all the ingredients until well combined.

Per Serving:

calories: 113 | fat: 10g | protein: 1g | carbs: 5g | fiber: 1g | sodium: 157mg

Pickled Onions

Prep time: 5 minutes | Cook time: 0 minutes | Serves 8 to 10

3 red onions, finely chopped
½ cup warm water
¼ cup granulated sugar

¼ cup red wine vinegar
1 teaspoon dried oregano

1. In a jar, combine the onions, water, sugar, vinegar, and oregano, then shake well and put it in the refrigerator. The onions will be pickled after 1 hour.

Per Serving:

calories: 40 | fat: 0g | protein: 1g | carbs: 10g | fiber: 1g | sodium: 1mg

Orange Dijon Dressing

Prep time: 5 minutes | Cook time: 0 minutes | Serves 2

¼ cup extra-virgin olive oil
2 tablespoons freshly squeezed orange juice
1 orange, zested
1 teaspoon garlic powder

¾ teaspoon za'atar seasoning
½ teaspoon salt
¼ teaspoon Dijon mustard
Freshly ground black pepper, to taste

1. In a jar, combine the olive oil, orange juice and zest, garlic powder, za'atar, salt, and mustard. Season with pepper and shake vigorously until completely mixed.

Per Serving:

calories: 284 | fat: 27g | protein: 1g | carbs: 11g | fiber: 2g | sodium: 590mg

Herbed Butter

Prep time: 10 minutes | Cook time: 0 minutes | Makes ½ cup

½ cup (1 stick) butter, at room temperature
1 garlic clove, finely minced
2 teaspoons finely chopped

fresh rosemary
1 teaspoon finely chopped fresh oregano
½ teaspoon salt

1. In a food processor, combine the butter, garlic, rosemary, oregano, and salt and pulse until the mixture is well combined, smooth, and creamy, scraping down the sides as necessary. Alternatively, you can whip the ingredients together with an electric mixer. 2. Using a spatula, scrape the butter mixture into a small bowl or glass container and cover. Store in the refrigerator for up to 1 month.

Per Serving:

⅛ cup: calories: 206 | fat: 23g | protein: 0g | carbs: 206g | fiber: 0g | sodium: 294mg

Versatile Sandwich Round

Prep time: 5 minutes | Cook time: 2 minutes | Serves 1

3 tablespoons almond flour
1 tablespoon extra-virgin olive oil
1 large egg
½ teaspoon dried rosemary,

oregano, basil, thyme, or garlic powder (optional)
¼ teaspoon baking powder
⅛ teaspoon salt

1. In a microwave-safe ramekin, combine the almond flour, olive oil, egg, rosemary (if using), baking powder, and salt. Mix well with a fork. 2. Microwave for 90 seconds on high. 3. Slide a knife around the edges of ramekin and flip to remove the bread. 4. Slice in half with a serrated knife if you want to use it to make a sandwich.

Per Serving:

calories: 354 | fat: 33g | protein: 12g | carbs: 6g | fiber: 3g | sodium: 388mg

Marinated Artichokes

Prep time: 10 minutes | Cook time: 0 minutes | Makes 2 cups

2 (13¾-ounce / 390-g) cans artichoke hearts, drained and quartered
¾ cup extra-virgin olive oil
4 small garlic cloves, crushed with the back of a knife
1 tablespoon fresh rosemary

leaves
2 teaspoons chopped fresh oregano or 1 teaspoon dried oregano
1 teaspoon red pepper flakes (optional)
1 teaspoon salt

1. In a medium bowl, combine the artichoke hearts, olive oil, garlic, rosemary, oregano, red pepper flakes (if using), and salt. Toss to combine well. 2. Store in an airtight glass container in the refrigerator and marinate for at least 24 hours before using. Store in the refrigerator for up to 2 weeks.

Per Serving:

¼ cup: calories: 228 | fat: 20g | protein: 3g | carbs: 11g | fiber: 5g | sodium: 381mg

Garlic-Rosemary Infused Olive Oil

Prep time: 5 minutes | Cook time: 45 minutes | Makes 1 cup

1 cup extra-virgin olive oil
4 large garlic cloves, smashed
4 (4- to 5-inch) sprigs rosemary

1. In a medium skillet, heat the olive oil, garlic, and rosemary sprigs over low heat. Cook until fragrant and garlic is very tender, 30 to 45 minutes, stirring occasionally. Don't let the oil get too hot or the garlic will burn and become bitter. 2. Remove from the heat and allow to cool slightly. Remove the garlic and rosemary with a slotted spoon and pour the oil into a glass container. Allow to cool completely before covering. Store covered at room temperature for up to 3 months.

Per Serving:

⅛ cup: calories: 241 | fat: 27g | protein: 0g | carbs: 1g | fiber: 0g | sodium: 1mg

Olive Mint Vinaigrette

Prep time: 5 minutes | Cook time: 0 minutes | Makes ½ cup

¼ cup white wine vinegar
¼ teaspoon honey
¼ teaspoon kosher salt
¼ teaspoon freshly ground black pepper

¼ cup extra-virgin olive oil
¼ cup olives, pitted and minced
2 tablespoons fresh mint, minced

1. In a bowl, whisk together the vinegar, honey, salt, and black pepper. Add the olive oil and whisk well. Add the olives and mint, and mix well. Store any leftovers in the refrigerator in an airtight container for up to 5 days.

Per Serving:

2 tablespoons: calories: 135 | fat: 15g | protein: 0g | carbs: 1g | fiber: 0g | sodium: 135mg

Red Pepper and Tomato Chutney

Prep time: 10 minutes | Cook time: 4 hours | Makes 2 to 3 cups

3 tablespoons rapeseed oil
1 teaspoon cumin seeds
4 garlic cloves, roughly chopped
1 large red onion, roughly chopped
2 red bell peppers, seeded and

roughly chopped
1 pound (454 g) fresh tomatoes
1 tablespoon malt vinegar
1 teaspoon salt
1 fresh green chile
¼ cup hot water

1. Heat the slow cooker to high and add the oil. 2. Add the cumin seeds and cook until they are fragrant. Then stir in the garlic and cook 1 to 2 minutes. 3. Add the onion, peppers, tomatoes, vinegar, salt, chile, and water. 4. Cook on low for 4 hours, until the peppers are soft and the tomatoes have burst. 5. Using an immersion or regular blender, purée, and then pour the chutney through a colander. 6. Put the chutney into a sterilized glass jar and leave to cool. When cooled, seal the jar. The chutney will keep for 2 weeks in the refrigerator.

Per Serving:

calories: 99 | fat: 7g | protein: 2g | carbs: 8g | fiber: 2g | sodium: 423mg

Sherry Vinaigrette

Prep time: 5 minutes | Cook time: 0 minutes | Makes about ¾ cup

⅓ cup sherry vinegar
1 clove garlic
2 teaspoons dried oregano
1 teaspoon salt

½ teaspoon freshly ground black pepper
½ cup olive oil

1. In a food processor or blender, combine the vinegar, garlic, oregano, salt, and pepper and process until the garlic is minced and the ingredients are well combined. With the food processor running, add the olive oil in a thin stream until it is well incorporated. Serve immediately or store, covered, in the refrigerator for up to a week.

Per Serving:

calories: 74 | fat: 8g | protein: 0g | carbs: 0g | fiber: 0g | sodium: 194mg

Herbed Oil

Prep time: 5 minutes | Cook time: 0 minutes | Serves 2

½ cup extra-virgin olive oil
1 teaspoon dried basil
1 teaspoon dried parsley
1 teaspoon fresh rosemary

leaves
2 teaspoons dried oregano
⅛ teaspoon salt

1. Pour the oil into a small bowl and stir in the basil, parsley, rosemary, oregano, and salt while whisking the oil with a fork.

Per Serving:

calories: 486 | fat: 54g | protein: 1g | carbs: 2g | fiber: 1g | sodium: 78mg

Zucchini Noodles

Prep time: 5 minutes | Cook time: 0 minutes | Serves 4

2 medium to large zucchini

1. Cut off and discard the ends of each zucchini and, using a spiralizer set to the smallest setting, spiralize the zucchini to create zoodles. 2. To serve, simply place a ½ cup or so of spiralized zucchini into the bottom of each bowl and spoon a hot sauce over top to "cook" the zoodles to al dente consistency. Use with any of your favorite sauces, or just toss with warmed pesto for a simple

and quick meal.

Per Serving:

calories: 27 | fat: 1g | protein: 2g | carbs: 5g | fiber: 2g | sodium: 13mg

Olive Tapenade

Prep time: 10 minutes | Cook time: 0 minutes | Makes about 1 cup

¾ cup pitted brine-cured green or black olives, chopped fine
1 small shallot, minced
2 tablespoons extra-virgin olive oil

1 tablespoon capers, rinsed and minced
1½ teaspoons red wine vinegar
1 teaspoon minced fresh oregano

1. Combine all ingredients in bowl. (Tapenade can be refrigerated for up to 1 week.)

Per Serving:

¼ cup: calories: 92 | fat: 9g | protein: 0g | carbs: 2g | fiber: 1g | sodium: 236mg

White Bean Hummus

Prep time: 10 minutes | Cook time: 30 minutes | Serves 12

⅔ cup dried white beans, rinsed and drained
3 cloves garlic, peeled and crushed

¼ cup olive oil
1 tablespoon lemon juice
½ teaspoon salt

1. Place beans and garlic in the Instant Pot® and stir well. Add enough cold water to cover ingredients. Close lid, set steam release to Sealing, press the Manual button, and set time to 30 minutes. 2. When the timer beeps, let pressure release naturally, about 20 minutes. Press the Cancel button and open lid. Use a fork to check that beans are tender. Drain off excess water and transfer beans to a food processor. 3. Add oil, lemon juice, and salt to the processor and pulse until mixture is smooth with some small chunks. Transfer to a storage container and refrigerate for at least 4 hours. Serve cold or at room temperature. Store in the refrigerator for up to one week.

Per Serving:

calories: 57 | fat: 5g | protein: 1g | carbs: 3g | fiber: 1g | sodium: 99mg

Appendix 1: Measurement Conversion Chart

MEASUREMENT CONVERSION CHART

VOLUME EQUIVALENTS(DRY)

US STANDARD	METRIC (APPROXIMATE)
1/8 teaspoon	0.5 mL
1/4 teaspoon	1 mL
1/2 teaspoon	2 mL
3/4 teaspoon	4 mL
1 teaspoon	5 mL
1 tablespoon	15 mL
1/4 cup	59 mL
1/2 cup	118 mL
3/4 cup	177 mL
1 cup	235 mL
2 cups	475 mL
3 cups	700 mL
4 cups	1 L

VOLUME EQUIVALENTS(LIQUID)

US STANDARD	US STANDARD (OUNCES)	METRIC (APPROXIMATE)
2 tablespoons	1 fl.oz.	30 mL
1/4 cup	2 fl.oz.	60 mL
1/2 cup	4 fl.oz.	120 mL
1 cup	8 fl.oz.	240 mL
1 1/2 cup	12 fl.oz.	355 mL
2 cups or 1 pint	16 fl.oz.	475 mL
4 cups or 1 quart	32 fl.oz.	1 L
1 gallon	128 fl.oz.	4 L

TEMPERATURES EQUIVALENTS

FAHRENHEIT(F)	CELSIUS(C) (APPROXIMATE)
225 °F	107 °C
250 °F	120 °C
275 °F	135 °C
300 °F	150 °C
325 °F	160 °C
350 °F	180 °C
375 °F	190 °C
400 °F	205 °C
425 °F	220 °C
450 °F	235 °C
475 °F	245 °C
500 °F	260 °C

WEIGHT EQUIVALENTS

US STANDARD	METRIC (APPROXIMATE)
1 ounce	28 g
2 ounces	57 g
5 ounces	142 g
10 ounces	284 g
15 ounces	425 g
16 ounces (1 pound)	455 g
1.5 pounds	680 g
2 pounds	907 g

The Dirty Dozen and Clean Fifteen

The Environmental Working Group (EWG) is a nonprofit, nonpartisan organization dedicated to protecting human health and the environment Its mission is to empower people to live healthier lives in a healthier environment. This organization publishes an annual list of the twelve kinds of produce, in sequence, that have the highest amount of pesticide residue-the Dirty Dozen-as well as a list of the fifteen kinds ofproduce that have the least amount of pesticide residue-the Clean Fifteen.

THE DIRTY DOZEN

- The 2016 Dirty Dozen includes the following produce. These are considered among the year's most important produce to buy organic:

Strawberries	Spinach
Apples	Tomatoes
Nectarines	Bell peppers
Peaches	Cherry tomatoes
Celery	Cucumbers
Grapes	Kale/collard greens
Cherries	Hot peppers

- *The Dirty Dozen list contains two additional itemskale/collard greens and hot peppers-because they tend to contain trace levels of highly hazardous pesticides.*

THE CLEAN FIFTEEN

- The least critical to buy organically are the Clean Fifteen list. The following are on the 2016 list:

Avocados	Papayas
Corn	Kiw
Pineapples	Eggplant
Cabbage	Honeydew
Sweet peas	Grapefruit
Onions	Cantaloupe
Asparagus	Cauliflower
Mangos	

- *Some of the sweet corn sold in the United States are made from genetically engineered (GE) seedstock. Buy organic varieties of these crops to avoid GE produce.*